# Boethius and Aquinas

# Boethius and Aquinas

## RALPH McINERNY

❋

THE CATHOLIC UNIVERSITY
OF AMERICA PRESS

Washington, D.C.

*Library of Congress Cataloging-in-Publication Data*
McInerny, Ralph M.
  Boethius and Aquinas / by Ralph McInerny.
    p.   cm.
  Bibliography: p.
  Includes indexes.
  ISBN 0-8132-0709-6 (alk. paper)
    1. Boethius, d. 524—Influence.   2. Thomas, Aquinas, Saint.
1225?–1274.    I. Title.
B659.Z7M35    1989
189—dc20                                           89-15705
                                                      CIP

# FOR JOSEPH BOBIK

*Princeps Thomistarum*

# Contents

# Preface

This book deals with the relation between St. Thomas Aquinas and Boethius. That "the last of the Romans and the first of the Scholastics" should have influenced Thomas has nothing distinctive about it: the same can be said of the vast majority of medieval masters. But there is more in the case of Thomas.

It is the rare theologian who does not invoke Boethius's definition of person and eternity, thereby exhibiting acquaintance, however secondhand, with the *Consolation of Philosophy* and the theological tractates. Thomas's affinity with Boethius is manifold. For one thing, unlike other theologians, he commented on works of Aristotle, among them *On Interpretation*, in the course of which he cites Boethius's comments, often to take exception to them. Nonetheless, his own massive effort in commenting on Aristotle owes much to techniques Boethius had passed on to the Latin West. More important, Thomas commented on two of Boethius's theological tractates, *De trinitate* (incomplete) and *De hebdomadibus*. It is with these that this book is chiefly concerned.

When in 1879 Leo XIII issued *Aeterni Patris*, thereby giving papal impetus to the modern revival of interest in St. Thomas Aquinas, the Holy Father saw Thomas not only for himself but as a lieutenant of Christian philosophy. Thomas was not regarded as a lonely figure, without antecedents and without epigones, but as a man of massive intellect and holiness in whom a multifaceted centuries-long cultural tradition achieved an impressive unity and from whom that perennial philosophy has been passed on. Thomas Aquinas might be the preeminent Doctor of the Church, but there were many doctors before him and there have been many since. Despite these assumptions of *Ae-*

*terni Patris*, subsequent study of Thomas tended to stress what was peculiar to his teaching rather than what he shared with others in the tradition in which he moved.

Indeed, in terms of modern prejudice, it was essential to point out how varied was the thought of men who nonetheless moved within the same tradition. The assumption that the Christian faith dictated a totally homogeneous interpretation of itself is not borne out by any close study of the medieval masters. If such diversity obtains when believers reflect on the truths of faith, it is scarcely surprising that interpretations of secular sources of knowledge should differ, sometimes dramatically. At times—the times in which Thomas lived—there was hostility among believers toward secular knowledge, and it was necessary to reconsider hasty judgments that had been made about the relation between the thought of Aristotle and articles of Christian faith. It is not too much to say that Thomas's intense and extensive commenting on the works of Aristotle saved the day for the view that, at bottom, reason and faith are complementary and that the speculations of pagans are a precious source for seeing what the world looks like to those for whom Revelation is a closed book. The condemnations of 1272 and 1277 are ample indication of the strength of the opposing party.

One of the ironies of the contemporary Thomistic school is that, despite Thomas's heroic efforts to save Aristotle, a chasm has been opened between the thought of Thomas and its Aristotelian sources. Indeed, it is not too much to say that there is an anti-Aristotelian animus in many presentations of the thought of Thomas. The same kind of isolation of Thomas from his sources can be found in most recent work on the relation between Thomas and Boethius.

Largely because of assertions made by Pierre Duhem, it has become commonplace to say that what Thomas finds in the text of Boethius is not there. Soon such eminent Thomists as Roland-Gosselin were agreeing that what Thomas took the Boethian text to mean could not be its meaning. Just as many doctrines Thomas found in Aristotle were said by Thomists not to be there, so too with Boethius. The Aristotelian claim is of course far more difficult to deal with than the Boethian. In this book, the focus is on what texts of Boethius mean and what Thomas took them to mean. I hope at least to open up the question and cast doubt on what has become received opinion. To a great extent, the dispute turns on the meaning of *Diversum est esse et id quod est*, the principal axiom in *De hebdomadibus*. Thomists have for so long been saying that the recognition of a real distinction between *esse* and essence not only characterizes the thought of Thomas, but that it is his achievement (no earlier thinker recognizing it) that they are bound to have trouble with passages in which Thomas attributes recognition of this distinction to others. That is what he does in his exposition of *De hebdomadibus* of Boethius.

Duhem maintained that the Boethian claim is to be taken to mean that there is diversity of essence and individual. The passage in which he argues this does not hold up under scrutiny. Of late, Boethian scholars of a Neoplatonic orientation have stoutly maintained that Boethius could not possibly have meant what Duhem takes him to mean. Thus, opening up the question entails a new look at Boethius as well as a new look at Thomas. The minimal claim of this study is that the denial that Boethius meant what Thomas takes him to mean must confront almost insuperable difficulties. It is simply no longer possible to put forward the Duhem view as if it were all but self-evident.

How important a part does Boethius play in the Thomistic synthesis? It would be absurd to suggest that he looms as large as Aristotle or Augustine or even the Pseudo-Dionysius. But whenever Thomas discusses a question on which Boethius wrote, he invariably gives his fellow Italian's views pride of place. For example, any discussion of divine and created goodness will feature the argument of *De hebdomadibus*. Those who regard the real distinction of *esse* and essence as the *clef de voûte* of Thomas's thought will correspondingly magnify Boethius's role, since Boethius is a major source of what Thomas has to say on that subject.

In order to make the points made in this study, it was necessary to touch on matters of far broader concern, for example, the nature and purpose of a Thomistic commentary. What is it that Thomas intends to do when he writes a commentary? His two commentaries on Boethius are of different literary form, that on *De hebdomadibus* an exposition of the text, line by line, word by word. That on *De trinitate* includes both an exposition of the text and questions and articles devoted to matters raised by the text. In short, it is like Thomas's commentary on the *Sentences* of Peter Lombard. Père Gauthier has made the somewhat surprising suggestion that Thomas's *Sententiae super Ethicum* are an exposition to which the second part of the *Summa theologiae* corresponds as questions on the text. It is less improbable to suggest that *ST*, Ia, qq. 5–6 and *Q. D. de veritate*, q. 21 complement the exposition of the *De hebdomadibus* as the second part of the *De trinitate* commentary complements the first part.

This volume has been a long time emerging from well over a decade of research aimed at writing "a book about Boethius," a project I had the temerity to announce in an article devoted to Boethius and Saint Thomas which appeared in the 1974 commemorative volume of *Rivista di filosofia Neo- Scolastica*. Originally I thought of presenting the thought of Boethius in all its scope to English readers, by which I mean of course readers of English. J. K. Sikes's book on Abelard and Gilson's on Augustine and Scotus suggested models of what I might do. A chapter on Boethius in Volume 2 of the *History of Western Philosophy* I undertook with my late colleague A. Robert Caponigri was the first fruits of my labors. The work I wrote on Thomas for the Twayne series on world authors dwelt on the role Boethius had played in the formation of Thomas's thought. And various papers, notably several read at the spring gatherings of medievalists in Kalamazoo at Western Michigan University, formed if only in my own mind pieces of the larger thing.

By 1974, I had made enough progress to permit me to refer in a footnote to a "work in progress, devoted to the thought of Boethius in its full scope." However, that same year appeared the imposing two volumes of Luca Obertello's *Severino Boezio*. Boethian studies would never be the same again. Here was a massive survey of the Boethian corpus along with the secondary literature on it accompanied by a full volume of bibliography. I will not say that my thunder had been stolen, since that would suggest that I could, then or now, achieve what Obertello had. But I did feel a bit deflated. My hopes began to revive when I considered that there are many who do not read Italian. And, after all, the book I planned was not at all like the one Obertello had written. And then in 1981 came the publication of Henry Chadwick's masterful book on Boethius.

Chadwick's book did, so much better than I ever could, what I had dreamt of doing that it forced a rethinking of my whole project. I leafed through the chapters I had written on Boethius's Quadrivial Pursuits and acknowledged that the world would not be a poorer place if they were never published. But it was not until 1985, after I resigned as Director of the Medieval Institute, that I saw my way clear. The book I would write would be a focused monograph on the relation between Boethius and Thomas Aquinas.

There are few who can read Thomas's two commentaries on Boethian works without being impressed by them. Crisp and clear, they already sound many of the themes of the later and more mature works and indeed many of his distinctive positions are found there as impressively put as they ever will be. Regarded as conveyors of Thomas's thought, the commentaries are held in high esteem, but are they good commentaries? That is, do they enable the reader better to fathom the text on which they comment?

I have mentioned that the views of Pierre Duhem became regulative of the discussion and, without having been subjected to any critical appraisal, were widely accepted. Even by Thomists!

It would of course be possible to embrace the content of the commentaries while acknowledging that what they say is in the text is not there, but that this is a curious position for a Thomist to be in seemed unrecognized. Indeed, Thomists were soon rhap-

sodizing over the way Thomas could find in texts things that
were not there. Non-Thomists, needless to say, described the dis-
crepancy otherwise.

The thesis of this book is simply stated: Boethius taught what
Thomas said he taught and the Thomistic commentaries on Boethius are without question the best commentaries ever written
on the tractates.

Another aspect of the opposition Thomists have thought to
find between Boethius and Aquinas has to do with the understanding of what Thomas himself means by the composition of
*esse* and essence in created things. This book will not enter fully
into that matter, only sufficiently to show that anyone who
thinks Thomists are of one mind, or explanation, about the "real
distinction" is grievously mistaken. That the diversity between
*esse* and *id quod est* is self-evident is one of the great overlooked
claims of *De hebdomadibus* and of Thomas's commentary on it.

The book I have come to write, then, is a monograph on the
relation between Boethius and his commentator. My thesis I
have stated. I will be content if this book, by subjecting received
opinion to severe scrutiny and criticism, opens up for reexami-
nation the relation between St. Thomas Aquinas and his great
predecessor and mentor Anicius Manlius Severinus Boethius.

It is pleasant to note here the cheerful and indispensable help
of Mrs. Alice Osberger, my administrative assistant in the
Medieval Institute and now in the Jacques Maritain Center.
Robert Anderson was of great help to me on earlier versions of
the effort and Brendan Kelly has been of enormous help in getting this final version ready for the press.

# Boethius and Aquinas

# Two Italian Scholars

## BOETHIUS: THE FIRST ROMAN SCHOLASTIC

Anicius Manlius Severinus Boethius (480–524) lived some seven hundred years before Thomas Aquinas (1225–1274). It may help to notice that almost exactly the same amount of time, seven centuries, separates us from St. Thomas as separated him from Boethius. The cultural, intellectual, religious setting of Boethius differed markedly from that of St. Thomas, accordingly, but both men played crucial roles in making the history of the West what it has been.

Boethius was a citizen of Rome under an Ostrogoth king as the Dark Ages closed in on Europe. Thomas was born in the Kingdom of Sicily, joined a new religious order, and was caught up in the exciting tumult of the still-new University of Paris. Boethius had a justified sense of living in an age of endings; Thomas lived when intellectual horizons were expanding with a rapidity that elicited conflicting reactions. One could continue this litany of the differences between the two men, but it is their profound similarities that also strike us.

Both were Catholics with a sense of intellectual mission. Boethius was aware that the kind of education he himself had received, as much Greek as Latin, had become all but impossible; fearful that the glory that was Greece might fade along with the grandeur that was Rome, he set himself to do something about it. Thomas Aquinas, confronted by a flood of new literature translated from the Arabic and Greek that carried disturbing implications for the Christian tradition, found the work that would fill his days. In lifetimes of forty-four and forty-nine years, respectively, separated by centuries, Boethius and Aquinas addressed a common task that can be summed up in the Boethian phrase: *fidem rationemque coniunge*: show the harmony of faith and reason.

## Boethius's Intellectual Project

The Boethius who comes before us at the outset of *The Consolation of Philosophy* is a man whose life has ended in debacle. His political career was cut short by the accusation of treason and in his cell in Pavia he smarts under the irony that the very Senate whose cause he championed has pronounced him guilty in his absence. He mordantly observes that a burner of churches and murderer of priests and other innocents would be better treated, and he awaits execution worried about his family and lamenting that the good are now terrorized while the wicked are in control. This opening self-defense, eloquent and moving, gives us a vivid sense of a very particular man. But we must not see here simply the fall of a Roman politician who tried to work with a barbarian king.

The philosophy in which Boethius seeks consolation is not the last refuge of a practical man fallen on evil days. Boethius had always heeded the advice of Dame Philosophy as she spoke through the works of Plato. His public career was founded on philosophical principle, a sense of what one who is granted the leisure for speculation owes to the public weal. It was the ideal of the Philosopher King that motivated Boethius—and to such disfavor he has come. In short, Boethius was a philosopher from first to last and even during his active career he was engaged in an intellectual task of superhuman proportions.

He tells us of it, almost as an aside, in the midst of his second commentary on Aristotle's *On Interpretation*, just before taking up the second book of the work.[1] One learns to look for these autobiographical tidbits, to listen for the voice of Boethius when

---

1. Which is said to have been written no earlier than 515. See L. M. De Rijk, "On the Chronology of Boethius' Works on Logic," which appeared as two parts, I and II, in *Vivarium* 2 (1964), pp. 1–49 and 125–161. There are chronological charts on pp. 159 and 161.

things were going well for him. At the outset of the first commentary on Porphyry's *Isagoge*, which De Rijk puts at 504 or 505, Boethius speaks of the violent southern wind which in winter kept him awake in his house on the Monte Aurelio. He decides to put his insomnia to good purpose and, urged by Fabius, turns his mind to introductory commentaries on learned books.[2] Ten years later, he sets down the statement of a literary project of breathtaking ambition. Paying deference to the labor and study of others, Boethius nonetheless thinks they failed to make clear the order and interrelationships of the various disciplines and he proposes to remedy that.

> I would put into the Roman tongue every work of Aristotle that has come down to us and write Latin commentaries on all of them. Whatever of the subtlety of the art of logic, the gravity of moral knowledge and depth of understanding in natural truth was written by Aristotle, I would by translating and commenting set out in an orderly way and clarify with commentaries. I would also put into Latin all the dialogues of Plato. That being done, I would then go on to bring into harmony the teachings of Aristotle and Plato and show, not as some do that they disagree in everything, but that in many and those the most important philosophical matters they are of one mind.[3]

All this he would do, he adds, if he is granted length of life and leisure in which to do it. No one with experience of such work,

2. "Hiemantis anni tempore in Aureliae montibus concesseramus atque ibi tunc, cum uiolenter auster eiecisset noctis placidam atque exturbasset quietem, recensere libitum est ea quae doctissimi uiri ad inluminandas quodammodo res intellectus densitate caligantissimas quibusdam quasi introductoriis commentariis ediderunt." *In Isagogen Porphyrii Commentorum*, Editionis primae, liber primus, 1, (ed. Samuel Brandt, *Corpus Scriptorum Ecclesiasticorum Latinorum* 48 [1906], pp. 3.1–4.3; *PL* 64, 9A.)

3. ". . . ego omne Aristotelis opus, quodcumque in manus venerit, in Romanum stilum vertens eorum omnium commenta Latinae oratione perscribam, ut si quid ex logicae artis subtilitate, ex moralis gravitate peritiae, ex naturalis acumine veritatis ab Aristotele conscriptum sit, id omne ordinatum transferam atque etiam quodam lumine commentationis inlustrem omnesque Platonis dialogos vertendo vel etiam commentando in Latinam redigam formam. his peractis non equidem contempserim Aristotelis Platonisque sententias in unam quodammodo revocare concordiam eosque non ut plerique dissentire in omnibus, sed in plerisque et his in philosophia maximis consentire demonstrem." *In librum Aristotelis Peri hermeneias commentarii*, secunda editio, II, 1 (ed. C. Meiser [1880], pp. 79.16–80.6; *PL* 64, 433C–D).

he says, would ever flinch from undertaking such a task. In what could not have been a leisured and was certainly not a long life, Boethius pursued this massively ambitious project. Rather than notice how little of it he brought to completion, we should marvel at what he did accomplish.

So far as we know, he translated nothing of Plato and, as for Aristotle, his work is confined to the Organon. But Boethius did translate the *Categories*, *On Interpretation*, the *Analytics*, the *Topics* and the *Sophistical Refutations*, although not all of these translations have come down to us. He wrote a commentary on the *Categories*, two on *On Interpretation*; he also wrote two commentaries on Porphyry's introduction to the *Categories*, the first making use of the Latin translation by Marius Victorinus, the second using his own translation. He wrote as well works on categorical and hypothetical syllogisms and on dialectical or topical differences besides commenting on Cicero's work on this last topic.[4]

The first thing to be said about Boethius's statement of his literary project is that, ambitious though it be, it does not begin to suggest the scope and extent of his writings. Besides the translations and commentaries of a logical sort, we find among the works of Boethius quadrivial pursuits as well. His *De institutione arithmetica* as well as his *De institutione musica* have come down to us, and he is said to have written on geometry and astronomy, too, but these have not survived. Besides these contributions to the liberal arts, Boethius wrote five short but extremely important theological tractates, the *opuscula sacra*, as well as his supreme literary achievement, *The Consolation of Philosophy*. The rough chronology of these works is first the

---

4. Cf. De Rijk, *op. cit.*; see too Luca Obertello, *Severino Boezio*, vol. 1 (Genova, Accademia ligure di scienze e lettere,1974), pp. 157–382 for a thorough discussion of Boethius's literary production and its transmission as well as the scholarly controversies attaching to these matters. Henry Chadwick, in his *Boethius* of 1984, provides a wealth of obiter dicta throughout his book. For example, he suggests that we find in the sixth book of Boethius's second commentary on the *Perihermeneias* a tailoring down of the project announced in the second book. See *passim* but on the point just mentioned p. 135.

mathematical, then the logical, next the theological and finally, of course, the *Consolation*. But this is quite rough, since his logical writings extend over the last twenty years of his life. We get a better sense of the energy of Boethius when we think of him engaged in the various genres simultaneously. It is not necessary to hold that Boethius set out with a clear notion of what he meant to do. He describes his effort in different ways at different times but always he seems drawn on by the implicit logic of what he has already done.

Nor should we overlook the fact that there were precedents aplenty for the task he undertook. He was not the first to dream of reconciling Aristotle and Plato, and various implementations of the dream would be known to those who read Greek. Indeed, Boethius's arithmetical work relies heavily on the writings of Nicomachus of Gerasa, and the influence of Ptolemy is added to that of Nicomachus in the work on music. Boethius is perfectly frank about this and it must not be thought that he was appropriating Greek thought and dishing it out in Latin as his own. Far better to say that he was turning into Latin what already amounted to Greek textbook summaries of received doctrine, a doctrine that "belonged" to Nicomachus no more than it did to Boethius. Furthermore, commenting on Aristotle was not a Boethian innovation. This was common practice among the Neoplatonists, especially those at Alexandria with whom, Pierre Courcelle has argued,[5] Boethius studied. We will see Boethius's setting down the canons of the commentary genre in passages that will greatly influence such later commentators as St. Thomas Aquinas. But these same canons can be found in Ammonius and in his teacher Porphyry. Porphyry also wrote commentaries on the dialogues of Plato, to say nothing of his having edited the *Enneads* of Plotinus. Boethius's literary effort, in this dimension of it, the dimension of the program in the second commentary on the *Perihermeneias*, reflects a long tradition among the Greeks.

5. Cf. Pierre Courcelle, *Late Latin Writers and Their Greek Sources*, translated by Harry E. Wedeck, (Cambridge, Harvard University Press, 1969), pp. 273–330.

Far from diminishing Boethius's accomplishment, these facts enable us to see how thoroughly he conveyed to the Latin reader the Greek intellectual tradition he sought to rescue.

The mode of authorship that emerges, with its dependence on earlier generations of writers, is no more open to the charge of plagiarism than the works in the Greek tradition on which it battens. Nor do such considerations turn the Boethian project into philosophical hackwork. Far from it. The commentaries of Boethius that we have, while obviously not made out of whole cloth and clearly dependent on Greek sources, represent a genuine if uneven achievement.

The overall intention of reconciling Aristotle and Plato is a familiar Neoplatonic one, where the reconciliation is *of* Aristotle *with* Plato, but we notice that Boethius, in stating his program, employs the Stoic division of philosophy into logic, ethics and natural science. Moreover, in coining the term *quadrivium,*[6] Boethius refers to Pythagoras, but transmits a way of gathering together disciplines that will define the pedagogical system of the Middle Ages until the introduction of the integral Aristotle, namely, the liberal arts curriculum. It is clear that Boethius occupies a tradition in which the various divisions of philosophy are regarded as reconcilable. He certainly employs a variety of them. St. Thomas will also find different divisions of philosophy complementary rather than competing.[7]

## Visions of Philosophy

When Dame Philosophy appears in Boethius's cell in the opening scene of the *Consolation,* there are embroidered on her gown two Greek letters, *theta* and *pi,* which stand for her dual though not equal concern with theoretical and practical questions. This division of philosophy, first adumbrated by Parmenides in the

6. Cf. *De arithmetica,* I, 1, PL 63, 1079D (. . . quasi quadrivio vestigatur . . .) and also the *De musica,* I, 1, ". . . unde fit, ut cum sint quattuor matheseos disciplinae . . . ," PL 63, 1167D–1168C.

7. Cf., for example, *In libros Ethicorum,* Bk. 1, lectio 1, n. 2, where the threefold division into rational, moral and natural philosophy is interpreted in such a way that "moral" stands for "practical" and "natural" for "theoretical."

metaphor of the spectator and participant,[8] and found in a more developed way in Plato, is elaborated by Aristotle with that prosaic precision we learn to expect from the Stagyrite. Sometimes Aristotle distinguishes both the theoretical and the practical from the poetic, the last referring to servile and laborious tasks aimed at transforming natural material.[9]

*Poesis* and *techne*, like the Latin *ars* which figures in the liberal arts tradition so dependent on Boethius, are ambiguous as between fine and servile arts, or, to take a cue from *De musica*, between the theory of an art and musical composition, on the one hand, and, on the other, playing: puffing the pipe, plucking the strings, beating the drum. The latter do not become a free man and thus are not liberal; they are for servants or slaves to do, hence servile.[10]

In the statement of his literary project, Boethius speaks of the logical art (*logicae artis*). His contemporary and kinsman, Cassiodorus Senator, will suggest a distinction between logic as science and logic as art,[11] and Boethius himself gets drawn into the question, contested by Stoics and Peripatetics, as to whether logic is part of philosophy or merely its instrument.[12] His solution is ingenious enough, but the problem would not even arise

8. Cf. Diogenes Laertius, *Lives of the Philosophers*, VIII, 8, in G. S. Kirk and J. E. Raven, *The Presocratic Philosophers*, (Cambridge University Press, 1957), p. 228, fragment 278: "Life, he said, is like a festival; just as some come to the festival to compete, some to ply their trade, but the best people come as spectators, so in life the slavish men go hunting for fame or gain, the philosophers for the truth."

9. *Metaphysics*, E, 1, 1025b25: "Therefore, if all thought is either practical or productive or theoretical. . . ." See St. Thomas, *in hoc loc.*, lectio 1, n. 1152–1155.

10. "Multo enim est majus atque altius scire quod quisque faciat, quam ipsum illud efficere quod sciat, etenim artificium corporale, quasi serviens famulatur. Ratio vero quasi domina imperat, et nisi manus secundum id quod ratio sancit efficiat, frustra fit. Quanto igitur praeclarior est scientia musicae in cognitione rationis, quam in opere efficiendi atque actu tantum, scilicet quantum corpus mente superatur!" *De musica*, I, 44, *PL* 63, 1195B–C.

11. Cf. *Institutiones*, ed. Mynors. For this great contemporary of Boethius, see *Cassiodorus*, by James J. O'Donnell (Los Angeles, University of California Press, 1979).

12. Cf. *In Porphyrii Isagogen*, editio secunda, *PL* 64, 73D–75A; Brandt, *ed. cit.*, I, 3, pp. 140.13–143.7. This is discussed in the next chapter.

for one who proposes logic, ethics and physics as the nets in which to catch the truths of philosophy.

In *De trinitate*, Boethius recalls the Aristotelian division of theoretical philosophy into natural science, mathematics and theology. St. Thomas interprets this as a straightforward instance of Aristotelian doctrine and expands and develops it accordingly in his commentary. That things are not so simple in Boethius's understanding of the threefold division of the theoretical will be seen in the next chapter.

At the beginning of his first commentary on Porphyry, Boethius tells Fabius that when Masters comment on a work there are six preliminary questions that must be dealt with.[13] Among those tasks is to say to which part of philosophy the work in question belongs. But Boethius discusses the nature of philosophy with reference to another of those preliminary tasks, oddly enough, that of showing the usefulness of the work. The *Isagoge* of Porphyry is a logical work and one's view of its usefulness will depend on one's view of the usefulness of logic generally. It is out of this discussion that eventually will come the question: Is logic a part of philosophy or preliminary to it? Which, of course, presupposes the biggest question of all: What is philosophy?

Philosophy is the love, study of, and in a way friendship with wisdom. Not of that wisdom which is involved in the knowledge and know-how of some arts and skills, but of that wisdom which, needing nothing else, is the living mind and primeval reason of all things. This love of wisdom on the part of the intelligent soul is an illumination by that pure wisdom and a kind of attraction and calling to it, such that the study of philosophy is seen to be the study of divinity and friendship with that pure mind.[14]

---

13. Boethius expresses these tasks both in Greek and Latin and is characteristically frank about his dependence on Greek sources.

14. "est enim philosophia amor et studium et amicitia quodammodo sapientiae, sapientiae uero non huius, quae in artibus quibusdam et in aliqua fabrili scientia notitiaque versatur, sed illius sapientiae, quae nullius indigens, uiuax mens et sola rerum primaeua ratio est. est autem hic amor sapientiae intellegentis animi ab illa pura sapientia inluminatio et quodammodo ad se ipsam retractio atque aduocatio, ut uideatur studium sapientiae studium diuinitatis et purae mentis illius amicitia." Ed. Brandt, p. 7.12–20.

This passage teems with tradition, recalling the etymological modesty of Pythagoras, the aspiring and divinizing effect of philosophizing stressed by Socrates and Plato—the study of death, the turning away from the things of this world—the knowledge of the divine that is an imitation of the peculiarly divine activity (Aristotle) and, of course, that initial rejection of the servile. There is also a distinctively Neoplatonic note, the concept of philosophy as a healing, a getting well, salvation: the soul's return to its origin. Does Boethius intend all these and other echoes or does he wish to select one strand from that great tradition and emphasize it?

### Philosophy and Theology

The vast translating and commenting project that Boethius undertook would seem to bear little relation to the fact that he was a Catholic. What he set out to do is what was done by Neoplatonists, most of them pagans, many of them ferocious foes of Christianity. This was less the case in Alexandria, where Boethius may have studied, and where Ammonius was possibly and John Philoponus certainly Christian. Does Boethius assume that philosophy is in the main compatible with Christian beliefs?

Henry Chadwick, in his magisterial work on Boethius, touches on the matter, though one may wonder whether the conflicts he suggests between Christianity and philosophy are unequivocally such.[15] But any real or apparent waffling on Boethius's part is not Chadwick's final view of the matter. "Nevertheless even in Boethius's Aristotelian commentaries there is a sense of keeping the pagan religious tradition at arm's length." [16]

Quite apart from problems which could arise for Boethius's religious faith from Neoplatonic philosophy, there is the consid-

15. Henry Chadwick, *Boethius: The Consolations of Music, Logic, Theology and Philosophy* (Oxford, Clarendon Press, 1981), p. 22. Chadwick mentions the use of "divine" to characterize the planets, and the distinction between such divine entities and those which are incorporeal.
16. *Ibid.*

erable fact that Theodoric was an Arian, that there was a split between the Eastern and Western churches on Christological matters, and not least that there were conflicts in Boethius's immediate circle due to accusations of immorality brought against Pope Symmachus which involved the bishops, the king and the Roman Senate. The theological tractates (the *opuscula sacra*) of Boethius relate in various ways to the tumultuous religious and theological world in which he lived.

The *opuscula sacra* raise but do not wholly illumine taxonomic problems of enormous interest and importance. It is in one of them, *De trinitate*, that Boethius recalls the threefold division of theoretical philosophy into natural science, mathematics and theology. It would appear that this division is recalled in order to locate and characterize the discussion under way, namely that of the Trinity. But the theology that is being distinguished from mathematics and natural science is a philosophical enterprise that can be and has been engaged in by pagans. Is theology in this sense capable of embracing discussions of the Trinity and of the union of the human and divine natures in Christ?

Consider what these tractates discuss. The first in the traditional ordering of them (which may not reflect the order in which they were written) asks, "How is the Trinity One God and not Three Gods?" The short name for this is *De trinitate*. The second asks "Whether Father, Son, and Holy Spirit may be Substantially Predicated of the Divinity?" The third, which is known as *De hebdomadibus*, asks "How Substances can be Good in virtue of their Existence without being Absolute Goods?" The fourth is a summary of Christian doctrine, *De fide Catholica*. The fifth, which may have been written first, is a treatise "Against Eutyches and Nestorius." Of these tractates, four are explicitly concerned with Christian doctrines; only *De hebdomadibus* looks to be a philosophical treatise, by which I mean a treatise that could conceivably have been written by a non-Christian.

In the prologue to his commentary on Boethius's *De trinitate*,

St. Thomas relates the five treatises to one another, sees them as a unified effort, and goes on to characterize the way in which Boethius treats matters of faith. A brief consideration of this here will give us the flavor of Thomas's reading of Boethius.

Thomas's prologue begins and ends with a verse from the Old Testament and is clearly occasioned by Boethius' opening statement that he has long pondered the problem he now proposes to treat.[17] Thomas picks up on *investigatam* and quotes from *Wisdom* 6:24 a line that includes *investigabo*.[18] The verbal connection is lost in the Douay, which renders the complete verse as "Now what wisdom is, and what was her origin, I will declare: and I will not hide from you the mysteries of God, *but will seek her out from the beginning of her birth, and bring the knowledge of her to light,* and will not pass over the truth." (I have italicized the portion Thomas quotes to establish the theme of his prologue). One purpose of the prologue is to characterize the activity in which Boethius is engaged in the tractate and Thomas moves from the verse taken to be echoed in the opening to a florilegium of scriptural passages which enable him to note that we humans must always move from creatures to God, this is our natural route to him, but that God in his mercy has given us another and safe way to knowledge of him, namely, the faith. In what we will see is his characteristic fashion, Thomas then distinguishes the philosophical approach to God from the theological. What we want to know from Boethius, then, is whether he recognized anything like that distinction.[19]

But first let us see how Thomas compares and orders the five Boethian tractates. The eternal generation of divine wisdom

17. "Investigatam diutissime quaestionem, quantum nostrae mentis igniculum lux diuina dignata est, formatam rationibus litterisque mandatam offerendam uobis communicandamque curaui tam uestri cupidus iudicii quam nostri studiosus inuenti." Rand and Stewart, p. 2, lines 1–5. Boethius is addressing Symmachus, his father-in-law, who raised him and saw that he got a classical education. Boethius tells us in the preface to the *De arithmetica* that, as Chadwick noted, Symmachus knew Greek as well as Latin.

18. "Ab initio nativitatis investigabo et ponam in lucem scientiam illius. . . ."

19. I am using *Expositio super librum Boethii De Trinitate* edited by Bruno Decker, second edition, (Leiden, E. J. Brill, 1959). The prologue is found on pp. 45–48.

from the Father within the Trinity provides the model for all other generations. (*Col.* 1:15) This yields a threefold division of the doctrine of the Boethian tractates. First, there is the consideration of the Trinity of persons, "from whose procession every other birth and procession is derived," in *De trinitate* dedicated to Symmachus, as well as in the second tractate concerned with the way of speaking of the Trinity (*de modo praedicandi*), dedicated to John, Deacon of the Roman Church (and possibly, according to Chadwick, the John who became pope in Boethius's last years). Second, there is a discussion of the procession of good creatures from the good God, in *De hebdomadibus*, also dedicated to John. Third, there is the restoration of creatures through Christ, a topic Boethius divides in two, first setting forth the faith taught by Christ whereby we are justified, in *De fide Christiana* (as Thomas calls it), and, second, considering how Christ is to be understood, that is, how two natures can belong to one person. This is the subject of that treatise the medievals knew as *De duabus naturis*, also dedicated to John.

But how does Boethius set about discussing the Trinity? Augustine has cited two ways in which this can be done, by authority or by argument (*per auctoritates et per rationes*), and he himself employed both. Some of the Fathers, like Hilary and Ambrose, discuss the matter solely on the basis of authority. "Boethius however chooses to proceed in the other way, namely by argument, presupposing what had already been accomplished by others through authority." [20]

Thomas seems to describe Boethius's procedure accurately enough. The tractates give us analyses of a somewhat austere kind, yet they presuppose what the Church teaches on the matters under discussion. Chapter 1 of *De trinitate* begins with a statement of the nature of the Church and more specifically with what the Church teaches about the Trinity.

There are many who claim as theirs the dignity of the Christian religion; but only that form of faith is valid which, both on account of the

20. *Ibid.* pp. 47.21–48.1.

universal character of the rules and doctrines affirming its authority, and because the worship in which they are expressed has spread throughout the world, is called catholic or universal. The belief of this religion concerning the Unity of the Trinity is as follows: the Father is God, the Son is God, the Holy Spirit is God. Therefore, Father, Son, and Holy Spirit are one God and not three Gods.[21]

The second tractate sets forth the following rule of procedure: "And I think that the method of our inquiry must be borrowed from what is admittedly the surest source of truth, namely, the fundamental doctrines of the Catholic faith." [22] Of course, the fourth tractate, On the Catholic Faith, proceeds per auctoritates. "The Christian Faith is proclaimed by the authority of the New Testament and of the Old." (p. 53, ll.1–2) Nonetheless, misunderstandings arise concerning what has been revealed, such as those of Arius and Sabellius, the Manicheans and Pelagius. These heresies have no grounding in the Old or New Testaments and of them can be said what Boethius says of the Pelagian denial of Original Sin: "the Catholic faith, as is known, at once banished [it] from its bosom." (p. 61, ll.116–7) False doctrines are recognized as heresy by their rejection by the church. And what is the church? "This Catholic church, then, spread throughout the world, is known by three particular marks: whatever is believed and taught in it has the authority of the Scriptures, or of universal tradition, or at least of its own proper teaching. And this authority is binding on the whole Church as is also the universal tradition of the Fathers, while each separate church exists and is governed by its private constitution and its proper rites according to difference of locality and the good judgment of each." (p. 71, ll.257–265) The bishops of Rome during Boethius's lifetime were insisting on their primacy in the Church and there is every reason to think that Boethius supported the papal claim.

21. Stewart and Rand, pp. 5–7.
22. So the Loeb edition of Stewart and Rand translates "uiamque indaginis hinc arbitor esse sumendam, unde rerum omnium manifestum constat exordium, id est ab ipsis catholicae fidei fundamentis" (p. 32, ll. 3–5).

Thus Thomas, by invoking Augustine's notion of a twofold approach to such topics as the Trinity, by way of authority and by way of reason, enables us to see that, while the first, second and fifth tractates proceed *per rationes*, they certainly presuppose, as Thomas noted, the way *per auctoritates* which is in fact exemplified by the fourth tractate. *De hebdomadibus* is theological only in the sense of the term also applicable to the work of philosophers who are not believers. The reasoning of the philosopher, we might say, does not presuppose authority. The reasoning about such matters as the Trinity and the dual nature of Christ which presupposes authority is never called theology in a special sense of the term, though the elements for the distinction between a philosophical or natural theology and the theology based on the authority of faith would seem to be implicit in Boethius. In Thomas it receives its most explicit and clear statement.

*The Problem of the* Consolation

What lifts Boethius to the front rank of cultural and literary importance is the *Consolation of Philosophy*. Without it, he would retain his importance as a major conduit through which achievements of Greek philosophy passed into the Latin West. His theological tractates would continue to enhance his status. However dependent on Augustine, they provided models of the application of philosophical analysis to the doctrines of faith that became the hallmark of Scholastic theology. But the *Consolation* crowns his achievement and adds an enigmatic note as well.

If Plato was the poet of philosophy and Aristotle its prose—not to say prosaic—stylist, Boethius in the *Consolation* shows himself able to embody abstract thought in a dramatic situation, a limit-situation, and one that is his own, not that of Socrates. The alternation of prose and verse in the five books feeds both our minds and our imaginations and conveys a sense of philosophy as comprehensive of both. The appeal is not only to our minds when they are on their best and most austere behavior, but to those longings and aspirations that brought us to philosophy in the first place. Both Plato and Aristotle pointed out that philosophy begins in wonder, in awe; it is only fitting that it should recover at its term an impassioned, half fearful, half hopeful response to reality. In the *Consolation*, philosophy becomes maternal, a stately yet anxious woman who appears to the devastated Boethius, unjustly accused, condemned to be executed in a particularly horrible way—first the knout, then beheading—and offers to lead him back to the consoling and salvific wisdom that the pressures of adversity have driven from him.

The intricate interplay of argument and imagery that constitutes the cumulative logic of the *Consolation* provides a vision of philosophy as a total answer to man's plight, and an answer man can achieve by his own efforts. It is this that brings us to the great problem posed by Boethius's literary production. Is the vision of philosophy operative in the *Consolation* compatible with Christian faith? What are we to make of a man who, in the extremity of misfortune, shows himself to be, in Dr. Johnson's phrase, *magis philosophus quam Christianus*? That the work is replete with pagan philosophy from a vast variety of sources is one thing—the same can be said of the commentaries on Porphyry and Aristotle—but it is the absence of any appeal to the author's faith that surprises. Some felt driven by this to deny the authenticity of the *opuscula sacra*, since they could scarcely say the *Consolation* is not by Boethius. But the *Anecdoton Holderi*[23] put an end to such speculation. Boethius was a Christian, a Catholic, a foe of Arianism, a defender of the faith, yet the *Con-*

---

23. H. Usener, *Anecdoton Holderi, ein Beitrag zur Geschichte Roms in ostgothishcer Zeit*, Bonn, 1877. See Chadwick, *op. laud.*, p. 7, and especially J. J. O'Donnell, *Cassiodorus*, (Los Angeles, University of California Press, 1978), pp. 259–266. The "excerpt from a book of Cassiodorus" describes Symmachus and then Boethius, attributing to the latter a *librum de sancta trinitate et capita quaedam dogmatica et librum contra Nestorium*, as well as works on logic and the mathematical disciplines, plus a bucolic poem. Missing from the list, of course, is the *Consolation of Philosophy*, but this fragment is taken to establish the identity of the author of the *opuscula sacra* and the translations and commentaries. O'Donnell suggests that the poetry attributed to Boethius is likely the early work mentioned at the outset of the *Consolation*.

*solation*, written when he was under sentence of death, betrays only the most obscure clues of his Christian faith.[24] Thus, if we seek a purely philosophical inquiry into the deepest and humanly most agonizing issues written by a believer but without appealing to his beliefs, the *Consolation* would answer. Those who deny such a work is possible have the *Consolation* to contend with. But others will wonder how Boethius, in the circumstances, could have so restrained himself. There have been many attempts to solve this puzzle. No solution makes it go away. It seems destined to remain a mystery.

In Boethius we have a Christian thinker who adopts his own version of the Neoplatonic project of bringing into harmony the two giants of fourth-century B.C. Athens. Involved in this project is the desire to bring together the Latin and Greek worlds, not only on the level of secular learning, but on the level of theology as well. We are thus confronted by a mind which seeks to make things hang together, to harmonize rather than unnecessarily to separate. The oft-quoted adage that Boethius is the last of the Romans and the first of the Scholastics tells us something essential about him. At times we find an adumbration of Thomistic style.[25] But there is, it is the purpose of this book to argue, a deeper affinity between the two Italian Catholic thinkers despite the some seven hundred years that separate them. Both men stand within, yet put their own mark upon, a tradition. Both men harmonize Aristotle and Neoplatonism, but differently. *Platoni uehementer assentior*, cries Boethius,[26] and it seems weak to

---

24. Étienne Gilson, in his *History of Christian Philosophy in the Middle Ages* (New York, Random House, 1955), p. 102, while allowing that Boethius in the *Consolation* does not seek direct support from Scripture, finds this unsurprising, since Dame Philosophy is speaking. "Let us however note the case, apparently unique, in Book III, prose 12, where Boethius says of the Sovereign Good that it 'reacheth from end to end mightily, and ordereth all things sweetly.'" He thinks this is undeniably a citation of *Wisdom* 8:1, so often quoted by Augustine. Gilson's judgment is characteristically sweeping. "Even when he is speaking only as a philosopher Boethius thinks as a Christian."

25. For example, in Chapter 7 of the fifth tractate, Boethius writes, "Contra quos respondendum est tres intelligi hominum posse status. . . ." Rand in a note observes that the phrase "has the true Thomist ring." Stewart and Rand, p. 122.

26. *Consolation*, III, pr. 12, opening line.

translate this, as has been done, by "I did very well like of Plato's doctrine" or "I agree fully with Plato." Why not let it say what it says? "I vehemently give my assent to Plato." Let us now turn to Thomas who might equally well have said, *Aristoteli uehementer assentior.*

## THOMAS AQUINAS: *LEGERE, PRAEDICARE, DISPUTARE*

The threefold task of the Master of Theology was to comment on texts, to preach and to dispute. That Thomas more than fulfilled his duty is clear from a glance at his collected works. A great many, perhaps the bulk, of his writings stemmed from his magisterial tasks. But before looking at the literary product of his teaching, a word should first be said about his education and then about where and when he functioned as teacher of theology.

Thomas was born in the family castle in Roccasecca in the Kingdom of Naples under the rule of Frederick II of Hohenstaufen in 1225. At about the age of five, in 1230, as the youngest son, he was presented to the Benedictine Abbey of Montecassino as an oblate. The monastery was the focus of armed struggle between papal and imperial troops. Thomas lived at Montecassino for about ten years and received his earliest schooling there. When the emperor again exerted pressure on the monastery, Thomas was sent to Naples where he studied the liberal arts and philosophy. Naples was an imperial university, a state university, a training ground for civil servants rather than clergy, all in all an anomaly in the medieval education of the time.[27] During the five years he studied in Naples, Thomas became acquainted with friars of the Dominican Order. Of not wholly unequal impor-

---

27. There were three major types of university in the thirteenth century: Naples, founded by Frederick II, Bologna, which was a corporation of students, and Paris—and most others—which were corporations of masters. See H. Rashdall's *Universities of Europe in the Middle Ages*, a new edition in three volumes by F. M. Powicke and A. B. Emden (Oxford, Clarendon Press, 1936); A. B. Cobban, *The Medieval Universities* (London, Methuen, 1975); A. L. Gabriel, *Garlandia: Studies in the History of the Mediaeval University* (Frankfurt a. M., Knecht, 1969). For later developments, see William J. Courtenay, *Schools and Scholars in Fourteenth Century England* (Princeton, 1987).

tance, he began the study of Aristotle's natural writings. The Hohenstaufens were patrons of Latin translations such as made by Michael Scot of Averroes's commentaries on Aristotle. Thus from the beginning of his university studies, Thomas confronted the new knowledge that was pouring into the West from Arabic, Jewish and Greek sources. His teacher, Peter of Ireland, introduced him to Aristotelianism well before Thomas studied under Albert the Great. When he was more or less twenty years of age, Thomas left Naples to join the Order of Preachers, the Dominicans.

Founded by Dominic de Guzman in 1215 in Toulouse to preach against the Albigensians, the Dominicans' role was soon expanded to preaching generally, for which serious study as well as prayer and a life of poverty, chastity and obedience were considered prerequisites. Dominic sent his men to universities to become proficient in sacred science. Thus it was that there were Dominicans at Naples. When Thomas joined the order, he was sent north to study but on the way was taken into custody by his family, who were not enthused by his joining this new band of religious. His brothers, putting his vocation to the ultimate test, introduced a prostitute into his room, but Thomas drove her away and fell to his knees in prayer. Testimony at his canonization process[28] indicates he was kept prisoner by his family for at least a year. He is said to have composed a work on fallacies and another on modal propositions (unrelated to the episode just mentioned) during this time.

When he resumed his journey north, he went either directly to Cologne or first to Paris and after several years to Cologne where he studied under Albert the Great. In 1248, Albert organized a House of Studies (*studium generale*) in Cologne and, if Thomas

28. Cf. *Thomae Aquinatis vitae fontes praecipuae*, a cura di P. Angelico Ferrua, O.P., Edizione domenicane, Alba, 1968. This useful volume contains the "Hystoria beati Thomae de Aquino" of Guglielmo di Tocco, the "Legenda sancti Thomae Aquinatis" of Bernard Gui, the canonization process, excerpts from Ptolemy di Lucca and others. See too *Friar Thomas d'Aquino* by James A. Weisheipl, O.P. (Garden City, NY, Doubleday, 1974), and Vernon J. Bourke, *Aquinas' Search for Wisdom* (Milwaukee, Bruce, 1965).

did first spend some years at the Parisian convent on the Rue St. Jacques, he went with Albert to Cologne at this time. There he heard Albert on the *Nicomachean Ethics* of Aristotle and on Pseudo-Dionysius's *The Divine Names*. We know this because we possess—the latter in Thomas's distinctive hand, the unreadable hand: *litera inintelligibilis*—reports on these lectures. It was likely in Cologne that Thomas was ordained priest. After four years in Germany, 1248–1252, he was sent to Paris to continue his studies.[29] Those studies consisted in close commenting on Scripture and the *Sentences* of Peter Lombard. Thomas arrived in Paris when the animosity of the secular masters toward the mendicants in their midst was reaching its peak. Indeed, after Thomas had become a Master of Theology, a year passed before he was permitted to occupy one of the Dominican chairs, the opposition overcome only by the interventions of the Pope.

Thomas's magisterial career is easily described. He delivered his inaugural lecture in the summer of 1256 and taught at Paris until 1259, when he returned to Italy, where he taught theology in various places in the Roman province of his order and was Regent Master in Rome and Viterbo until 1268.[30] Thomas's second Paris regency extends from 1269 to 1272 when he confronted the issue of Latin Averroism.[31] Thomas returned to Italy

29. Young men entered the Faculty of Arts at the age of fourteen or fifteen and pursued a course of some six years in duration. The Master of Arts was thus a man in his very early twenties. The Faculty of Arts was the avenue into the other faculties, those of Theology, Law and Medicine. Thomas seems never to have been a student of arts at Paris. The theology was extremely long, involving six years as *auditor*, during which one heard lectures for four years on Scripture and for two years on the *Sentences* of Peter Lombard. After an examination, the fledgling theologian began at least cursory lectures on the Bible. Weisheipl holds that Thomas was a *cursor biblicus* under Albert in Cologne and that, when he came to Paris in 1252, he embarked on a four-year period as *baccalarius Sententiarum*. See *op. cit.*, pp. 53–92.

30. Weisheipl has extended discussions of this period in chapters IV and V of his *Friar Thomas D'Aquino, op cit.* Needless to say, there is controversy about the details of every period in the life of Thomas, but Weisheipl mentions the main alternatives to his own judgments.

31. Or Heterodox Aristotelianism, as Van Steenberghen prefers to call it: See Fernand Van Steenberghen, *La Philosophie au XIIIe Siècle* (Louvain, Publications Universitaires, 1966), especially pp. 357–412, but the whole latter part of

in 1272 and was appointed regent of studies at Naples, thus ending his Dominican career where it had begun. A mystical experience brought his writing to an end.[32] He was on his way to the Council of Lyon when he fell ill, and he died in the Cistercian monastery at Fossanova, south of Rome, on March 7, 1274.

## The Writings of Thomas

The vast literary production of Thomas can be sorted out in a variety of ways.[33] Weisheipl, in his catalogue of the authentic works of Thomas, discusses the matter at some length and ends by adopting the classification followed in the *New Catholic Encyclopedia*.[34] This divides the works into theological syntheses, academic disputations, expositions of Scripture, expositions of Aristotle, other expositions, polemical writings, special treatises, expert opinions, letters, liturgical works and sermons and doubtfully authentic works.

Given the threefold task of the theologian, we might imagine

---

the book is concerned with the controversy. See Luca Bianchi, *L'errore di Aristotele: La polemica contro l'eternita del mondo nel XIII secolo* (Florence, La Nuova Italia, 1984).

32. See Josef Pieper, *The Silence of St. Thomas*, tr. J. Murray, D. O'Connor (New York, Pantheon, 1957).

33. When we speak of the writings of St. Thomas, we should be aware that he dictated a good number of his works, that some exist as reports by others, not all of which were reviewed by Thomas. We have holographs of Thomas which exhibit his terrible handwriting, the rightly called *litera inintelligibilis*. Doubtless it was this fact, as well as the prolific nature of his genius, that led to the assignment to him of fellow Dominicans like Reginald of Piperno as secretaries. Cf. Antoine Dondaine, *Secrétaires de Saint Thomas* (Rome, Editori di S. Tommaso, S. Sabina 1965), 2 volumes, the second of which consists of illustrative plates.

34. Cf. Weisheipl, *op. laud.*, pp. 356–405. He intends his catalog to complement and not supplant that of Eschmann, which is included in Etienne Gilson's *The Christian Philosophy of St. Thomas Aquinas* (New York, Random House, 1956), pp. 381–439. The Parma edition of the *Opera Omnia* (1852–73) in twenty-five volumes, and the Vives *Opera Omnia* in thirty- four volumes (Paris, 1871–82), both of which include the invaluable *Tabula Aurea* of Peter of Bergamo (1473), are still necessary because the Leonine Edition, commissioned by Leo XIII in 1880, has yet to be completed, though in recent years there has been a spate of volumes. On the composition and classification of the works, see M.-D. Chenu, *Introduction à l'étude de Saint Thomas d'Aquin* (Montreal, Institut d'études medievales, 1950).

classifying the works as expositions, disputations and sermons. This would leave out a sizeable portion of the works, however, most notably the commentaries on Aristotle and various Neoplatonic writers. A feature of these works is that, while their author was a theologian, it is impossible to characterize the works as theological. The fact is that Thomas is the author of an extensive philosophical production. It is convenient, accordingly, to take the division of the writings into philosophical and theological as basic.

*Philosophical Writings.* The very first work of Thomas may well be that *On Modal Propositions*, thought to have been written in 1244–5 as a letter to fellow students at Naples while Thomas was being detained by his family at Roccasecca. A work *On Fallacies* had the same addressees and was written at the same time and place. At Paris, before he became a Master in 1256, Thomas wrote *On Being and Essence* and *On the Principles of Nature*. It can be disputed whether such works as *On the Rule of Princes*, written in Rome about 1267, and that *On Separate Substances* can be classified as philosophical. In any case, there are independent philosophical treatises from the pen of Thomas. But by far the bulk of his philosophical writings consists in the commentaries on Aristotle that he wrote during the last half dozen or so years of his life. Thomas wrote commentaries on the following works of Aristotle: *Perihermeneias* (incomplete), *Posterior Analytics, Physics, De coelo et mundo, On Generation and Corruption, On Meteors, De anima, On Sense and the Sensed Object, On Memory and Reminiscence, Metaphysics, Nicomachean Ethics* and *Politics* (incomplete). This enormous production, accomplished in so compressed a period of time, went on while Thomas was working on *Summa theologiae* and engaged in the controversies of the second Parisian professorship. I discuss at some length in the next chapter the significance of these commentaries, their character, and their relation to the thought of Thomas.

Such commentaries on Neoplatonic works as that on the *Book on Causes* (which Thomas correctly discerned to be excerpted from the *Elements of Theology* of Proclus) and that on Pseudo-Dionysius's *On the Divine Names* can be classified as philosophical.

Such polemical works as that *On the Unicity of Intellect Against the Averroists* and *On the Eternity of the World* should be classified among Thomas's philosophical writings since they reveal his attitude toward the text of Aristotle. Thomas wrote as well a little work *On the Motion of the Heart* and another *On the Mixing of Elements*, yet another *On Buying and Selling on Time*. His works on casting lots, on consulting astrologers, and the hidden operations of nature may be mentioned here, as well as the little work *How to Study* (*De modo studendi*).

As for the expositions that particularly interest us, those on Boethius, the one dealing with *On the Trinity* is of course theological, while that on *De hebdomadibus* is philosophical.

*Theological Writings.* Thomas's work *On the Sentences* of Peter Lombard, the compendium in four books by the twelfth century bishop of Paris, has its origin in Thomas's work as bachelor of theology at Paris. Some of his biblical commentaries may date from his student days as well, but not all. There is a self-styled literal exposition on *Job*, commentaries on the *Psalms* (1–54), on *Isaiah*, on *Jeremiah* (incomplete) and another on the *Lamentations* of Jeremiah. The *Golden Chain* (*Catena Aurea*) is a continuous gloss on the four Gospels gleaned from the Latin and Greek Fathers and undertaken at the wish of Pope Urban IV. There are commentaries on *Matthew* and *John,* though these were taken down by another, the latter by Reginald of Piperno, a fellow Dominican. Thomas commented on all the *Epistles of St. Paul.*

The *Summa contra gentiles*, in four books, was written at the behest of St. Raymond Penafort, as an aid to Dominican missionaries preaching against Moslems, Jews and Christian heretics in Spain, and is dated 1259–64 by Weisheipl. The great unfinished *Summa theologiae* was begun after Thomas returned to Italy, perhaps in 1266. The First Part was completed in 1268. The Second Part spanned the years 1269–72, the second Parisian regency, the *prima secundae* finished about 1270 and the *se-cunda secundae* in 1272. The Third Part, never finished, was begun at Naples in 1272. Thomas also began but did not complete a *Compendium of Theology* for his companion Reginald of Piperno; the work is placed late in his life, perhaps also written at Naples. These three summations of theology did not flow naturally from Thomas's teaching task, but were undertaken as special efforts.

The *Disputed Questions* and the *Quodlibetal Questions* are fairly direct results of Thomas's magisterial activity. The former include the massive collection *On Truth*, other extensive collections such as those *On Evil* and *On God's Power*, as well as briefer disputes on *The Cardinal Virtues*, *On the Virtues in General*, *On Spiritual Creatures*, *On Charity*, and shorter ones *On Fraternal Correction*, *On the Union of the Incarnate Word*, and *On Hope*. There is no more disputed question than when and where the public discussions on which these works are based took place. It is safe to say that the task of disputation covers the whole of Thomas' magisterial career, at Paris and in Italy. The 12 quodlibetal questions have also been the subject of much discussion as to the place and date of their occurrence. There is no question as to the time of year, since this academic exercise was scheduled for Christmas and Easter. Weisheipl divided them into two groups, according to the two Parisian periods.[35]

It is clear from what we have said that some of Thomas's writings explicitly address the Latin Averroist controversy. He also wrote against the secular masters who attacked the religious vocation of the mendicants. *Against Those Impugning the Cult of God and Religion* is one of these, dating from perhaps 1256, and *On the Perfection of the Spiritual Life* and *Against those who would Prevent Boys from Entering Religion*, which were likely written in 1270 and 1271 are instances of this genre. He also compiled for Pope Urban IV in 1263 a work *On the Errors of the Greeks*, meaning the Eastern church. He wrote a work on

35. See Weisheipl, *op. cit.* pp. 367–68.

the faith directed against Saracens, Greeks and Armenians at the request of the Cantor of Antioch in 1264.

But enough. There emerges a picture which in its way complements that of Boethius. Although a layman and statesman, Boethius was caught up in ecclesiastical and theological disputes, rubbed elbows with the great of his day, combined an active life with a life of study. The world of St. Thomas some seven hundred years later was enormously different from that of Boethius. The papacy had become a political as well as a religious force; the elements of ancient learning Boethius and others had put into Latin and refurbished from time to time from other sources had grown into a tradition of education, at first monastic, its tone set by the Vivarium of Cassiodorus Senator, then urban, in cathedral schools after Charlemagne. Secular learning was all but equated with the seven liberal arts, and the liberal arts were seen chiefly as a propaedeutic to the study of Scripture.[36] The tradition has been called Augustinian, but it was of course influenced by others of the Christian Fathers, both Latin and Greek. The twelfth century, which has received so much attention of late, saw the consolidation of that tradition in such massive efforts as the codification of law, the *Glossa Ordinaria*, and efforts like that of Peter Lombard in his *Sentences*. But there were signs of upheaval as well, such dramatic conflicts as that of Bernard of Clairvaux and Peter Abelard, but equally important disputes concerning the nature of monasticism.[37] And the work of expanding the medieval literary arsenal by translations from the Greek and Arabic quickened.

## The Condemnation of 1270

The introduction of Aristotle into the West presented both an opportunity and a threat, and at times it was the threat that seemed most obvious.[38] The Faculty of Arts exhibits obvious

36. See *The Seven Liberal Arts in the Middle Ages*, edited by David L. Wagner (Bloomington, Indiana University Press, 1983).

37. See for example John Van Engen, *Rupert of Deutz* (Berkeley, University of California Press, 1983).

38. See Fernand Van Steenberghen, *Aristotle and the West* (Louvain, Nau-

links to the long tradition of medieval education, since it was sometimes styled the Faculty of the Seven Liberal Arts.[39] The introduction of Aristotle's *Ethics* and *Metaphysics*, to name only two, presented problems for a curriculum based on the liberal arts since the subject matters of these works cannot be reduced to any of the traditional arts.[40] But it is not for reasons of curricular strain that a prohibition against the reading of Aristotle, whether public or private, was issued in 1210. In 1215, the papal legate drew up a body of statutes as guidance for the masters which forbade lectures on the physical and metaphysical books of Aristotle. The point of such prohibitions was the real or apparent conflict between the newly discovered philosophical works and the Faith. But if courses were not to be based on these works, the prohibition was to last only until they had been examined and purged from heresy. It is obvious, then, that the works had to be studied.

The matter was complicated because of the way in which Aristotle came to Northern Europe. At Toledo, Christian and Jewish and Arabic scholars collaborated in turning works from Arabic into Latin.[41] Not only did the text of Aristotle get translated but along with it various commentaries and explanations, notably those of Averroes and Avicenna. Whether the *Commenta-*

weaerts, 1970), and *Saint Thomas and Radical Aristotelianism* (Washington, D.C., the Catholic University of America Press, 1980).

39. The twelfth-century antecedents to the University of Paris were the cathedral school of Notre Dame and the monastic schools of Ste. Geneviève and St. Victor. John of Salisbury, in his *Metalogicon*, gives us a vivid picture of the Parisian situation in the century prior to the founding of the university.

40. This is not to say that the interpretation of the range of an art was not commodious. For example, under Grammar, the study of the poets and historians flourished. At Paris, however, this was not the case in the Faculty of Arts, where the emphasis was on logic.

41. In the translator's prologue of Avicenna on the *De anima* is found this famous description of the technique of translation. "Habetis ergo librum, nobis praecipiente et singula verba vulgariter proferente, et Dominico Archidiacano singula in latinum convertente, ex arabico translatum: in quo, quicquid Aristoteles dixit in libro suo de anima, et de sensu et sensato, et de intellectu et intellecto, ab auctore libri sciatis esse collectum; unde, postquam, volente Deo, hunc habetis, in hoc illos tres plenissime vos habere non dubitetis." *Avicenna Latinus, Liber De Anima I-II-III*, critical edition by S. Van Riet (Louvain, E. Peeters, 1972), p. 4, 11, 21–26. See Rashdall, vol. 1, pp. 356–361.

*tor* was correct in his interpretation of the *Philosophus* thus became a matter of importance. Matters came to a head during St. Thomas's second Paris regency in the so-called Condemnation of 1270, more precisely thirteen propositions condemned by Stephen Tempier, Bishop of Paris, on December 10, 1270. Here they are.

1. That the intellect of all men is one and the same in number.

2. That this is false or inappropriate: Man understands.

3. That the will of man wills or chooses from necessity.

4. That all the things which are done here below depend upon the necessity of the celestial bodies.

5. That the world is eternal.

6. That there never was a first man.

7. That the soul, which is the form of man as a human being, is corrupted when the body is corrupted.

8. That the soul separated after death does not suffer from corporal fire.

9. That free will is a passive power, not active; and that it is moved necessarily by appetite.

10. That God does not know things in particular.

11. That God does not know other things than himself.

12. That human actions are not ruled by divine Providence.

13. That God cannot give immortality or incorruptibility to a corruptible or mortal thing.[42]

The idea of the condemnation is that the propositions condemned are contradictories of propositions believed to be true on the basis of faith. Clearly, if one believes $p$ to be true, he by that very fact believes $-p$ to be false. It is impossible for a proposition and its contradictory to be simultaneously true. If then philosophy—Aristotle—taught as true any of the thirteen propositions, there are two relevant possibilities. Either Aristotle is

---

42. *Chartularium universitatis Parisiensis*, I, 486–87. The translation of the 13 propositions is taken from Lynn Thorndike, *University Records and Life in the Middle Ages* (New York, Columbia University Press, 1949), pp. 80–81.

right, and Christianity wrong, or vice versa. Presumably everyone would agree on this.

Unfortunately, not everyone did. Much scholarly ink has been spilled over the question as to whether or not the Two Truths Theory was actually held by anyone, say by Siger of Brabant. The theory would have it that a proposition could be true for faith while its contradictory opposite is true in philosophy. One thing is clear and that is that contemporaries, St. Thomas Aquinas notably among them, understood certain masters to be holding this theory. It is of course incoherent, being as straightforward a violation of $-(p \cdot -p)$, the Principle of Contradiction, as one could wish. It is also impious, since it suggests that God proposes for our belief as true propositions whose contradictory opposites we can know to be true.[43]

If we rule out this "solution" to the conflict, there are several policies to adopt. One would be to accept as good money what Aristotle is said to have taught, and if the thirteen propositions just quoted are a fair sample of his doctrine, to warn against him as a threat to the truth. It may not be entirely unfair to St. Bonaventure to say that he adopted this policy. What is clear is that he never commented on any work of Aristotle. The policy adopted by Thomas, as is suggested by his writing, was considerably different.

Already at Naples Thomas had been made aware of the "new" learning coming in from Islam as well as directly from the Greek.[44] In Albert he had a master who devoted himself to a

43. Adhuc autem gravius est quod postmodum dicit: "per rationem concludo de necessitate, quod intellectus est unus numero; firmiter tamen teneo oppositum per fidem." Ergo sentit quod fides sit de aliquibus, quorum contraria de necessitate concludi possunt. Cum autem de necessitate concludi non possunt nisi verum necessarium, cuius oppositum est falsum impossibile, sequitur secundum eius dictum quod fides sit de falso impossibili, quod etiam Deus facere non potest: quod fidelium aures ferre non possunt. *De unitate intellectum* n. 267, ed. Marietti.

44. Almost simultaneously with translations made in the quite complicated Toledan manner, translations began to be made directly from the Greek. Indeed, a plurality of Latin versions of given works of Aristotle began to circulate, and one of the concerns of students of a commentary on Aristotle is to figure out which, if any one, of these versions was being used.

vast paraphrase of the Aristotelian corpus. In his earliest writings Thomas already exhibits a receptive and welcoming attitude toward Aristotle and indeed toward philosophical learning generally. Beginning in Italy several years before his return to Paris for his second three-year stint as *Magister regens* in a Dominican chair of theology, Thomas began the massive task of subjecting the writings of Aristotle to a painstaking line-by-line reading. During a period when, as the above list of writings and the following chronology[45] show, he was more than fully engaged in several other important duties, as well as continuing writing the *Summa theologiae*, the Angelic Doctor commented on a majority of the works of Aristotle. This one achievement would have been sufficient to gain him immortality. We will be saying more of the nature of these commentaries in the next chapter; suffice it for now to recall the pithy comment which occurs in Pico della Mirandola. *Sine Thoma Aristoteles mutus esset.* Without the Thomistic commentaries, Aristotle would remain a closed book.

What is of present importance is the relation of this effort to the situation at Paris created by heterodox Aristotelianism and the theological reactions to it. Consider propositions (1), (2) and (7) in the list condemned by Etienne Tempier. Do these represent the thought of Aristotle? Thomas's negative answer is based on a close reading of the text of *De anima*. Both his commentary on that work as well as the polemical opusculum *De unitate intellectus contra averroistas* establish the correct understanding of Aristotle. Correctly understood, the teaching of Aristotle is not only compatible with the Faith, but is of immense philosophical and theological import.

Consider proposition (5). Did Aristotle hold that the world is eternal? Yes. Once Thomas felt that the eternity of the world was taught by Aristotle only as an opinion, but he explicitly rejected this later.[46] Aristotle held that the world never had a beginning; it is a datum of Faith that the world and time had a beginning.

---

45. Appendix A.
46. Cf. *In VIII Physicorum*, lectio 2, n. 986.

Both positions cannot be true. If what Christians believe to be true is true, then Aristotle taught what is false. But Thomas does not leave the matter there. In *De aeternitate mundi contra murmurantes*, he rejects the position that the proposition that the world has always existed is not only false but also incoherent, expressing what could not be true. Thomas disagrees. There is nothing self-contradictory in the claim that the world is eternal. Thus, its falsehood is contingent, not necessary—contingent on the fact that God chose to create the world in time although he could have created an eternal world. Bonaventure, by contrast, argued that the concept of an eternal world is impossible.[47]

It is difficult to overestimate the importance of Thomas's successful defense of the philosophy of Aristotle. What had seemed a threat became an unequivocal part of the intellectual patrimony, the autonomy of natural reason was acknowledged, and the method of theology was elaborated under the influence of the Aristotelian ideal of science with new rigor and precision. The history of western thought would have been profoundly different if Thomas had not shown the middle path between heterodox Aristotelianism and theological obscurantism.

The precise nature of Thomas's achievement in his commentaries on Aristotle is a matter of debate. For far too long, followers of Thomas have treated these commentaries as of little value in understanding their master. Indeed, there has been an amazing tendency on the part of Thomists to drive a wedge between Aquinas and Aristotle. This is a profound mistake. For our purposes, it is important to realize that the negative estimate of Thomas's commentaries on Aristotle has carried over to his commentaries on Boethius. There is almost a consensus that Thomas failed to understand the meaning of the Boethian texts and that his commentaries convey a doctrine which is only tenuously connected with the text being commented on.

It is to these matters that we must now turn.

47. Cf. Bonaventure, *In II Sententiarum*, dist. 1, pars 1, art. 1, q. 2, Respondeo, Florence, 1938, vol. 2, p. 15 ff.

# PART ONE

# The Art of the Commentary

# CHAPTER I

# Commenting on Aristotle

The most obvious point of contact between St. Thomas and Boethius is the commentaries the former wrote on the latter. As has been noted, we have an incomplete commentary on the *De trinitate* and a complete exposition of the *De hebdomadibus*. Discussions have arisen as to the similarities between the thought of Thomas and Boethius, and such discussions are most pointed when they refer to a Boethian text and a comment of Thomas on it. As we will see, Thomists have adopted a very cavalier attitude toward Thomas's commentaries on Boethius, particularly that on the *De hebdomadibus*. It has become commonplace to suggest that what the Thomistic commentary says the Boethian text says is not true, yet somehow this does not lead to what one might think is the obvious judgment on Thomas as commentator.

An explanation of their odd discipleship might be had if these Thomists held a theory of commenting as a recognized convention according to which such fundamental discrepancies were simply the order of the day. On the face of it, however, it seems unlikely that when one man set out to explain the book of another he meant to do anything else than that. We shall need to know, in short, what commentaries are and what Thomas set out to do when he commented on Boethian tractates.

To write a commentary in the thirteenth century was to adopt a literary genre, not to invent one, and among the chief influences on the genre is none other than Boethius himself. We remember that in setting forth his literary project, Boethius planned to put the whole of Aristotle into Latin and then comment on it. "*Ego omne Aristotelis opus quodcunque in manus venerit, in Romanum stylum vertens, eorum omnium commenta*

*Latina oratione perscribam. . . ."* [1] Those commentaries formed part of the patrimony of medieval education. The theory of commenting which is thematically discussed as well as exemplified in them is of enormous importance for understanding what Thomas himself thought a commentary is. Indeed, as we shall see, Thomas will in his own Aristotelian commentaries sometimes take issue with Boethius's interpretation by appealing to the commonly understood task of the commentator.

Thus we must first turn our attention to the Boethian commentaries and to the remarks we find there as to the canons of the genre. Boethius is quite consciously adopting a well-known genre among the Greeks and making it available to the Latins. Once we have achieved some clarity on what Boethius thinks the task of the commentator is, we can put the same question to Thomas, with particular reference to his commentaries on Boethius.

## BOETHIUS AS COMMENTATOR

Boethius's first commentary on the *Isagoge* of Porphyry is described in the second as meant for beginners in logic whereas the second is for the advanced.[2] Chadwick, who feels[3] this is an afterthought some five years later, claims that the second is really no more demanding than the first, but leaves untouched the question why there should be two. Then again, why should there be any?

The answer lies in the project Boethius had set himself, one that if it were well carried out would make the need for Greek works a thing of the past.[4] But just getting the great treasure of logic and ethics and natural philosophy into Latin was not enough: *id quodam lumine commentationis illustrem:* I shall

---

1. *PL* 64, 433C.
2. See Meiser, p. 154, l. 4.
3. Henry Chadwick, *Boethius,* p. 132.
4. "Quocirca multum profecisse videbor, si philosophiae libris Latina oratione compositis per integerrimae translationis sinceritatem, nihil in Graecorum litteris amplius desideratur." *PL* 64, 71A = Meiser, p. 135, ll. 8–13.

clarify it with commentary.[5] This task beyond translation would
have been suggested to him by the practices of Greek culture.
Boethius's own techniques as a commentator are learned from
Greek predecessors. Indeed, much of the recent discussion on the
Boethian commentators has to do with their relation to their
Greek counterparts. Pierre Courcelle was not the first to describe
what Boethius is doing as plagiarism.[6] It would be a considerable
diversion from my purposes to examine in detail the house of
cards Courcelle constructs in order to deprive Boethius of any
claim on our attention as a serious thinker in the area of logic.
The apodictic ring of his assertions can only be explained by the
flimsiness of his evidence. It would of course be another matter
if his judgment of Boethius as largely a plagiarizer were widely
shared. Fortunately it is not. That being said, no one can read
Courcelle without gain.

## Prolegomena to Commentaries

At the beginning of his first commentary on Porphyry, based
on the Latin translation of Marius Victorinus, Boethius refers to
*didascalicis quibusdam* that expositors or commentators use to
induce docility in the minds of students.

Then I said [the work pretends to be a dialogue between Boethius and
Fabius], altogether there are six things that masters first set down in
any exposition. For they first teach what is the *intention* of the work,
which they call its *skopos*; second, what its *usefulness* is, which the
Greeks call *kresimon*; third, what is its *order*, which they call *taxin*;
fourth, whether it is indeed a work of the author, which they usually
express as *gnesion*; fifth, what is the title of the work, named by the
Greeks *epigraphein*. (When the intention of any work is dealt with

5. PL 64, 433D.
6. Pierre Courcelle, *Late Latin Writers and Their Greek Sources*, translated
by Harry E. Wedeck (Cambridge, Harvard University Press, 1969). Boethius on
the *Categories*: ". . . although he plagiarizes Porphyry, as Bidez has shown, he
feels obliged to arrange the schema in six points, whereas Porphyry discussed
only three." (p. 287) Not that Courcelle is singling out Boethius. "Can we not
always imagine, when we know the procedure of the Greek commentators of
Aristotle and their endless and mutual plagiarism, that this resemblance in the
texts is explained by a common source?" (p. 294) "Mutual plagiarism" is a
somewhat puzzling charge, if it is a charge.

clumsily, its intention too will be discussed by those less skilled.) Sixth, the part of philosophy to which the work belongs, given its intention, is discussed, something expressed in the Greek phrase *eis poion meros philosophias anagetai*. All these then it is usual to ask about and deal with in the case of any philosophical work.[7]

Boethius assures Fabius that without the bridge of Porphyry's introduction Aristotle simply could not be understood, and doubtless a close commentary on it is equally requisite for understanding the Aristotelian text.[8]

We will come back to see how Boethius fulfills this sixth task, but first let us make a survey of the beginnings of his commentaries in the light of what he has told us a commentator should always do.

The second commentary on Porphyry, this one on the text of Boethius's own translation, does not of course repeat the six prolegomenal points. Rather, Boethius leads into the work circuitously by mentioning the three powers of the soul, the vegetative, sensitive and mental or rational, with the first serving the second and both serving the third. "This [the third] is wholly constituted in reason, which is taken up either with the firmest conception of present things, the understanding of what is absent, or the inquiry into what is unknown."[9] Our overall task is twofold,

---

7. "Tunc ego: Sex omnino, inquam, magistri in omni expositione praelibant. praedocent enim quae sit cuiuscumque operis intentio, quod apud illos *skopos* uocatur; secundum, quae utilitas, quod a Graecis *kresimon* appellatur; tertium, qui ordo, quod *taxin* uocant; quartum, si eius cuius esse opus dicitur, germanus propriusque liber est, quod *gnesion* interpretari solent; quintum, quae sit eius operis inscriptio, quod *epigraphein* Graeci nominant. in hoc etiam quod intentionem cuiusque libri insollerter interpretarentur, de inscriptione quoque operis apud quosdam minus callentes haesitatum est. sextum, est id dicere, ad quam partem philosophiae cuiuscumque libri ducatur intentio, quod Graeca oratione dicitur *eis poion meros philosophias anagetai*. haec ergo omnia in quolibet philosophiae libro quaeri conuenit atque expediri." Meiser, p. 4.17–5.10 = *PL* 64,9B–C. In the twelfth century, Hugh of St. Victor will use the term *Didascalicon* as title for one of his most important works.

8. Boethius will describe his own treatise, *De syllogismo Categorico*, as a bridge (*quodammo pontem ponere*—*PL* 64,793C), the very term he uses to describe the *Isagoge*. Cf. Brandt, p. 5.13: *introductionis pons*.

9. "eadem tota in ratione constituta est eaque uel in rerum prasentium firmissima conceptione uel in absentium intelligentia uel in ignotarum inquisitione uersatur." Meiser p. 137.6–8 = *PL* 64,71D–72A.

first to know, then to act in accord with knowledge. But there is a great danger that we might equate the way we think with the way things are. Boethius uses the following example. In calculating, there is a one-to-one correspondence between digits and things counted. But it is not so in reasoning. There is a danger not only of reasoning badly about things but of thinking the process of reasoning is identical with the real. We must then first learn to reason well in the various modes of reasoning, namely, discovery and judgment.[10]

Having written two commentaries on Porphyry, Boethius turns to the *Categories* itself, which he will first explain in an undemanding way. Having said that, he turns immediately to the *intentio operis*. The human race alone can impose names on the things that are, but we also have names for our names, such as "name" itself. The second obviously presupposes the first imposition (*prima positio*). "Man is a name." In the *Categories*, Boethius says, things are dealt with not in their proper natures but as signified by names.[11] Such words of second imposition as *genus* and *species*, already discussed by Porphyry in the *Isagoge*, will be brought into play. "Therefore the intention of this work is to treat of words signifying things insofar as they are signifying." [12]

It will expedite matters, Boethius says, if he follows Porphyry closely here. (Such a disclosure ought to be kept in mind when charges of plagiarism are bandied about.) Having discussed the intention of the work, Boethius goes on to note its usefulness, its order, its title and author.[13] And of course, since we are told it is a logical work, we know which part of philosophy it pertains to. If he meant to write a second commentary on the *Categories*, we do not have it. But he tells us that in it he will discuss the intention, usefulness and order of the work.[14]

---

10. *Ibid.*, pp. 138–139 = *PL* 64,72–73.
11. *PL* 64,154.
12. "Est igitur hujus operis intentio de vocibus res significantes, in eo quod significantes sunt, pertractare." *PL* 64,160A.
13. *PL* 64,161B.
14. *PL* 64,160A. "Est vero in mente de intentione, utilitate et ordine, tribus

The first commentary on the *Perihermeneias* announces that it is the first of two and that difficult matters will be postponed until the second.[15] Boethius says he will briefly discuss the intention of the work and he does so by discussing its title, noting that the work deals only with *interpretationes* which are true or false and not with commands and the like. Not all the preliminaries come into play here and those that do seem aspects of a single consideration rather than a series of separate matters.

The second commentary begins with references to a number of Greek commentators. Alexander was prompted to write his commentaries because he found himself in disagreement with existing ones. Boethius notes the tack taken by Vetius Praetextatus of simply putting into Latin the commentary of Themistius on the *Analytics*. Since no one so far as he knows has provided a continuous commentary on the *Perihermeneias*—he means in Latin—he has taken on that task. Whereupon he plunges immediately into what he calls an exceptionally subtle book because of its brevity and succinctness.

The first thing Aristotle must do is define *vox* or expression and, in discussing this, Boethius fulfills some of the prolegomenal tasks. He contrasts the intention of this book with that of the *Categories*[16] as well as noting the different treatment of speech in the *Poetics* and the *Perihermeneias*.[17] We get a much fuller discussion of the interpretative speech that will not be discussed in this work. The five kinds of speech are *deprecativa* or prayerful, *imperativa*, *interrogativa*, *vocativa* and *enunciativa*. Only the last is susceptible of truth or falsity and it alone is the subject of this work.

At this point, Boethius mentions Theophrastus and the Stoics (who have done much with complex propositions) and gives us a florilegium of views of commentators, Alexander, Aspasius,

questionibus disputare, videlicet in alio commentario quem componere proposui de eisdem categoriis ad doctiores."

15. Meiser, p. 32, l. 3.
16. See Meiser, p. 7, ll. 25 ff.
17. Meiser, p. 8, l. 7.

Porphyry, Andronicus. Boethius takes issue with Alexander's view that the title of the work is defective because it does not deal with *interpretatio* or *hermeneia* in general, agreeing with Porphyry's defense. He accepts Alexander's rejection of Andronicus's opinion that this work is not Aristotle's. To Boethius it is clear that, just as the *Perihermeneias* presupposes the *Categories*, so it is presupposed by the *Analytics*. It will thus be seen that Boethius indirectly takes up the six prolegomenal points.

In his commentary on Cicero's *Topica*, Boethius begins with a dedication to Patricius, notes that Marius Victorinus devoted four books of commentary to this work of Cicero's, suggests that a task remains for him to do, and then moves to Cicero's *proemium*, about which he says this.

Omne proemium, quod ad componendum intendit auditorem, ut in rhetoricis discitur, aut benevolentiam captat, aut attentionem praeparat, aut efficit docilitatem. . . .

As one learns in rhetoric texts, every proemium that aims at winning over its hearer seeks to obtain goodwill, prepares attentiveness, or produces aptness for learning. . . .[18]

We will see Thomas keeping an eye out for such proemial notes in the introductory portions of the works on which he comments. It is interesting that Boethius contrasts his own commentary on Cicero with that of Marius Victorinus by saying that, unlike the latter, he will not get bogged down in the examination of isolated words but try to give a sense of the whole.[19] If Boethius will sometimes reject the interpretations of other commentators, he will do so because there is a reasonable basis in the text to reject them. Sometimes, however, that basis is sought in more general views. Every effort is made to understand what the text is saying because, the assumption is, what the text is saying is true. A man who took on the literary project that Boethius did, whose ultimate objective was to show that Aristotle and

18. *PL* 64,1042D. Trans. Eleonore Stump, *Boethius In Ciceronis Topica* (Ithaca, Cornell University Press, 1988), p. 22.
19. *PL* 64,1044C.

Plato were in agreement with one another, is not likely to think a text of Aristotle is in disagreement with itself or with other writings of Aristotle.

In the logical works, Boethius as commentator urges a particular ordering of those books. Clearly, Porphyry's *Introduction to the Categories* should be read before the *Categories*, and this is to give Porphyry pride of place among the commentators. Plato and Aristotle are *the* authors and thus possess *auctoritas*, a term that Boethius applies to Porphyry himself.[20] After the *Categories* come the *Analytics*.[21] With such stress put on the order among different Aristotelian works, we are not surprised by the attention paid to the internal order of a work.

As someone joining a long distinguished line and having the added task of putting the authoritative texts into Latin, it is hardly surprising that Boethius would look to his predecessors. One would be stunned not to find the similarities which have led to excessive judgments such as those we find in Courcelle. The point of the commenting endeavor is not to come up with a novel and personal reading, but to get the text right.

It is the text, the *opus*, that is the center of attention and it is approached almost with reverence. The working assumption is that the text contains the truth and the reader's task is to find it. We remember that one of the aims of the proemium was to produce docility in the reader.

## The Sixth Didascalicon

Given the similarities between Ammonius and Boethius that were pointed out by Brandt,[22] it is worth noting that what Ammonius mentions as the sixth preliminary thing to be done by the commentator is to divide the text into chapters.[23] Boethius,

---

20. PL 64,814C. See Chadwick, *op. cit.*, p. 134.

21. Just as in the *Perihermeneias* Aristotle concentrates on the simple proposition, so in the *Analytics* he concentrates on syllogisms made up of simple propositions. The former is ordered to the latter. PL 64,397D–398A.

22. Cf. CSEL, 48, pp. VII–XXVII. Also cf. Luca Obertello, *Severino Boezio* (Genova, Academia ligura di scienze e lettere, 1974), p.530.

23. Ammonius, *In Categorias*, ed. Busse, p. 8, l. 6.

we recall, gave as the sixth task assigning the work in question to the appropriate part of philosophy. Ammonius is emphasizing the internal order of the text whereas Boethius is emphasizing the overall philosophical order which illuminates the text. It is just this question as to the appropriate part of philosophy that creates a difficulty when the work to be commented on is a logical one.

Is logic a part of philosophy? Any answer to the question clearly depends on what we mean by "philosophy" and what we mean by "logic." We have at least a preliminary notion of the first from the Introduction, and the preceding paragraphs had things to say about the contents of logical works. Nonetheless, it seems well to get clearer on the nature of logic.

Our chronology in the appendix makes it clear that Boethius was concerned with logic throughout his career; his logical writings include translations, commentaries and independent treatises. As to what logic is, we know from the above that for Boethius logic comprises a vast but ordered set of discussions, not quite all of which have been the subjects of Aristotelian works. The goal or telos of the study of logic is to get clear about arguments, about syllogisms. Syllogism is discussed in a number of works but the basic doctrine is laid out in the *Prior Analytics*.

Thus it is that those wishing to learn logic should first read this book (*Categories*). The whole of logic is concerned with the nature of syllogism which is a conjunction of propositions, but propositions are made up of words and that is why it is of the first importance for the meaning of science to know what words mean.[24]

A syllogism is made up of propositions, but before considering the peculiar syllogistic conjunction of propositions and the role propositions play as premises or conclusions, we should first study the proposition itself, especially insofar as it is the carrier

24. "Hinc est quod ad logicum tendentibus primus hic liber legendus occurit, idcirco quod cum omnis logica syllogismorum ratione sit constituta, syllogismi vero propositionibus jungantur, propositiones vero sermonibus constent, prima est utilitas quid quisque sermo significet, propriae scientiae diffinitione cognoscere." *PL* 64,161B.

of truth or falsity. The proposition, however, is made up of terms, and these can be discussed either with regard to the roles they play in propositions—as subject or predicate—or in themselves. Terms as such are expressive of things, so that to know the meaning of a term is, ideally, to know the definition of a thing. The *Categories* is seen as part of the logic of definition.[25] The order referred to here is not simply that of the dependence of the complex on its components; it is also a pedagogical order.[26]

When logic is said to prepare a way (*quasi quandam uiam parat*),[27] we will be put in mind of the liberal arts and indeed Boethius immediately discusses the relation of logic to grammar and rhetoric. Although he never calls these a *trivium*, he fashioned the term *quadrivium* to cover the mathematical arts: arithemetic, geometry, music and astronomy.[28]

What is logic about? "Every account of discourse, what the old Peripatetics called logic, is divided into two parts, one of discovering, the other of judging. That part which instructs and purifies judgment, called Analytic by them, we can call the Resolutive, and that which serves the capacity for discovering is called Topics by the Greeks and *Localis* by us."[29] How exactly

25. Here is a good summary statement: "quoniam categoriae ad propositiones aptantur, syllogismi de propositionibus componuntur, apodictici uero uel dialectici syllogismi in logicae artis disciplina uertuntur, constat quoque categorias, quae ad propositiones syllogismosque pertinent, logicae scientiae esse conexas. quare introductio quoque in categorias ad logicam scientiam conuenieter aptabitur." Brandt, pp. 15, ll. 15–21. Boethius's own *Liber de divisione* is a contribution to the logic of definition. PL 64,875–892.

26. This is clear throughout the discussion of *ordo* that begins on Brandt, p. 12, l. 17 and continues through p. 15.22. A neat summary is found on p. 14, lines 18–23: "sic igitur cum ante apodicticam dialecticamque rem syllogistica praelegatur, ante syllogisticam in propositionibus primus labor sit. ante propositiones in categoriis pauca desudent, ante categorias quae generibus, speciebus, differentiis, propriis accidentibusque censentur, ordo est de his ipsis rebus pauca praelibare." The reiteration of *ante* and the prefix *prae* underscores the temporal progression.

27. Bra:dt, p. 10, ll. 7–8.

28. PL 63,1079D, *De arithmetica*, and PL 63,1168C, *De musica*.

29. *De differentiis topicis*, 1173B: "Omnis ratio disserendi, quam logicen Peripatetici veteres appellavere, in duas distribuitur partes, unam inveniendi, alteram judicandi. Et ea quidem pars quae judicium purgat atque instruit, ab illis analyt-

are we to characterize such concerns? Boethius, we remember, contrasted calculation or counting and logic by suggesting that while there is a necessary fit between the counting and the counted, it would be a big mistake to think that rigor of reasoning implies rigor in the things reasoned about. We must not equate *sermo* and *natura*.[30] It has been said that Neoplatonic logic differed from the Aristotelian in being more formal and less tied to ontology.[31] Luca Obertello, on the other hand, seems to say that since the *Categories* is not a logical work, Boethius's interpretation of it as logical misses its point. We do seem to be told conflicting things by Boethius. On the one hand, the *Categories* is concerned with the types of things; on the other, it forms part of the art of reasoning.

Consider the following lengthy passage which occurs very early in Boethius's commentary on the *Categories*.

The human race alone can impose names on the things about us which are what they are chiefly by the proper constitution of their nature. Thus it happens that for each of the things man's mind grasps he can fashion a name. For example, he calls this body "man," that "stone," this "wood" and another "color." Whatever generates another out of itself he calls "father" and assigns its own name to the measure of magnitude, calling it "two feet" or "three feet," and so in like manner with other things. Once names have been fashioned, he turns his attention to the properties and figures of words, and he calls "noun" that form of word which can be inflected in cases and that which is distributed in tenses the "verb." That then is the first imposition of names through which he designates objects of intellect or sense; the second consideration whereby each property and form of names is looked at—such that the first imposition is the very name of a thing, as for example when something is called a man, and then the very word "man" is said to be

---

ice vocata, a nobis potest resolutoria nuncupari. Ea vero quae inveniendi facultatem subministrat, a Graecis topice, a nobis localis dicitur."

30. *PL* 64,72D–73A: "Hic vero magnus est error: nec enim sese res ut in numeris, ita etiam in ratiocinationibus habet. In numeris enim quidquid in digitis recte computantis evenit, id sine dubio in res quoque ipsas necesse est evenire: ut si ex calculo centum esse contigerit, centum quoque res illi numero subjectas esse necesse est: hoc vero non aeque in disputatione servat; nec enim quidquid sermonum decursus invenerit, id natura quoque fixum tenetur."

31. Cf. A. C. Lloyd, "Neoplatonic Logic and Aristotelian Logic," *Phronesis*, I, (1955–56), pp. 58–72 and 439–53.

a name—does not refer to the signification of the term but to its figure, namely, that it can be inflected in cases. Therefore, the first imposition of the name is according to the signification of the word, but the second is such that names are designated by other names.[32]

First and second order naming, then, with some words signifying things, other words being the names of words. Boethius reserves the term *signification* for the relation between name and thing. The contrast is variously expressed: *prima positio* and *secunda positio*, *nomina rerum* and *nomina nominum*. Names in the first sense are appelatives or are said to have *appelatio*, the second do not.

With this made clear, Boethius can now tell us what the intention of the *Categories* is.

The intention of this book is to dispute concerning the first names of things and the words signifying things, not insofar as they are formed according to some property or figure, but insofar as they are significant.[33]

The discussions of the *Categories* are about substance, quantity, quality, relation, and so on, but these words will not be discussed in terms of the properties of nouns but with reference to the real

32. "Rebus praejacentibus, et in propria principaliter naturae constitutione manentibus, humanum solum genus existit, quod rebus nomina posset imponere. Unde factum est ut sigillatim omnia prosecutus hominis animis singulis vocabula rebus aptaret. Et hoc quidem, verbi gratia, corpus hominem vocavit, illud vero lapidem, aliud lignum, aliud vero colorem. Et rursus quicunque ex se alium genuisset, patris vocabulo nuncupavit. Mensuram quoque magnitudinis proprii forma nominis terminavit, ut diceret bipedale est, vel tripedale, et in aliis eodem modo. Omnibus ergo nominibus ordinatis, ad ipsorum rursus vocabulorum proprietates figurasque reversus est, et hujusmodi vocabuli formam, quae inflecti casibus possit, nomen vocavit; quae vero temporibus distribui, verbum. Prima igitur illa fuit nominum positio, per quam vel intellectui subjecta vel sensibus designaret. Secundo consideratio, qua singulas proprietates nominum figurasque perspicerent, ita ut primum nomen sit ipsum rei vocabulum: ut, verbi gratia, cum quaelibet res homo dicatur. Quod autem ipsum vocabulum, id est homo, nomen vocatur, non ad significationem nominis ipsius refertur, sed ad figuram, idcirco quod possit casibus inflecti. Ergo prima positio nominis secundum signficationem vocabuli est, secunda vero ut aliis nominibus ipsa nomina designarentur." *PL* 64,159A–C.

33. "In hoc opere haec intentio est, de primis rerum nominibus et de vocibus significantibus disputare, non in eo quod secundum aliquam proprietatem figuramque formantur, sed in eo quod significantes sunt." *PL* 64,159C.

things they are used to designate. Of course, anyone who set out to discuss whatever real things are signified by human language would be embarked on an endless task. If the number of things is infinite, it looks as though the number of words signifying them would be equally infinite, but *infinitorum scientia nulla est*: the infinite cannot be known by the human mind. This is why Aristotle intends to discuss not the infinity of things that might be signified but rather the ten categories of things.[34] Horse, man, wood, rock, stone, animal can all be called substance. So, too, quantity and quality and the others can tame infinity in their genera. But how does "Man is a substance" differ from "Man is a noun"?

Therefore what we call the ten categories are genera of the infinity of things signified by words, but since all words signify things, which are signified by the word as signifying, they necessarily signify the genera of things. So, to conclude our discussion of its intention, we should say that in this book are treated the first words signifying the first genera of things insofar as they are signifying.[35]

This is the passage that not unsurprisingly gives Obertello trouble, but before discussing that let us summarize what we now know of Boethius's conception of logic.

The aim of logic is argument, and the syllogism is its form. Logic cannot just begin with argument, however, but must go into its proximate and remote constituents. The propositions which enter into arguments can be discussed apart, and the words which enter into propositions can be discussed apart. The logic of terms taken alone is the logic of definition and the *Categories* deals with incomplex things. In this way, the work would seem to form part of logic. Does this give us a way of distin-

---

34. Actually Aristotle in the *Sophistical Refutations* says that it is just because language is not infinite as is reality that it enables us to master the real.

35. "Ergo decem praedicamenta quae dicimus, infinitarum in vocibus significationum genera sunt, sed quoniam omnis vocum significatio de rebus est, quae voce significantur in eo quod significantes sunt, genera rerum necessario significabunt. Ut igitur concludenda sit intentio, dicendum est in hoc libro de primis vocibus, prima rerum genera significantibus in eo quod significantes sunt, dispositum esse tractatum." *PL* 64,161A.

guishing the logician's and the grammarian's concern with language?

Boethius, as we have noted, distinguishes logic, grammar and rhetoric. He speaks of the logical art as that which enables us to achieve truth by way of correct discourse and to avoid the error due to fallacy. In the first commentary on Porphyry, Boethius says that logic deals with genus, species, difference, property and accident, but these are also said to be useful to the grammarian when he distinguishes the parts of speech. The five predicables are also of use to the rhetor.[36] Elsewhere he says that "the grammarian treats any part of speech differently from the logician, much as the mathematician and natural philosopher treat line and surface differently." [37] Perhaps this could be developed to say that, just as the natural philosopher's concern with the line must take into account its properties in nature (e.g. moist, cool, smooth) whereas the geometer ignores them, so too the concern with *prima nomina* must take into account the things that are signified by them, but this is not so with *nomina nominum*. The logician would then be concerned with language as significant of real things, the grammarian with syntactical matters.

Luca Obertello holds that the *Categories* is a work in ontology, although he finds the text ambiguous. It begins with a discussion of homonyms and synonyms—equivocals and univocals—and Obertello finds the "text unclear whether it means to speak of words or of things." [38] He surveys the commentators and singles out Jamblichus who holds that the *Categories* treats at once of words, things and thoughts. Words are considered as signifying things, and things as they are manifested through language and thought is what establishes the relation between word and thing.[39] Obertello concludes: "The *Categories* consequently is not primarily a work of logic but of ontology (that is to say, a

---

36. PL 64,12C. Cf. Eleonore Stump, "Boethius's Works on the *Topics*," *Vivarium*, XII, 2 (1974), pp. 77–93.
37. *Introductio ad syllogismos categoricos*, PL 64,762C.
38. *Severino Boezio*, Vol. I, p. 592.
39. *Ibid.*, p. 594.

work which investigates existing things in their real relations); nonetheless, it is obvious that such research affords precious elements of logical theory, since the principles of reality are also principles of discourse."[40] It is not easy to understand such an identity. Are the starting points of talk and the starting points of reality the same? Obertello gives discourse a fairly central role in Aristotle's understanding of what he is doing while contrasting Aristotle's view with that of Boethius.

Aristotle considers *things* insofar as they are spoken of and become objects of discourse; Boethius, on the other hand, considers *names* insofar as they are *res significantes*, that is, insofar as they signify things, indicate them, designate them, manifest them. In the first case, reality must be defined as "that which is indicated by the name" and, in the second, the name as "that which indicates reality."[41]

Although the contrast is verbally clear, it is by no means clear what difference it is supposed to make: the thing signified by the name and the name signifying the thing would seem to imply one another so thoroughly that it makes little difference where one begins. Unless of course the contrast is between a consideration of the things meant by words but not as meant by words and a consideration of words that mean things but not as meaning things. But this does not seem to be what Obertello has in mind. This is important because he is saying that Boethius is mistaken about the very nature of the *Categories*. If Obertello cannot clarify what the *Categories* is really about, his charge becomes idle. He makes another try at stating the opposition between Aristotle's and Boethius's understanding of the nature of the *Categories* with reference to a passage in the *prooemium*.

40. "Le *Categorie* non sono pertanto e primariamente un'opera di logica, ma di ontologia (ossia un'opera che indaga le cose existenti nel loro rapporti reali); e peraltro ovvio che tale ricerca fornisce dei preziosi elementi alla teoria logica, poiche i principii della realta sono anche i principi del discorso." *Ibid*, p. 594.

41. ". . . Aristotele consideri *le cose* in quanto vengono dette e sono oggetto di un discorso; Boezio considera invece *i nomi* in quanto *res significantes*, ossia in quanto significano le cose, le indicano, le designano, le manifestano. Nel primo caso la realta deve essere definita come 'cio che e indicata dal nome' nel secondo il nome come 'cio che indica la realta.'" *Ibid*.

Alluding to the distinction Boethius makes between names of first and second imposition, Obertello remarks that it is obvious that names are not just names, that is, "every name has an intrinsic intentional reference to the reality which corresponds to it." [42] He regards the categorial classification of names as in a certain way a categorial classification of beings. Quoting this passage, "since things are the signification of any name, the genera of things necessarily signify what are signified by names insofar as they are signifying," Obertello feels there must be a missing premise, namely, that there is a biunivocal correspondence between things and words, between reality and language. [43] Here is the argument Obertello apparently has in mind.

(1) There is a biunivocal correspondence between words and things.

(2) *Omnis significatio vocum de rebus est.*

From which follows:

(3) *Quae voce significantur, in eo quod significantes sunt, genera rerum necessario significabunt.*

Not only is Obertello's supplied premise of no help in deriving the conclusion, its meaning is unclear. It could mean "Whatever relations are found among things are found among words, and vice versa," but this makes (2) somewhat otiose and, in any case, the conclusion would then be something like: "The relations among the words that signify them are matched by the things signified." How can Boethius arrive at the conclusion that words, as significant, necessarily signify the genera of things? Doubtless by employing the premise he explicitly sets down in the text: The ten categories are the genera of the infinite significations of words. Boethius's argument is as follows:

(1*) *Decem praedicamenta quae dicimus, infinitarum in vocibus significationum genera sunt,*

42. *Ibid.*, p. 599.
43. The passage from Boethius is *PL* 64,161A; the reference to Obertello is p. 599.

(2) *sed quoniam omnis vocum significatio de rebus est,*

(3) *quae voce significantur in eo quod significantes sunt, genera rerum necessario significabunt.*

There is no need to supply a premise in order to help Boethius make his point. This is not a small point; it is profoundly important. Chief among the real things signified by *prima nomina* are the categories or genera of things. That is as flat a statement as one could ask that genera are real. Obertello ignores this essential feature of the argument since he is in pursuit of a contrast between Aristotle and Boethius that never clearly emerges.[44]

Obertello's appeal to the *prooemium* of the commentary on the *Categories* in search of further clarity on Boethius's conception of logic yields mixed results. The distinction between names of things and names of names seems to suggest a difference between the grammarian's and the logician's concern with language, but because of the use of the example of the different accounts of noun and verb that we find in *On Interpretation*, a logical work, the contrast does not wear its meaning on its face. What seems clear is that Boethius is telling us that in the *Categories* we are concerned with things talked about and not our talk about them. Obertello oddly finds this formalistic (*filogistica mentalità*) and contrasts it with Aristotle's ontological intention, but Obertello never succeeds in manifesting this contrast.

What is truly important is that Boethius claims that among the real things signified by words are genera. Taken at face value, this claim amounts to a solution of the problem of universals of

44. Immediately after stating the premise he imagines the argument of Boethius needs, Obertello writes, "Questo non e diverso da cio che avrebbe detto Aristotele (e che in realta disse, anche nelle *Categorie*). Tuttavia in Boezio l'accento e diversamente posto. Aristotele parte dalla ricognizione della realta, che e sempre un *primum* anteriore al linguaggio. La sua occupazione e di far emergere le strutture dell'essere, al di la e al di sopra (o al di sotto—l'immagine e altrettanto vicina al pensiero di Aristotele) del linguaggio: 'ogni significazione delle voce riguarda le cose,' e non piu 'delle cose che sono dette, le une son dette di un soggetto' (*Categories*, 1a20). Il nocciolo della questione per Boezio sta dunque nel problema della significazione: le parole, o voci significanti 'in quanto sono significanti' (o, per tradurre meglio 'in cio che sono significanti') 'significheranno necessariamente i generi delle cose.'" *Ibid.*, p. 599.

a decidedly realistic sort, but more on that shortly. For now, it seems clear that it is the *Categories* that is difficult to describe, either as logical or as ontological, something reflected in the vacillations of Obertello and DeRijk.[45]

The claim that the significations of words in their first use or imposition are things (*nomina rerum*) suggests comparison with Boethius's discussion of the famous passage in the *Isagoge* where the status of such universals as genus and species is asked about. Before turning to that, however, we must first complete our discussion of the status of logic. Is it to be accounted a part of philosophy or merely its instrument? Boethius examines arguments on both sides and then attempts an adjudication.

*Logic Is a Part of Philosophy.* Those who hold logic to be a part of philosophy ground their position in the following arguments. It is beyond doubt that philosophy has two parts, a speculative and an active. It is equally indubitable that logic constitutes a third part of philosophy. This is an appeal to the Stoic division of philosophy into physics, ethics and logic. Only philosophy is concerned with natural science, that is, with speculative philosophy, and only philosophy is concerned with morals and other matters pertaining to active science. It is equally true that only philosophy is concerned with logic. Therefore, by parity, logic must be part of philosophy. This means that a discipline is a part of philosophy if it is the concern of philosophy alone. Logic fulfills the condition. Therefore . . .

But a difficulty arises. Is logic really a distinct discipline?

There is no doubt that logic is a discipline distinct from natural science and moral science because of the nature of its subject. For logic treats of propositions and syllogisms and other like things, something which cannot be said either of the part [of philosophy] which considers things rather than talk, nor of the active part which looks to morals.[46]

45. Cf. L. M. De Rijk, *The Place of the Categories of Being in Aristotle's Philosophy* (Assen, Netherlands, Van Gorcum, 1952). "The logical and ontological side of the doctrine of the categories are wholly interwoven for Aristotle." (p. 88) Perhaps what De Rijk meant to say is that *what* is categorized is real, but *categorizing* is logical.

46. "Dubium non est quin logica disciplina a naturali atque morali suae ma-

Boethius says that this is to distinguish the various parts of philosophy with reference to their goals or ends. Earlier he had made explicit what the ends of speculative and practical philosophy are. "The one indeed seeks to know the natures of things by way of a determinate notion of inquiry, whereas the other seeks first to acquire knowledge that we might then act with moral seriousness." [47] The end of logic is specified negatively: it is not concerned with the natures of things nor with putting into practice knowledge of what is to be done. Put more positively, logic is concerned with discourse (*oratio*).

Boethius is here recounting one side of a controversy but nothing he says in his own name conflicts with this characterization of logic. Logic does not have as its goal knowledge of the things that are, the natures of things. This does not seem to sit well with his characterization of the intention of the *Categories*. In that logical work, Aristotle is said to be concerned with *prima nomina* only insofar as they signify real things. Among the real things signified by such names are the genera of things. The genera of things, however, would seem to pertain to discourse, since a genus has been defined by Porphyry as that which is said of many specifically different things.

Boethius seems to hold two incompatible views of logic. Moreover, as we shall see, the view expressed in the commentary on the *Categories* is clearly at variance with the solution to the problem of universals Boethius advances in his second commentary on Porphyry.

*Logic Is Not a Part of Philosophy.* Those who hold that logic is not a part, but only an instrument of philosophy, argue as follows. The end of logic is not like the ends of speculative and active philosophy. Both look to their proper ends, knowledge of

---

teriae proprietate distincta sit. Etenim logicae tractatus est de propositionibus atque syllogismis et caeteris hujusmodi, quod neque ea quae non de oratione sed de rebus speculatur, neque activa pars quae de moribus invigilat, aeque praestare potest." *PL* 64,74A.

47. "Unum quidem, ut rerum naturas inquisitionis certa ratione cognoscat; alterum vero, ut ad scientiam prius veniat quod post gravitas moralis exerceat." *Ibid.,* 72B–C.

things, rules of life, respectively, and the one is not confused with the other.

The end of logic, however, cannot be isolated but is in a certain way linked to and constricted by the other two parts. An argument brings us to knowledge of some sort or other, either of what is true or of what is likely, but this science of arguments is referred either to knowledge of things or to discovering things which in the practice of morality lead to happiness.[48]

The aim of logic is thus absorbed into the end of speculative or moral inquiry since the end of successful argumentation is either the true or the likely about the things that are or concerns what is conducive to happiness. Having no distinct end of its own, logic cannot be an independent part of philosophy but is merely its instrument.

*Boethius Adjudicates the Dispute.* Boethius feels this dispute can be amicably settled provided that nothing prevents logic from having both the status of part of philosophy and that of serving an instrumental function with regard to the other two parts. In short, he sees merit on both sides of the dispute and is anxious to appropriate the insights of the opposed camps.

Insofar as logic has an end of its own and is studied only by philosophy—accepting both criteria for being a part of philosophy supplied by the disputants—logic will be part of philosophy. Insofar as logic, because of its end, is useful to the other two parts, it will be an instrument. What is the end of logic? "Est autem finis logicae inventio judiciumque rationum: the aim of logic is the discovery and appraisal of arguments."[49] Boethius feels an analogy may be helpful. We need not wonder that logic is at once a part of philosophy and an instrument of the other parts since a similar observation must be made when the parts

48. "Logicae vero finis esse non potest absolutus, sed quodammodo cum reliquis duabus partibus colligatus atque constrictus est. Scire enim quemadmodum argumentatio concludatur, vel quae vera sit, quae veresimilis, ad hoc scilicet tendit, ut vel ad cognitionem rerum referatur haec rationum scientia, vel ad invenienda ea quae in exercitium moralitatis adducta beatitudinem pariunt." *Ibid.*, 74C.
49. *Ibid.*, 74D.

of the body are referred to soul. A part of the body is, of course, a part, but it is also an instrument of the soul; hence our talk of the organic body. Hence too the use of the Greek term *organon* (instrument) to cover all the logical writings of Aristotle. The hand is used for dragging, the eye for seeing, and both parts are instruments of another part, the soul. So too the discipline of logic is a particular part of philosophy yet is also an instrument through which the truth of philosophy is achieved.[50]

Throughout this discussion, Boethius accepts the description of logic as concerned not with things but with discourse or argumentation. This is scarcely compatible with his characterization of the *Categories*, a logical work, as being concerned not with the forms and figures of language, but with language as significant, that is, as designating things. Now, if the *Categories* is not a logical work, as Obertello says it is not, there is no problem. But it is perfectly clear that Boethius considers it a logical work. It discusses things necessary for propositions, which in turn are constituents of arguments, which are the chief concern of logic. The problem is complicated when we find Boethius listing genera among the things signified by *primae voces*, since this entails that genera are things. But elsewhere Boethius gives an account of genera offered by Alexander of Aphrodisias according to which genera are not things.

We will consider the celebrated problem of universals in the next chapter. But first, let us see what Thomas Aquinas has to say about the nature of logic.

## St. Thomas and the Nature of Logic

Thomas commented on two Aristotelian logical works, the *Perihermeneias* (incomplete) and the *Posterior Analytics*. The *prooemia* he wrote to these commentaries provide succinct statements of his teaching on the nature of logic.

Thomas begins the proemium to his commentary on the *Perih-*

---

50. "Ita quoque logica disciplina pars quaedam philosophiae est. Suppellex vero est, quod per eam inquisita veritas philosophiae vestigatur." *Ibid.*, 75A.

*ermeneias* by citing the *De anima* to the effect that there is a twofold activity of mind, one which is called the understanding of indivisibles or simples whereby the essence of a thing is grasped, and another which consists of composing and dividing.

To these a third operation is added, namely reasoning, whereby reason proceeds from what is known to inquire into what is unknown. Of these operations, the first is ordered to the second (because there can only be composition and division of apprehended simples) and the second is ordered to the third (because it is from some known truth to which it assents that intellect proceeds to accept with certitude unknown things).[51]

Logic bears on each of these mental operations, Aristotle's *Categories* being concerned with the first, the *Perihermeneias* with the second, the *Prior Analytics* and the Aristotelian works following on it with the third operation. Having placed the work, Thomas then begins to speak of the *Perihermeneias* as such.

In the *prooemium* to his commentary on the *Posterior Analytics*, Thomas gives a far more detailed statement of the subdivisions of logic and their correlation with Aristotelian works. Noting that it is characteristic of human beings that they live by art and reason, Thomas reminds us of Aristotle's definition of art as *"certa ordinatio rationis quomodo per determinata media ad debitum finem actus humani perveniant*: the fixed guidance of reason whereby human acts achieve their ends in a definite way."[52] Reason directs external acts and the activities of the lower powers but is also capable of directing its own activity.

For it is proper to the intellectual part that it reflect on itself: understanding understands itself and reason can reason about its own activity. The consequence of reason's reasoning about manual activity is the

---

51. "Additur autem et tertia operatio, scilicet ratiocinandi, secundum quod ratio procedit a notis ad inquisitionem ignotorum. Harum autem operationum prima ordinatur ad secundam: quia non potest esse compositio et divisio nisi simplicium apprehensorum. Secunda vera ordinatur ad tertiam: quia videlicet oportet quod ex aliquo vero cognito, cui intellectus assentiat, procedatur ad certitudinem accipiendam de aliquibus ignotis." *In libros Peri Hermeneias Expositio*, n. 1.

52. *In libros Posteriorum Analyticorum Expositio*, n. 1.

art of making or building whereby a man in an easy and orderly fashion performs such acts. In much the same way an art is needed to direct reasoning activity itself so that a man can engage in the act of reasoning in an orderly way, easily and without error. This art is logic, that is, the science of reasoning.[53]

Logic is the "art of arts" since it is directive of the very activity of reason itself; insofar as there are different acts of reason, there are corresponding parts of logic. But there are three acts of reason, Thomas notes, one of which is the understanding of simple and incomplex things as when the mind grasps what a thing is. Aristotle's *Categories* deals with the directing of this activity. The *Perihermeneias* is concerned with the mental activity of composing and dividing where truth or falsity is had. The third act of reason is the reason it is called reason. This is discursive activity, moving from one thing to another in such a way that the first makes the second known.[54]

Thomas suggests that there is an analogy of sorts between activities of reason and natural activities, unsurprising of course since art imitates nature. In nature some things occur necessarily, without fail, whereas others come about for the most part and thus some rarely, when nature fails. And so it is in reasoning: sometimes it is characterized by necessity, achieving truth without fail; sometimes it concludes what is usually though not necessarily true; sometimes reason fails to arrive at the true because of a defect of some principle which should govern it.

The part of logic which serves the first process is called the judicative part because judgment is certitude of knowledge. Because a certain knowledge of effects can only be had by resolving them into their first principles this part is called the analytic or resolutive. The certainty of judgment had through resolution comes either from the *form* of syllo-

53. "Hoc enim est proprium intellectivae partis, ut in seipsam reflectatur: nam intellectus intelligit seipsam et similiter ratio de suo actu ratiocinari potest. Si igitur ex hoc, quod ratio de actu manus ratiocinatur, adinenta est arts aedificatoria vel fabrilis, per quas homo faciliter et ordinate huiusmodi actus exercere potest; eadem ratione ars quaedam necessaria est, quae sit directiva ipsius actus rationis, per quam scilicet homo in ipso actu rationis ordinate, faciliter et sine errore procedat. Et haec ars est *Logica*, idest rationalis scientia." *Ibid.*, nn. 1–2.

54. *Ibid.*, n. 4.

gism alone, to which the *Prior Analytics* which deals with syllogism as such is devoted, or from the *matter* as well because it makes use of *per se* and necessary propositions. The *Posterior Analytics* which treats of demonstrative syllogism is devoted to this.[55]

The process of reason which only for the most part arrives at truth is served by the inventive part of logic, for discovery is not always characterized by certitude. And just as in natural events which do not occur necessarily there is a range of frequency, so is it with mental activity which falls short of necessary truth.

Sometimes this process produces faith or opinion because of the probability of the propositions from which it proceeds. The process of reasoning is ordered to concluding a given proposition and excluding its contradictory. Opinion is had when the mind is completely committed to one side of a contradiction, to *p* as opposed to − *p*, but with uneasiness that the opposite could be true. Such reasoning is dialectical. Aristotle's *Topics* concerns reasoning of this kind.

Sometimes what is arrived at is not opinion, but only a suspicion that one side of the contradiction is true and the mind is more inclined to that. Aristotle's *Rhetoric* deals with this kind of discourse.

Sometimes only an intimation inclines the mind to one of contradictories thanks to a representation, as a certain food becomes abominable to a person because it is presented in a certain way. Aristotle's *Poetics* is concerned with his kind of discourse, it being peculiar to the poet to incline us to the virtuous by way of a fitting representation.[56]

Such are the parts of logic and the Aristotelian works corre-

55. "Pars autem Logicae, quae *primo* deservit processui, pars *Iudicativa* dicitur, eo quod iudicium est cum certitudine scientiae. Et quia iudicium certum de effectibus haberi non potest nisi resolvendo in prima principia, ideo pars haec *Analytica* vocatur, idest resolutoria. Certitudo autem iudicii, quae per resolutionem habetur, est, vel ex ipsa *forma* syllogismi tantum, et ad hoc ordinatur liber *Priorum Analyticorum*, qui est de syllogismo simpliciter; vel etiam cum hoc ex *materia*, quae sumuntur propositiones per se et necessariae, et ad hoc ordinatur liber *Posteriorum Analyticorum*, qui est de syllogismo demonstrativo." *Ibid.*, n. 6.

56. ". . . nam poetae est inducere ad aliquod virtuosum per aliquam decentem repraesentationem." *Ibid.*, n. 6. See my *Rhyme and Reason: St. Thomas and*

sponding to them. But is there not a kind of mental activity analogous to a failure of nature? Yes. Aristotle deals with it in his *Sophistical Refutations*.

In both these *prooemia*, it is clear that Thomas identifies the author and places the work in question within the wider context of logic. Its usefulness is made clear. The intention of the *Perihermeneias* is to consider enunciative speech which is either true or false. Thomas cites Boethius for the meaning of *interpretatio* and indeed the earlier Latin commentator is a felt presence throughout Thomas's commentary.[57] Like his great predecessor, Thomas is interested in previous commentaries, not in order to develop an independent and original position, but in order to understand the text. But Thomas does not always cite Boethius with approval.[58] Perhaps the most fundamental demand that

---

*Modes of Discourse*, The Aquinas Lecture, (Milwaukee, Marquette University Press, 1981).

57. *In I Periherm.*, prooemium, n. 3. The discussion in lectio 2 of the phrase *passiones animae* that Aristotle here uncharacteristically uses for concepts, prompting Andronicus to doubt the work's authenticity, is clearly dependent on Boethius. This is clear from the mention of Alexander and Porphyry.

58. He invokes Boethius (and Ammonius) for the way in which a word like *nothing* can be a name, though a name means something (lectio 4, n. 48). He thinks Boethius's explanation of why the verb is said to signify *eorum quae de subiecto vel in subjecto* is good, but proposes one he thinks is better (lectio 5, n. 60). He rejects Boethius's claim that the unity and plurality of speech (*oratio*) is taken from the thing signified, whereas simple and compound are drawn from language (lectio 8, n. 101). The basis for the rejection is important. *Sed haec expositio non videtur secundum intentionem Aristotelis* (n. 102). Boethius's explanation is not in keeping with what has gone before. Boethius's suggestion that when Aristotle says "significant speech is of that which is or of that which is not" he is not defining it but dividing it is rejected in favor of Porphyry's taking of this as a definition. But then, taking into account what Ammonius says, he says it is neither a definition nor a division. And then he remarks on Aristotle's procedure. "Est autem considerandum quod artificiossime procedit: dividit enim genus non in species, sed in differentias specificas. Non enim dicit quod enunciatio est affirmation vel negatio, sed *vox significativa de eo quod est*, quae est differentia specifica affirmationis, vel *de eo quod est*, in quo tangitur differentia specifica." (Lectio 8, n. 108). In lectio 14, he makes clear that his discussion of possibility and necessity with reference to Diodorus, the Stoics, and Philo depends on Boethius's commentary. And, after discussing a very subtle exposition of the text, he feels it distorts rather than explains. "Et ideo simplicio et magis conveniens litterae Aristotelis est expositio Porphyrii quam Boetius ponit; secundum quam expositionem attenditur similitudo et dissimilitudo secundum consequentiam affirmativarum ad negativas." (*In II Periherm.*, lect. 2, n. 222.)

Thomas makes of an interpretation is that it be consistent with the text as a whole.

It is instructive to ask St. Thomas what he took a *prooemium* to be and to glance at those he wrote to his own commentaries. "One who writes a *prooemium* intends to do three things, first, elicit a favorable attitude from the reader, second, to make him docile, third, to make him attentive. A favorable attitude is engendered by showing the usefulness of the knowledge, docility, by showing the order and division of the treatise, attentiveness, by being told how difficult the science is. All three of which Aristotle does in the *prooemium* of this treatise." [59] But before remarking on Aristotle's prefatory remarks, Thomas has made some of his own, locating the *De anima* within natural science by appealing to a principle Aristotle lays down at the outset of the *Physics*.[60] At the outset of his commentary on the *Physics*, Aristotle speaks of the procedure of any science and Thomas takes the occasion to discuss the way theoretical sciences are divided and thus to locate natural philosophy. He then takes up Aristotle's own *prooemium*, where the principle that we must

59. "Qui enim facit prooemium tria intendit. Primo enim ut auditorem reddat benevolum. Secundo ut reddat docilem. Tertio ut reddat attentum. Benevolum quidem reddit, ostendendo utilitatem scientiae: docilem, praemittendo ordinem et distinctionem tractatus: attentum attestando difficultatem tractatus. Quae quidem tria Aristoteles facit in prooemio huius tractatus." *In I de anima*, lectio 1, n. 2. Dante, in the famous dedicatory letter to Can Grande, writes: "Sex igitur sunt que in principio cuiusque doctrinalis operis inquirenda sunt, videlicet subiectum, agens, forma, finis, liber titulus, et genus philosophie." Dante Alighieri, *Tutte le Opere* (Florence, a cura Luigi Blasucci, 1981), Epistola XIII, n. 6, p. 343.

60. The natural order of learning is to move from the common and confused to the specific and distinct. Thomas frequently invokes that precept in his *prooemia*. At the outset of his commentary to the *De anima*, he first applies it to metaphysics, saying that in that endeavor we first consider what is common to being as being and then what is proper to whatever being, which seems a clear instance of *obscurum per obscurius*. Does Thomas think one taking up the *De anima* for the first time has already read the *Metaphysics*? We will return to that point in the text. The study of the soul, the principle of living being, a type of physical substance, is seen to follow upon considerations of physical substance as such—that is, to come after the *Physics*. *Ibid.*, lectio 1, n. 1.

begin with the general and only gradually become specific in a given subject matter is introduced. Thomas makes explicit how this works out in natural philosophy, attaching the names of particular Aristotelian works to the subdivisions of the science.[61] Such situating of a work about to be read obviously fulfills the threefold prooemial intention.[62]

The *prooemium* to the commentary on the *Metaphysics* is a remarkable performance that explains why the science about to be studied is called, variously, theology, metaphysics and first philosophy. It begins with the statement that there is an order among the sciences. "All sciences and arts, however, have a single aim, man's perfection, which is his happiness. That is why one of these must be regulative of all the others and rightly takes the name of wisdom. For it is the role of the wise to order." *Nam sapientis est alios ordinare.*[63] A pedagogical order, a fitting order of studying the various sciences, emerges from such considerations, and in his *prooemium* to his commentary on the *Liber de causis* Thomas gives an extended statement of it. "Hence it is that the chief intention of philosophers was to arrive at knowledge of the first causes by way of what they considered in everything else. They put knowledge of first causes last, accordingly, assigning it to the end of one's life, beginning first with logic, which treats the mode of the sciences, proceeding second to mathematics of which even boys are capable, third to natural philosophy which relies on experience and thus needs time,

61. Cf. *In I Physic.*, lectio 1. In his commentary on the *De sensu et sensato*, Thomas gives a detailed arrangement of the parts of life science and the corresponding Aristotelian works (lectio 1, nn. 1–7), and, in his commentary on the *De generatione et corruptione*, the most detailed statement of the divisions and subdivisions of Aristotelian natural science.

62. The opening of the commentary on the *Nicomachean Ethics*, with its distinction of four orders, is a remarkable arraying of the theoretical, practical, logical and artificial orders. Having located the moral order thus, he then goes on to subdivide it and to locate the *Ethics* more properly. The procedure is a good example of that zeroing-in envisaged by the Aristotelian principle: from the general to the particular.

63. "Omnes autem scientiae et artes ordinantur in unum, scilicet ad hominis perfectionem, quae est eius beatitudo. Unde necesse est, quod una earum sit aliarum omnium rectrix, quae nomen sapientiae recte vindicat. Nam sapientis est alios ordinare." *In libros Metaphysicorum, prooemium.*

fourth to moral philosophy of which youths are not fitting students, and last turning to divine science which considers first causes." [64] The point of this is to locate the *Liber de causis* in metaphysics. The *prooemium* to the commentary on the *De divinis nominibus* is careful to locate the work among other writings of Denis.

If one had to single out the major characteristic of Thomas as commentator it would be his displaying of the order of the text. Order is a principle of intelligibility. It is the mark of the wise man to order.

I will have other more specific things to say of Thomas as commentator in Part Two. I now move on to the discussion of universals which will establish further points of contact between Boethius and St. Thomas.

64. "Et inde est quod philosophorum intentio ad hoc principaliter erat ut, per omnia quae in rebus considerabant, ad cognitionem primarum causarum pervenerint. Unde scientiam de primis causis ultimo ordinabant, cuius considerationi ultimum tempus suae vitae deputarent: primo quidem incipientes a logica quae modum scientiarum tradit, secundo procedentes ad mathematicam cuius etiam pueri possunt esse capaces, tertio ad naturalem philosophiam quae propter experientiam tempore indiget, quarto autem ad moralem philosophiam cuius iuvenis esse conveniens auditor non potest, ultimo autem scientiae divinae insistebant quae considerat primas entium causas." *In librum de causis*, Saffrey edition (Fribourg, 1954), p. 2. There is also a magnificent Marietti edition by C. Pera (Turin, 1955). Pera locates the *prooemium* within lectio 1, nn. 1–9.

CHAPTER 2

# *Altissimum negotium:* Universals

Porphyry wrote his Introduction or *Isagoge* to the *Categories* of Aristotle in order to deal with what came to be called the five predicables: genus, species, difference, property and accident. Without prior knowledge of these, Porphyry felt, it would be very difficult for a beginner to follow Aristotle's book. Given that purpose, Porphyry did not want to make his introduction itself overly demanding. Thus it was that he set aside an issue of great moment in order to get immediately to work.

Now concerning genera and species I beg off asking whether they subsist or are in mere understanding alone, whether subsisting they are corporeal or incorporeal, and whether they are separate from or in sensible things. A discussion of this sort is most profound and falls to a far more demanding inquiry.[1]

This small paragraph has generated a veritable flood of commentary and discussion. Indeed, it is difficult to find in the history of western thought a passage of comparable length that has had so vast an effect. A discussion too difficult and demanding to undertake now? What better bait to snare the commentator could there be?

If Boethius respects Porphyry's tantalizing demur in his first commentary on the *Isagoge*, he deals at some length with the three questions in the second commentary. This is not to say that he ignores the problem on the first occasion. We will be looking

---

1. "Mox de generibus et speciebus illud quidem, sive subsistant, sive in solis nudis intellectibus posita sunt, sive subsistentia corporalia sint an incorporalia, et utrum separata a sensibilibus an in sensibilibus posita: et circa haec consistentia dicere recusabo. Altissimum enim negotium est hujusmodi, et majoris egens inquisitio." Text as found in Boethius, *PL* 64,82A–B.

at both treatments if only because the first is usually ignored in favor of the more developed second commentary.

The Problem of Universals consists of three questions which can be stated as disjunctions. Genera and species, the subject matter of the *Isagoge*,

(1) *either really subsist* or exist in the mind alone
(2) are either corporeal or *incorporeal*
(3) either exist separately from bodies or are conjoined with them.

It can be seen that the second disjunction presupposes that the first has been settled in favor of the emphasized option. So too the second disjunction is settled as indicated. This is why the problem of universals is often equated with the question formed from the third disjunction.

### THE FIRST COMMENTARY ON PORPHYRY

*The First Question*

"Prima est quaestio, utrum genera ipsa et species vere sint, an in solis intellectibus nuda inaniaque fingantur: the first question is whether genera and species themselves truly are or are empty and inane fabrications of thought alone."[2] Note how Boethius weights the question by employing a debunking language calculated to stir up opposition in Fabius (his interlocutor in this dialogue commentary) and prompt the right answer. Do genera and species really exist or are they empty and useless mental constructs? Fictions, products of dreams . . .

Boethius begins by distinguishing two parts of our soul, sense and intellect. Through the objects of the senses the quality of sensed things is grasped and from this, by way of speculation, conceived, thereby paving the way for the incorporeal. I see a number of men, and I know that I *see* them; recognizing them as men, I claim to *understand*.

2. *Ibid.*, 19A.

Intelligence, strengthened as it were by knowledge of sensible things, raises itself to sublimer understanding, conceiving the species of man, which contains individual men and falls under the genus animal "and it understands this incorporeal thing which it takes from its corporal particulars first sensed and understood in single men."[3] For we must think of the species man (*hominem quidem illum specialem*), which we all gather together within the ambit of the name, as incorporeal, since it is conceived by mind and intelligence alone. Mind using sensible things as stepping stones ascends to higher understanding of primordial and incorporeal beings.

But mind is not only an artist enabling us to gain understanding of incorporeal things by way of sensible things, it is also the source of fabrications and lies. Such fantastic notions as that of the centaur, the hybrid of horse and man, are constructed by the mind. That is why Porphyry wonders whether genera and species are fanciful like the centaur or are drawn from singulars and understood to be the essence and constitution of things.

If you consider the truth and wholeness of things, there is no doubt they truly are. For since all things which truly are require these five in order to be, you cannot doubt that these five are truly understood to be. They are however linked to and in some wise conjoined and compact with all things. For why does Aristotle dispute concerning the first ten words signifying the genera of things, or collect their properties and differences, and discourse chiefly about their accidents, if not because he sees these as deep in things and as it were made one with them? This being so, there is no doubt they truly are and are grasped in a certain consideration of soul.[4]

---

3. ". . . et illud incorporeum intelligit, cujus ante particulas corporales in singulis hominibus sentiendis et intelligendis assumpserat." *Ibid.*, 19A.

4. "Sed si rerum veritatem atque integritatem perpendas, non est dubium quin verae sint. Nam cum res omnes quae verae sunt, sine his quinque esse non possint, has ipsas quinque res vere intellectas esse non dubites. Sunt autem in rebus omnibus conglutinatae et quodammodo conjunctae atque compactae. Cur enim Aristoteles de primis decem sermonibus genera rerum significantibus disputaret, vel eorum differentias propriaque colligeret, et principaliter de accidentibus dissereret, nisi haec in rebus intimata et quodammodo adunata vidisset? Quod si ita est, non est dubium quin verae sint, et certa animi consideratione teneantur." *Ibid.*, 19C–D.

Mind is here depicted as a fashioner of true concepts but as well the producer of such fictions as the centaur. Genera and species are to be distinguished from such notions as that of centaur. Of the centaur it might be said that there is no such beast save in the mind of the one considering it. To consider it aright is to consider it as something fashioned by the mind of man, having no counterpart in reality.

"Man" on the other hand has a real counterpart which is in some way united with and stuck to the things out there. So too "substance" is meant to refer to things unfashioned by our mind. Only the negative side of Boethius's response is fairly clear: genera and species are not fictions as the centaur is. The positive side of what he is saying is desperately obscure.

### The Second Question

Having settled that genera and species truly subsist, the question arises, are they corporeal or not? No one doubts that genera and species are incorporeal, Boethius assures Fabius, though they are not grasped by the senses and must be clarified by mind.

The incorporeal has priority of nature over the corporeal since bodies are the effects of incorporeal causes. But if the incorporeal is thus prior to the corporeal, the reverse cannot obtain. Take the case of the genus, substance. Its species are corporeal and incorporeal. How could the species "incorporeal" be included in the genus if that genus were itself corporeal?[5] As an argument, this taxes the mind. Indeed, throughout this first discussion of universals we find Boethius failing to distinguish between the conceptual content, e.g., substance, man, and so on, and that content's being predicable in one way or another, that

5. "Quod si corporale esse genus, nunquam sub eo species incorporea poneretur." *Ibid.*, 20A. Martin M. Tweedale, in his *Abailard on Universals* (New York, 1976), a book which could serve as a guide on how not to do the history of medieval philosophy, seems not to have read Boethius very carefully, since he triumphantly makes this Boethian point against Boethius. I have in mind pp. 66–67, but consider Tweedale's overture. "I must warn the reader from the start that what we are about to examine is a confused, vague and disorderly piece of philosophical writing." (p. 63) The warning his reader takes is not likely to be the one Tweedale intends.

is, its being common or universal, a distinction that he himself makes further along in the discussion of this second question.

How can a genus, which is incorporeal, contain as its species the corporeal as well as the incorporeal? How in general does a genus contain the differences which divide its species? "How, it is asked, if animal understood alone is neither rational nor irrational, can these differences occur in its species, not being beforehand in their genus?"[6] If the genus contains the differences and the differences are contraries, the genus would be an impossibility, something at once corporeal and incorporeal, rational and irrational.

The solution is to say that the differences are in the genus potentially, but not actually, the differences being things it can account for without being identical with them.[7] Boethius promises to clarify this in the second book of his commentary. One answer to the second question, then, is that the genus is neither corporeal nor incorporeal in itself but may have as species the corporeal and incorporeal because they are effects it can cause.

But isn't there a way in which one can say that genera and species themselves are incorporeal? Let us take the genus substance and distinguish the consideration of it as substance—as that which enjoys autonomous existence—from the consideration of it as a genus—as that which is predicated of many specifically different things. The latter consideration focuses on the fact that the substance has species under it. Again, taking its putative species, corporeal and incorporeal, e.g., man and God, we can consider these precisely as falling under the genus. So too the differences two-footed and four-footed can be considered as such or as differences, that is, as dividing a species.

And the same can be said of property. We can talk about laughter in itself, so to say, or as a property, that is, as a distin-

6. "Quaeritur si animal solitario intellectu neque rationale neque irrationale sit, unde hae differentiae in speciebus natae sint, quae in genere ante non fuerant?" *Ibid.*, 20A.
7. "Ita ergo genus tale est, ut ipsum neque incorporale neque corporale sit, utrumque tamen ex se possit efficere." *Ibid.*, 20C.

guishing accident of the species man. In short, Boethius is proposing a distinction between things (a) considered in themselves, and (b) considered as genera, species, differences, properties and accidents. Things themselves may be corporeal or incorporeal, but for things to have species under them or a genus over them, for example, is indubitably to focus on something incorporeal.

Boethius does not exploit this distinction here and, indeed, he can be read as more or less groping his way through this discussion of the second question. From suggesting that genera and species must be incorporeal because they are grasped by intellect rather than by sense, he argues for the priority of the incorporeal over the corporeal because the former is the cause of the latter. Then he argues that the genus substance must be incorporeal because one of its species is corporeal. If the genus were corporeal, it could not be prior to its other species, the incorporeal, because the incorporeal is prior to the corporeal, and not vice versa. Therefore the genus cannot be corporeal and it is the fact that it produces the corporeal as a species that entails that the genus is incorporeal.[8] But if the genus contains two such species it must be both and thus be both corporeal and incorporeal, which is impossible. Unless, of course, we say that the genus contains these differences *vi et potestate*. Then we can say that the genus is neither corporeal nor incorporeal. But this pushes the question onto the species. If the genus substance is neither corporeal nor incorporeal, one of its species is corporeal. Is the species then corporeal?

Perhaps we can distinguish the thing in itself from the thing as genus or species or property or difference or accident. Then "to be said of many numerically different things" may sometimes be true of corporeal things and sometimes of incorporeal things, e.g., sometimes true of man and sometimes true of isosceles triangle. But however it may be with the thing that is a genus, to

8. "Nam quia incorporeorum prima natura est, potest res incorporea parens esse quodammodo corporeae." *Ibid.*, 20A.

consider it as a genus is to concentrate on something indubitably incorporeal.

### The Third Question

The very raising of this question indicates that the answer to the preceding question is that genera and species are incorporeal. We would not ask if corporeal things exist separately from or in conjunction with bodies: they would *be* bodies. The question is asked rather because incorporeal things relate differently to bodies. Some (a), like God and the soul, are completely unaffected by bodies, but some (b) are such that they cannot exist apart from bodies, like the edges of bodies.[9] Some things (c), like (human?) soul, are sometimes found in bodies but they can exist apart. The third question, then, amounts to this: in which of these three classes are the five predicables to be put?

It would seem that they fall in the class of things that are sometimes found in bodies and sometimes apart. When bodily things are divided as genera into species and their properties and differences are named there is no doubt that they are bodily things. By the same token, incorporeal things are also divided as genera into species.

If so there is no doubt that these five are of the same kind, that they can be separate from bodies and can be joined to bodies, such that if they are joined with bodies they are inseparable from them. If conjoined to incorporeals they are never separated from them. Thus they contain both in themselves.[10]

If genera and species and differences and properties and accidents are found in both corporeal and incorporeal things, they

9. "Sed dicam breviter terminos me dixisse extremitates earum quae in geometria sunt figurarum: de incorporalitate vero quae circa terminos constat, si Macrobii Theodosii doctissimi viri primum librum quem de Somno Scipionis composuit in manibus sumpseris, plenius uberiusque cognosces." *Ibid.*, 22B.

10. "Quod si hoc est, non est dubium quod quinque haec ex eodem sint genere, quod et praeter corpora separatum esse possit, et corporibus jungi patiatur, sed ita ut si corporibus juncta fuerint, inseparabilia a corporibus sint. Si vero incorporalibus, nunquam ab incorporalibus separentur, et utrasque in se contineant." *Ibid.*, 21C.

are not confined to corporeal things. Boethius concludes with a divided answer. When genera and species and so forth are found conjoined to bodies they are incorporeal in the way terms (lines, points, surfaces) of bodies are incorporeal (as not being themselves bodies) and can never be apart from bodies.[11] When, on the other hand, they are found in incorporeal things (the genera and species of incorporeal things), they, like soul (!), are never conjoined with body.[12] Thus, genera and species fall in class (c).

It is easy to be dissatisfied with this first Boethian treatment of the three questions that make up the problem of universals. Yet each question elicits from him some interesting distinction or argument. Thus, in handling the first question he seeks to clarify the difference between fictions and concepts of real things. Important as that distinction is, however, its use here leaves us with the suggestion that "genus," "species," "man," and "animal" are all alike included in a class opposed to one that includes "centaur." But what then are the differences between man and animal, on the one hand, and species and genus, on the other?

In discussing the second question, Boethius invokes a distinction between considering man as man and considering man as a species. Presumably, what emerges from the first consideration (e.g., that man is composed of matter and form) will differ from what emerges from the second (e.g., is predicated of many numerically different things). How can the differences between these two considerations be formally characterized? To be told that the second is concerned with the incorporeal is unhelpful and runs into problems when the *things* that happen to be species are incorporeal.

The way things that are distinguished from bodies may always exist separately from bodies, or sometimes separately, or never separately, is interesting and important. How disappointing then for Boethius to conclude that the genera and species of corporeal

11. "Quae nunquam discedit a corpore." *Ibid.*, 21D.
12. "Qui nunquam corpori copulatur." *Ibid.*, 21D.

things are like those incorporeal things that never exist apart
from bodies, whereas the genera and species of incorporeal
things are like the incorporeal things that never exist in conjunction with bodies. Quite apart from the difficulty that there are
geometrical genera and species as well as physical ones, thus
giving us an unaccounted-for class of the five predicables, Boethius's solution seems altogether too Solomonian. Is it something
wholly different for an incorporeal thing to be a genus than it is
for a corporeal thing when both are considered *insofar as they
are genera*? Would it not be true of both that, as genera, they
have species under them? And must that claim be explained differently in the two cases? We are not told. And from what we
are told it is difficult to guess what Boethius's answer would be.

### THE SECOND COMMENTARY ON PORPHYRY

The discussion of the vexed text in Porphyry occupies three-
and-a-half columns in the Migne edition of Boethius's first commentary, four columns in the second commentary. The difference
between them is not a quantitative one. The more advanced and
profound discussion Boethius intended to characterize his second commentary does not, in the matter of universals, manifest
itself in length as well as depth; indeed the second commentary
as a whole is only slightly longer than the first. The first commentary occupies columns 9–70 of Volume 64; the second, columns 71–158. The difference, if there is one, must lie in the quality of the discussion. With respect to Boethius's treatment of the
problem of universals, our expectations of the second commentary are not disappointed.

This second discussion divides into three parts: first, a clarification of the questions; second, the making of some important
distinctions; third, the solution. Let us have the text before us in
Boethius's translation of it.

Mox de generibus et speciebus illud quidem, sive subsistunt, sive in solis
nudis intellectibus posita sint, sive subsistentia corporalia sint an in sen-

sibilibus posita, et circa haec consistentia, dicere recusabo. Altissimum enim negotium est hujusmodi, et majoris egens inquisitionis.[13]

## Clarification of the Questions

Whatever is understood by mind may be distinguished into that which, established in the nature of things, is conceived by the intellect and described for itself by reason, and that which, since it does not exist, is depicted by empty imagination. If this division is exhaustive, we can ask of genera and species whether, in understanding them, we are dealing with things that are, from which we form a true concept, or are only amusing ourselves by forming empty images of things that do not exist. Assuming genera and species are the former, another and more difficult question awaits which manifests the supreme difficulty of discerning and understanding the nature of genus itself. Whatever exists is either corporeal or incorporeal, so genera and species must fall into the one class or the other. Which class contains genus, the corporeal or incorporeal? We can scarcely claim to know what genus is if we cannot assign it to its appropriate class, but of course to settle that question does not end the matter.

If we say that genera and species are incorporeal, the mind is besieged by another difficulty. Do these incorporeal entities, genera and species, subsist with bodies or apart from them? There are, as it happens, two forms of the incorporeal: the one kind can be apart from bodies and endure separate from bodies and their corporeality, for example, God, mind, the soul; the other kind, although incorporeal, cannot exist apart from bodies, for example, lines, surfaces, numbers, singular qualities.[14]

This clarification of the third question amounts to paring down the tripartite distinction of the first commentary to a bipartite one. Boethius apparently no longer thinks it useful to mention things which can exist either with bodies or apart from them, a distinction which was, in any case, fuzzy before, since

---

13. PL 64,82A.

14. "Quas tametsi incorporeas esse pronuntiamus, quod tribus spatiis minime distenduntur, ita tamen in corporibus sunt, ut ab his divelli nequeant aut separari, aut si a corporibus separata sint, nullo modo permaneant." Ibid., 83A.

soul was cited to exemplify it, yet soul, there as here, is mentioned along with God as something never involved with body.
In the first commentary, we would have to distinguish between
kinds of soul, one a sort of Neoplatonic hypostasis, the other a
principle animating this body or that. In the second commentary,
Boethius seems to confine soul to the hypostatic level. Speaking
generally, we can say that he moves with crisp authority through
this clarification of Porphyry's questions without the groping
that characterized the first discussion.

## Working Up the Difficulties

Before attempting to answer these questions, Boethius suggests that certain difficulties and doubts be noted. He does this
by proposing the following thesis:

Genera and species either are and subsist or they are only products of
understanding and cogitation: but genera and species cannot exist.[15]

There are two kinds of concepts: concepts of things that are, or
idle fancies constructed by the mind having no counterpart in
reality. If genera and species do not exist, they must perforce be
idle fancies. But on what basis is real existence denied to genera
and species?

"Anything simultaneously common to many cannot in itself
be one."[16] What is common to many things, especially when one
and the same thing is found as a whole simultaneously in many,
cannot be one. However many species there are, in each of them
is found one and the same genus, and not in such a way that
each species has some part of it, rather each species at one and
the same time has the whole genus. It cannot be in several things
simultaneously and as a whole and be something numerically
one. But if the genus is not numerically one, it cannot exist, since
whatever exists is one.

This difficulty, reminiscent of the *Parmenides*, strikes at the

15. "Genera et species aut sunt et subsistunt, aut intellectu et sola cogitatione
formantur, sed genera et species esse non possunt." *Ibid.*, 83A.
16. "Omne enim quod commune est uno tempore pluribus, id in se unum esse
non poterit." *Ibid.*, 83B.

very notion of the genus as *unum in pluribus*, some one thing
that is found in many. If it is found in many, it cannot be one; if
it is not one, it cannot exist. If it is not found in many, it is not a
genus. The same difficulty can be raised about the species.

We are being given some sense of why such universals as genera and species constitute a problem. In the first commentary,
the questions were treated as if they were irreverent murmurings
that must be quickly set aside. Nor were the questions linked to
the chief feature of that of which genera and species are types,
the universal. The universal is something one said of many. Boethius is now confronting the difficulties that arise from that description. If it is one, how can it be many? If it is many and not
one, how can it be?

What would happen if we were to say that genera and species
are not units but manifolds? One consequence, Boethius argues,
is that there could then be no ultimate genus. His reasoning is
complicated but comes down to this. The point in looking for a
genus is to overcome multiplicity, to reduce it to unity, and the
same is true of the species. The species *man* expresses something
that is common to this man, that man, and so on. The genus
*animal* expresses something common to man, horse, gnu and so
on. If now, *ex hypothesi*, the generic name and the specific name
simply refer to the many, as if "animal" *meant* man and horse
and gnu and so on, and "man" *meant* Horst and Horace and
Homer and so on, what led us to seek a genus or species, namely,
to overcome mere multiplicity, would goad us on to finding a
genus that expressed the similarity and not merely the multiplicity. But what is true of one genus is true of them all and we could
never arrive at a supreme genus. The genus is supposed to express a similarity among the many: if that similarity is simply
dissolved back into manyness, we may think of the consequence
as an endless search for what *will* express the similarity of the
many. Or we may simply say that the notion of genus is being
rejected. There just is not something one that is common to
many.

This unwelcome consequence will turn us back to the possibility that the genus is numerically one, but then it is difficult to see how it can be common. That is, having confronted the charge that genus, if common to many, cannot be one, we now confront the difficulty that, if the genus is one, it cannot be common to many. Either way the concept of a genus seems to be incoherent since the elements of its description are incompatible: the genus is something *one* that is *common* to many species.

There are of course ways in which something numerically one can be common to many, but none of them answers to our concept of genus. For example, a numerically one thing can relate to its many parts, but no part would be the whole. To be a pie is common to all its pieces but not to any one of them. Further, a single entity can be used by many, as several members of a family might share a car. But they cannot all drive it at the same time, only in series. Yet another example: many can simultaneously share the same whole thing, as each member of the audience sees the same show at the same time. But the show is not common to them as constituting what they are.

Genus cannot be common to its species in any of these ways, for it must be so common that the whole be in each at the same time and such that what is common can form and constitute their substance. Wherefore if it is neither one, because it is common, nor many since then we would have to seek another genus of the multitude, it seems that genus in no wise exists, and the same must be said of the other [predicables].[17] Yet another difficulty is devised from the conception of truth. If genera and species and the rest are grasped in concepts alone, and concepts are drawn from things (*ex re subjecta fiat*) and express how they are or how they are not, a concept without a corresponding thing would be empty indeed and certainly no understanding could be based upon it. If on the other hand genera and species and the rest are drawn (*veniat*) from things such that things are understood as they are, they would not be mere concepts but would be grounded in reality and derive their

---

17. "Genus vero secundum nullum horum modum commune esse speciebus potest: nam ita commune esse debet, et ut totum sit in singulis, et uno tempore, et eorum quorum commune est constituere valeat et conformare substantiam. Quocirca si neque unum est, quoniam commune est, neque multiplex, quoniam ejus quoque multitudinis genus aliud inquirendum est, videbitur genus omnino non esse, idemque de caeteris intelligendum est." *Ibid.*, 83D–84A.

truth from it. But there is a third possibility. What if the concepts of genus and species are indeed drawn from things that exist but do not express these things as they are? Such conceptions would be indeed vain since they would be false: they would amount to understanding things otherwise than as they are.[18]

Given these reasons for thinking that genera and species cannot exist, since they purport to be a one in many and this has been argued to be impossible, and given further that if they are concepts of things, they are systematic falsifications of the things conceived, it is no wonder, Boethius observes, that so much care has been expended in disputing about these five predicables. They seem to concern things that are not and to be devoid of truth. Boethius's reader now has a far livelier sense of the nature of the dispute that Porphyry declines to discuss and he looks forward eagerly to the solution that Boethius, relying on Alexander of Aphrodisias, proposes.

### The Solution

Must we say that any understanding of a subject thing, a real thing, is false and vacuous if it is not an understanding of the thing as it exists? Boethius thinks not, so long as we have in mind the distinction between conjoining and dividing. False opinion requires that some conjunction be made. "Were one to compose and conjoin in his mind that which nature does not permit to be linked, no one would deny this to be false: for example, were someone in imagination to join horse and man and fashion a centaur."[19]

Understanding together, putting together in mind and imagination, what are separate in reality, gives rise to falsity. Taking apart or dividing in the mind what are together in reality does not have the same result. "But if it comes about through division or abstraction that the thing is not as it is understood, the under-

18. ". . . id est enim falsum quod aliter atque res est et intelligitur." *Ibid.*, 84B.
19. "Si enim quis componat atque conjungat intellectu id quod natura jungi non patiatur, illud falsum esse nullus ignorat: ut si quis equum atque hominem jungat imaginatione, atque effigiet centaurum." *Ibid.*, 84C.

standing is not false." [20] This is Boethius's first use of the term
"abstraction" in discussing universals and it is used as a synonym for "divide."

There are many things which have their being in other things, from
which they either can in no way be *separated* or, if they be separated,
could in no way subsist. That this might be manifest to us in a well
known example: the line is something in body and what it is it owes to
body, that is, it retains its existence through body. This can thus be
made clear: if it were *separated* from body it would not subsist. For
who has ever by any of his senses grasped a line *separated* from body?
But the soul, when it grasps things confused and mixed up with bodies
in themselves, *distinguishes* them by its own power and thought. All
such incorporeal things having their being in body we grasp by our
senses along with bodies; but the soul in whose power it is to compose
the unjoined and to *dissolve* the composed so *distinguishes* what are
passed on by the senses as confused and conjoined with bodies that it
sees and speculates on the incorporeal nature in itself and without the
bodies in which it is concretized. [21]

In this text, "distinguish" is apparently a synonym for "divide"
and "abstract." In any case, we are speaking of an activity per-
formed by the mind. There are things, Boethius writes, which
cannot be separated: that is, they are such that one cannot *be*
apart from the other. Sensation respects this togetherness; mind,
however, is able to abstract one thing from another—e.g., line
from body—and consider it in this absolute and abstract condition. Concretely the line has its existence in the kind of body

20. "Quod si hoc per divisionem et abstractionem fiat, not ita quidem res sese
habet, ut intellectus est, intellectus tamen minime falsus est." *Ibid.*
21. "Sunt enim plura quae in aliis suum esse habent, ex quibus aut omnino
*separari* non possunt, aut si *separata* fuerint, nulla ratione subsistunt. Atque ut
hoc nobis in pervagato exemplo manifestum sit, linea in corpore est aliquid, et
id quod est corpori debet, hoc est, esse suum per corpus retinet, quod docetur
ita: si enim *separata* sit a corpore non subsistit; quis enim unquam sensu ullo
*separatam* a corpore lineam cepit? Sed animus cum confusas res permistasque
corporibus in se a sensibus cepit, eas propria vi et cogitatione *distinguit*. Omnes
enim hujusmodi res incorporeae in corpore suum esse habentes sensus cum ipsis
nobis corporibus tradit: at vero animus, cui potestas est et disjuncta componere
et composita *dissolvere*, quae a sensibus confusa et corporibus conjuncta tradun-
tur, ita *distinguit* ut in incorpoream naturam per se ac sine corporibus in quibus
est concretur, et speculetur et videat." *Ibid.*, 84C–D.

perceived by sense and cannot exist separately from it. Thus abstraction or division or distinction is a mental activity thanks to which a thing that cannot exist apart from another is conceived independently of, in abstraction from, that other.

There is more. The thing thus conceived apart is incorporeal and what it is conceived in abstraction from is body. Body is what is grasped by the senses. The senses lay hold of lines along with the bodies they perceive, presumably as their edges. Who has ever seen a line apart from a body?

A line by definition has length but no width. What permits this abstraction to avoid being false is the fact that what is abstracted from the corporeal is in itself incorporeal. This "in itself" does not amount to the claim that such an incorporeal thing can exist apart from body. Therefore, it must only mean that it can be considered, speculated about, defined, without body entering into the consideration, speculation or definition.

So far so good. What Boethius is saying casts light on his understanding of the ontological status of mathematicals; it evokes what he had to say about the three kinds of incorporeal thing in his first discussion of the passage from Porphyry. But this discussion is only a preliminary to solving the problem of the status of such universals as genus and species.

Genera and species and the others are found either in corporeal things or in incorporeal things: (a) and if the mind comes upon them in incorporeal things it has right off an incorporeal understanding of genus; (b) if however it beholds the genera and species of corporeal things, it bears off as is its custom the nature of incorporeals from bodies and considers it alone and pure and as very form. When mind grasps things mixed with bodies, dividing incoporeals it considers and speculates on them.[22]

22. "Genera ergo et species caeteraque vel in corporeis rebus, vel in his quae sunt incorporea, reperiuntur: (a) et si ea in rebus incorporeis invenit animus, habet illico incorporeum generis intellectum; (b) si vero corporalium rerum genera speciesque prospexerit, aufert (ut solet) a corporibus incorporeorum naturam, et solam puramque et in seipsa forma est contuetur. Ita haec cum accipit animus permista corporibus, incorporalia dividens speculatur atque considerat."

On the assumption that genera and species are in themselves incorporeal, we are to think of them as sometimes conjoined with incorporeal, sometimes with corporeal, things. In either case, presumably, the genera and species are other than that with which they are conjoined, whether corporeal or incorporeal.

This is not as clear as it might be because of the *illico*—right off, on the spot, straightaway—used in the first instance. The misleading suggestion there is that when they are conjoined with incorporeal things there is no need to distinguish, divide, abstract, genera and species from those things. Indeed, these verbs have been tied to the split between the corporeal and incorporeal. That is why they come into play in the case where genera and species are conjoined with corporeal things (*aufert* and *incorporalia dividens speculatur*). One longs for an example here. One misses the distinction of the first commentary between considering something in itself and insofar as it is a genus. Can incorporeal things be considered in themselves or insofar as they are genera and species? Here Boethius speaks of considering the incorporeal genera and species in abstraction from corporeal things with which they are conjoined: *et solam puramque ut in seipsa forma est contuetur*. It is the occurrence of "form" in the phrase that puzzles. The abstraction of genera and species is spoken of as if it were a matter of abstracting form from bodily conditions. The chosen and familiar analogy of the line does little to dissipate this impression.

Boethius's immediate concern is to argue that this consideration of genera and species in abstraction from bodies with which they are conjoined is not productive of falsity.

No one will say that we have a false thought of line when our mind grasps it apart from body even though it cannot be apart from body. Not everything the mind grasps of things around us otherwise than as they exist is thought to be false (as was said above). It is he who does this by way of composition who commits a falsehood, as when joining man and horse he thinks the centaur to exist. But as for him who does this in divisions and abstractions and assumptions from the things in which they are, not only is he not guilty of falsity, it is only in the understanding of what is proper to the thing that truth is found. Such things exist in corporeal and sensible things, but they are understood apart from sensibles in order that their nature may be seen and what is proper to them may become comprehended.[23]

This is a clearer statement than the former one to which it refers. To understand something otherwise than it is (*aliter quam sese habent*) is ambiguous: sometimes it is false because it amounts, so to say, to a bad picture of what is, putting together things that do not exist together; sometimes it is true because it amounts to considering a thing apart from conditions which do not belong to its very nature. To consider incorporeal things without considering the corporeal condition in which they exist is not a false, but an abstract, consideration. This abstract or intellectual consideration will enable us to see what is truly proper to the incorporeal nature. Since all this is aimed at elucidating genera and species, we want to know if to be a genus or to be a species is a property of a nature considered abstractly or whether it *is* the nature considered abstractly. But that second possibility would unequivocally call into question the presumed distinction between incorporeal genera and species and incorporeal things to which they are conjoined. Boethius blurs this distinction almost in the course of making it.

Therefore when genera and species are thought of, from the singular things in which they exist their likeness is collected, as when from singular men dissimilar from one another the similarity of humanity is

23. "Nemo ergo dicant falsam nos lineam cogitare, quoniam ita eam mente capimus quasi praeter corpora sit, cum praeter corpora esse non possit. Non enim omnis qui ex subjectis rebus capitur intellectus aliter quam sese ipsae res habent, falsus esse putandus est (ut superius dictum est) ille quidem qui hoc in compositione facit falsus est, ut cum hominem atque equum jungens putat esse centaurum. Qui vero id in divisionibus et abstractionibus atque assumptibus ab his rebus in quibus sunt efficit, non modo falsus non est, verum etiam solus intellectus id quod in proprietate verum est invenire potest. Sunt igitur hujusmodi res in corporalibus atque in sensibilibus rebus. Intelliguntur autem praeter sensibilia, ut eorum natura perspici et proprietas caleant comprehendi." *Ibid.*, 85A–B.

taken, which similitude when thought by mind and truly seen becomes a species, and, further, when the similarity found in diverse species, which can only be in those species or in their individuals, becomes genus. Thus all these exist in singulars. Universals are thought and the species is thought to be nothing else than the substantial similitude collected by mind from numerically different individuals, and the genus the understood similitude collected from species. When this similitude is in singulars it becomes sensible, when in universals it becomes intelligible. Likewise when it is sensible, it is in singulars; when it is understood, it becomes universal. They subsist then in sensibles and are understood apart from bodies. Nothing prevents two things in the same subject from being diverse in notion, as the convex and concave line, which are captured by different definitions and the understanding of them differs yet they are always found in the same subject. It is always line which is either concave or convex. So too with genera and species, there is one subject of singularity and universality, but in one way, when it is understood, it is universal, and in another, when it is sensed in the things in which it exists, it is singular. With this, I think, the question is settled. For these genera and species subsist indeed in one mode and they are understood in another; they are incorporeal but joined to sensible things they subsist with sensible things. They are understood apart from bodies, as subsisting in themselves and as not having being in other things.[24]

24. "Quocirca cum et genera et species cogitantur, tunc ex singulis in quibus sint eorum similitudo colligitur, ut ex singulis hominibus inter se dissimilibus humanitatis similitudo, quae similitudo cogitata animo veraciterque perspecta fit species, quarum species rursus diversarum considerata similitudo, quae nisi in ipsis speciebus aut in earum individuis esse non potest, efficit genus, itaque haec sint quidem in singularibus. Cogitantur vero universalia, nihilque aliud species esse putanda est, nisi cogitatio collecta ex individuorum dissimilium numero substantiali similitudine, genus vero cogitatio collecta ex specierum similitudine. Sed haec similitudo cum in singularibus est, fit sensibilis, cum in universalibus, fit universalis. Subsistunt ergo circa sensibilia, intelliguntur autem praeter corpora, neque enim interclusum est ut duae res eodem in subjecto non sint ratione diversae, ut linea curva atque cava: quae res cum diversis diffinitionibus terminentur, diversusque earum intellectus sit, semper tamen in eodem subjecto reperiuntur; eadem enim cava linea eademque curva est. Ita quoque generibus et speciebus, id est singularitati et universalitati unum quidem subjectum est, sed alio modo universale est cum cogitatur, alio singulare cum sentitur in rebus his in quibus habet esse suum. His igitur terminatis omnis (ut arbitror) quaestio dissoluta est. Ipsa enim genera et species subsistunt quidema alio modo, intelliguntur vero alio modo, et sunt incorporalia, sed sensibilibus juncta subsistunt in sensibilibus. Intelliguntur vero praeter corpora, ut per semetipsa subsistentia, ac non in aliis esse suum habentia." *Ibid.* 85B–86A.

This long and difficult passage contains Boethius's solution to the problem of universals. First, we are given an example. That which individual men have in common, that thanks to which they are similar as men, is collected from them, abstracted, divided, distinguished, to constitute the species, humanity or man. The similarity among species is abstracted, divided, distinguished, from them and gives rise to the genus, say, animal. Both the specific and generic similarities exist in singular things, but are considered apart from them, such that singularity does not enter into their definitions.

Second, Boethius, on the basis of this example, provides us with some definitions. The species is a thought (*cogitatio*) collected (abstracted, divided, distinguished, drawn) from the substantial similarity of numerically dissimilar individuals. The genus is a similitude collected from species.

Such similitudes enjoy two different conditions: in singulars they are sensible, when understood they are universal. Genera and species subsist in sensible things but are understood apart from bodies. We are to think of some one thing from different points of view as the same line can be considered concave or convex and be defined differently though it is one and the same line. Thus, what is considered apart from body is the same thing that subsists in body. *Singularity and universality are different states of the same thing*. To return to Boethius's example, one and the same humanity can be considered abstractly or in singulars. This suggests that our earlier difficulty can be set aside. We found it difficult to decide whether Boethius was identifying the abstract nature and the universality that pertains to it as abstract. The long text we have just quoted distinguishes between the abstract nature, on the one hand, and the universality and singularity which attach to it as considered and as it subsists, respectively. From this point of view, *abstraction is a precondition of universality and not identical with it*.

We must make this distinction between the abstract nature and its being universal as abstract. The example of the abstract nature given is humanity and this same humanity subsists in individuals. Thus it would have to be the case that what is true of the nature is true of the individuals having that nature as having that nature. If to be a species were part and parcel of that nature, then Socrates would have to be a species. To be a species cannot be, as Boethius seemed to suggest earlier, a constituent of the abstract nature considered per se. Whatever is a constituent of the nature per se must be true of the individuals in which that nature subsists. If man is risible, Socrates is risible. But though man is a species, Socrates is not.

Boethius may thus be said to provide the means for making a distinction he does not always sufficiently honor in his text. The abstract natures, man, animal, can be dubbed species and genus respectively. But we do not want to identify the nature and its universality. Thus when Boethius says of the *Categories* that they consider *primae voces* as signifying, that is, as designating things that are, we must distinguish.

"Substance" and "animal" and "man" are examples of *primae voces* and designate or signify what is found in *res subjectae*. But insofar as substance is called a category, a supreme genus, insofar as animal is called a subalternate genus and man a species, we are not talking of aspects of these natures found in *res subjectae*. Rather we are calling attention to a consequence of their being thought of by an abstracting mind. "Category" and "genus" and "species" are not *primae voces*, nor do they seem to be the *secundae voces* of the *prooemium* to the commentary on the *Categories:* they are not grammatical terms. But they are closer to grammatical terms than they are to being *primae voces*. No doubt this is the source of the thought expressed by Obertello, a widely held thought, to the effect that the *Categories* is an odd mixture of the ontological and the logical. But as soon as we see the difference between *what* is categorized and category, we see a way out of the confusion. The former is real, the latter is a feature of our thinking. Logic always presupposes the real, for it is known reality that is ordered, affirmed, denied, inferred, and the like. To see the real through the lens of such mental ordering is characteristic of logic in the classical sense.

Only when logic is identified with a pure formalism thought to be independent of the way the world is will this conception of logic seem odd.

When we understand logic as Aristotle did it is plain that the *Categories* is a logical work.

### ST. THOMAS AND UNIVERSALS

In an early work, the *De ente et essentia*, Thomas asks what the relation of essence is to genus, species, and difference and, in the course of developing an answer to that question, he gives us both his reply to the problem of universals and his conception of the nature of logic.

He has defined "essence" as that whereby something is a being, has noted that in natural things the essence comprises both matter and form, and has distinguished matter as it enters into the definition of an essence from matter as the principle of individuation. The essence is that which is expressed by the thing's definition and tells us what sort of thing the individual having that essence is. It is of essence so understood that Thomas asks: How does it relate to genus, species and difference?

Having seen what is meant by the word "essence" in the case of composite substances, we must see how it relates to the notion of genus and species and difference.[25] That which is called a genus or species or difference is predicated of singular individuals, which suggests that these attach to essence not as abstractly expressed, e.g., by way of terms like "humanity" and "animality." Abstract terms signify the essence *per modum partis,*[26] such that I can distinguish in Socrates his humanity from other things true of him. But when I say that Socrates is a man, I predicate the term of all, not just a part, of him.

Similarly, it cannot be said that the notion of genus or species belongs to essence as to something existing apart from the singulars, as the Plato-

25. Cf. *De ente et essentia*, cap. III, (ed. Leonina), lines 1–4. "Viso igitur quid significetur nomine essentie in substantiis compositis, uidendum est quomodo se habeat ad rationem generis, speciei et differentie."
26. Cf. *ibid.*, line 8.

nists say, because then genus and species would not be predicated of the individual; Socrates cannot be said to be something separate from himself nor would that separate entity contribute to knowledge of this singular thing. Therefore the notion of genus or species must belong to essence insofar as it is signified in the manner of a whole, as by the name "man" or "animal," as implicitly and indistinctly containing all that is in the individual.[27]

Given the fact that genus and species and difference are among the five predicables discussed by Porphyry in his *Isagoge*, it is not surprising that Thomas, in asking how essence is related to them, should provide us with his answer to the problem of universals.[28] Already in these preliminary remarks, he is guided by the Porphyrian definitions. The genus and species are *predicated*, the genus of many specifically different things, the species of many numerically different things. Both, then, relate to individuals. This is clue enough that they attach to essence as this is predicated of individuals *and* that, insofar as the essence expresses what individuals are, that whatness cannot be separate from the individuals.

In order to grasp the relation between essence and universal, we must take note of the fact that essence or nature can be considered in two ways, either in what Thomas calls an absolute consideration or with respect to its existence in this mode or that. Nothing is true of the nature absolutely considered save what pertains to it per se.

For example, animal and rational belong to man as man as do other things that enter into his definition; but white or black, or any other such thing that is not part of the notion of humanity, does not belong to man insofar as he is a man.[29]

---

27. "Similiter etiam non potest dici quod ratio generis vel speciei conueniat essentie secundum quod est quaedam res existens extra singulari, ut Platonici ponebant, quia sic genus et species non praedicarentur de hoc indiuiduo; non enim potest dici quod Sortes sit hoc quod ab eo separatum est, nec iterum illud separatum proficeret in cognitionem huius singularis. Et ideo relinquitur quod ratio generis uel speciei conueniat essentie secundum quod significatur per modum totius, ut nomine hominis uel animalis, prout implicite et indistincte continet totum hoc quod in indiuiduo est." Ibid., ll. 13–25.

28. Cf. *ibid.*, ll. 6–7: "ratio universalis," i.e., ratio generis et speciei.

29. "Verbi gratia homini in eo quod homo est conuenit rationale et animal et alia que in diffinitione eius cadunt; album vero aut nigrum, uel quicquid huius-

A somewhat surprising consequence of this is that it is not true to say of essence or nature that it is one or many; taken by itself, absolutely considered, Thomas holds, it is neither.[30] If to be many were of the essence of the nature, it could never be one as it is one in Socrates; and if to be one as it is in Socrates were of the essence of the nature, then Socrates and Plato (and other putative individuals) would actually be the same one.

In another way, it [essence] is considered according to the being it has in this or that individual and, so considered, something can be predicated of it *per accidens* by reason of the individual in which it is, as man is said to be white because Socrates is white, though this does not belong to a man because he is a man.[31]

Thomas here gives a distinctive statement of the difference between *per se* or essential and *per accidens* or incidental predication: something predicated essentially is true because of what the thing is; something predicated accidentally happens to be true of the thing not because of what it is but because of the individual in which the whatness is found.

To be one or many is incidental or accidental to the nature or essence. So too, to exist in one way or another is incidental to the essence.

This nature however has a twofold existence, one in singulars, another in the mind, and accidents are true of it according to both modes of existence. In singulars indeed it has a multiple existence according to the diversity of the singulars.[32]

---

modi quod non est de ratione humanitatis, non conuenit homini in eo quod homo." *Ibid*, ll. 32–37.

30. "Unde si queratur utrum ista natura sic considerata possit dici una uel plures, neutrum concedendum est, quia utrumque est extra intellectum humanitatis, et utrumque potest sibi accidere." *Ibid.*, ll. 37–40.

31. "Alio modo consideratur secundum esse quod habet in hoc uel in illo: et sic de ipsa aliquid predicatur per accidents ratione eius in quo est, sicut dicitur quod home est albus quia Sortes est albus, quamuis hoc non conueniat homini in eo quod est homo." *Ibid.*, ll. 45–51.

32. "Hec autem natura habet duplex esse: unum in singularibus et aliud in anima, et secundum utrumque consequuntur dictam naturam accidentia; in singularibus etiam habet multiplex esse secundum singularium diuersitatem." *Ibid.*, ll. 52–56.

Thomas continues in a way that seems merely repetitive of what he has already said of oneness and manyness with respect to the essence, concluding that "it is evident that man's nature absolutely considered abstracts from any existence, but in such a way that it does not make precision from any of them."[33] It is not difficult to understand what it means to say that the nature exists in singulars, but what does it mean to say that it exists in the mind or soul? Having just recalled the concept of a nature's being considered absolutely, Thomas writes:

> The notion of universal cannot be said to pertain to the nature so considered, because unity and community are of the notion of the universal, but neither of these belong to human nature according to its absolute consideration.[34]

If community belonged to the nature as such, then community would belong to anything having that nature, but Socrates who is a man is not shared or general or universal but individual. If community is not said of the individual because it does not belong to the nature *per se*, community or universality must be incidentally true of the nature, said of it *per accidens*.

> Similarly too it cannot be said that the notion of genus or of species is accidental to human nature because of the existence it has in individuals, because human nature is not found in individuals with the kind of unity that makes it something one belonging to all, as the notion of universal requires. One solution is left: the notion of species is accidental to human nature as it exists in the intellect.[35]

What Thomas is suggesting, thus far, then, is this. Consider the difference between such sentences as these:

33. ". . . patet quod natura hominis absolute considerata abstrahit a quolibet esse, ita tamen quod non fiat precisio alicuius eorum." *Ibid.*, ll. 68–70.

34. "Non tamen potest dici quod ratio uniuersalis conueniat nature sic accepte, quia de ratione uniuersalis est unitas et communitas; nature autem humane neutrum horum conuenit secundum absolutam suam considerationem." *Ibid.*, ll. 73–77.

35. "Similiter etiam non potest dici quod ratio generis uel speciei accidat nature humane secundum esse quod habet in indiuidiis, quia non inuenitur in indiuidiis natura humana secundum unitatem ut sit unum quid omnibus conueniens, quod ratio uniuersalis exigit. Relinquitur ergo quod ratio speciei accidat nature humane secundum illud esse quod habet in intellectu." *Ibid.* ll. 82–90.

(1) Man is rational.
(2) Man is tan.
(3) Man is a species.

The problem of universals becomes: how do sentences of type (3) differ from the others? And there are of course any number of other examples we might have used:

(3a) Man is a predicate.
(3b) Man is a subject.
(3c) Man is universal.

And, beyond retaining the same grammatical subject, man, we might have given, as the same type of sentence as (3), such sentences as:

(4) Rational animal is the definition of man.
(5) The middle term in the argument is rational.
(6) The predicate of the conclusion is the middle term of the syllogism.
(7) The second valid mood of the first figure of the syllogism derives a universal negative conclusion from the conjunction of a universal negative and a universal affirmative.

The point of adding (3a), (3b), (3c) and (4), (5), (6) and (7) is to make it clear that we will find in Thomas's solution to the problem of universals his notion of the nature of logic in general. Universality is just the sort of thing that interests the logician and universality thus falls to the same subject matter as the things mentioned in (4)–(7).

(1) is an example of what Thomas means when he speaks of something pertaining to the essence as such, *per se*, absolutely considered. Rational enters into the definition of man, is true of it *per se*, and thus is true of each of the things of which man is predicated. That is, the following inference holds:

Man is rational.
Manlius is a man.
Manlius is rational.

Whatever is true of the essence as such is true of anything in which that essence is found. This provides us with a contrast between (1) and (2), since this inference does not hold:

Man is tan.
Manlius is a man.
Manlius is tan.

(2) is true, if it is, because someone like Manlius, who is a man, is tan and, as it happens, Manlius is not that man. The tan person that may, if only for purposes of a philosophical example, prompt us to say that [a] man is tan, is Edgar Rice Burroughs, say. But Edgar is not tan just by virtue of the fact that he is human, but because he has been diligently sunning himself in Tarzania, California. He happens to be tan. There was a time when although he was human he was pale as a ghost and there may very well come a time when his pallor will appal. For the nonce, however, it happens, it is contingently true, that Edgar Rice Burroughs has a tan. Unlike the first inference, where something true of the essence is necessarily true of the individual(s) in which the essence is found, in the second inference something is said of the essence because it happens to be true of one (or more) of the individuals in which the essence is found. With this distinction before us, Thomas feels that we have a first grasp of the status of universals.

Among the universals mentioned by Porphyry in setting down the problem of universals is species. Species shows up in (3). But what of the following inference?

Man is a species.
Manlius is a man.
Manlius is a species.

We do not want to say that an individual is a universal because this would render the description of the universal incoherent.

A universal is something said of many; a species is one nature said of many individuals. This can scarcely mean that some individual is identical with a plurality of other individuals; such identity is precisely the denial of the plurality. So, if species is a universal, and it is, Manlius, an individual, cannot be a species. This means that our third inference is unlike our first and like our second.

The second inference took off from a claim about a nature that was true because some individual having that nature happened to have a certain quality. Or, as Thomas put it, something is true of the essence because of its existence in individuals, an existence which does not pertain *per se* to the essence. To be a universal, he is suggesting, relates to the nature somewhat in that way; it is not true of the nature *per se*, but because of a certain mode of existence of the nature. What mode of existence? Existence in the intellect.

In the intellect human nature itself has an existence abstracted from all individuating marks; it has therefore a notion uniform to all individuals outside the mind, insofar as it is equally the likeness of all and leads to knowledge of each of them insofar as they are men. Because it has this relation to all individuals, the intellect fashions the notion of species and attributes it [to the nature].[36]

In order to be related to many, the nature must be something one. As found in individuals, the nature is many, not one, so they cannot be said to have numerically the same nature. But sameness demands unity. And we do want to say that individual humans have the same nature. Such talk requires that the real similarity between the individuals be grasped by the mind in one concept whose content relates to all the individuals in which it is exemplified. To call the nature universal is to relate a known essence to the many individuals in which the essence is found. Of course the concept in the mind is a particular one.

Although this understood nature has the note of universality as it is compared to things outside the mind, because it is one likeness of all,

36. "Ipsa enim natura humana in intellectu habet esse abstractum ab omnibus indiuiduantibus; et ideo habet rationem uniformem ad omnia indiuidia que sunt extra animam, prout equaliter est similitudo omnium et ducens in omnium cognitionem in quantum sunt homines. Et ex hoc quod talem relationem habet ad omnia indiuidua, intellectus adinuenit rationem speciei et attribuit sibi. . . ." *Ibid.*, ll. 91–99.

as it exists in this mind or that it is a particular understood species. . . . [T]he universality of this form is not due simply to its existence in the intellect, but insofar as it is referred to things as their likeness.[37]

Universality does not characterize the concept as concept nor is it part of the conceptual content; that is, it is neither a psychological property nor a constituent of the nature or essence. Thus, if true of the nature, as in such claims as (3), it is only incidentally true of it, thanks to an accident following on its existence in the mind. The notion of universal refers precisely to the relation between the nature as understood and a plurality in which the nature is found. Thomas provides this commentary on our third inference.

Because human nature absolutely considered is predicated of Socrates and to be a species does not pertain to it according to its absolute consideration but is one of the accidents that follow on its existence in the intellect, the term species is not predicated of Socrates, as if we might say Socrates is a species, something that would necessarily happen if the notion of species pertained to man according to the existence it has in Socrates, or according to its absolute consideration, that is, as man: whatever belongs to man as man is predicated of Socrates.[38]

The notion of a species is of something one said of many numerically different individuals. "To be said of" or "to be predicated" does not pertain to the nature absolutely considered, as if it were a constituent of it, nor to the nature as found in individuals, e.g., Socrates, as if (3) above were the very same sort of remark as (2). For a nature or essence to be predicated, to be a universal,

---

37. "Et quamuis hec natura intellecta habeat rationem, uniuersalis secundum quod comparatur ad res extra animam, quia est una similitudo omnium, tamen secundum quod habet esse in hoc intellectu uel in illo est quedam species intellecta particularis. . . . quia non est uniuersalitas illius forme secundum hoc esse quod habet in intellectu, sed secundum quod refertus ad res ut similitudo rerum." *Ibid.*, ll. 102–13.

38. "Et quia nature humane secundum suam absolutam considerationem conuenit quod predicetur de Sorte, et ratio speciei non conuenit sibi secundum suam absolutam considerationem sed est de accidentibus que consequntur eam secundum esse quod habet in intellectu, ideo nomen speciei non predicatur de Sorte ut dicatur Sortes est species: quod de necessitate accideret si ratio speciei conueniret homini secundum esse quod habet in Sorte, uel secundum suam considerationem absolutam, scilicet in quantum est homo; quicquid enim conuenit homini in quantum est homo predicatur de Sorte." *Ibid.*, ll. 120–134.

to be a species, to be a middle term, and so on is something that happens to it as a result of being known by such a mind as ours. Such things as species and universal are relations established by the mind in knowing natures and essences. Such relations ride piggy-back on natures as known and if the nature or essence conceived is a likeness of things and is thus a means of knowing them it is called a *first intention*. Logical relations, like universality, since they attach to such first intentions as accidents, are called *second intentions*.

Most of the puzzles that have exercised philosophers in the matter of universals remind one of the third instance of inference above, the one that sought to move off from (3) as one can from (1). From the fact that man is a species and Socrates is a man, it does not follow that Socrates is a species. Why not? Because (3) predicates of the essence an accident that inheres in it as it is known by the human mind. But it is the nature or essence that can be predicated of Socrates, not all the accidents that nature has in the mind. So too in Socrates the nature takes on other accidents that cannot be confused with the previous set. With such precisions as these in mind, the question as to whether or not the *Categories* is a logical or metaphysical work is easily answered. The difficulty seemingly arises because it is rightly recognized that "substance" and "quantity" and "quality" and the like are names of first intention, that is, they are imposed to signify real natures or essences. But when substance is said to be a genus, it is taken to be something one predicated of many specifically different things. Where is it one? If we think of an ontological unit existing independently of individuals, a sort of superindividual to which material individuals relate by a *real* relation, well then, of course, we seem to be engaged in a description of the way things are and thus in ontology. But Thomas regards that as a simple mistake. The nature is made one in the required sense by the human mind, which expresses in one concept the real similarity of the material individuals. This nature, absolutely considered, does not contain as a constituent either existence in individuals or existence in the mind. Indeed, it does not contain as a constituent either numerical oneness or numerical plurality. The mind, reflecting on this content and relating it to the many individuals in which that content is found, establishes the relation of universality. So *that to which universality attaches* is a real nature or essence, that is, a conceptual content expressive of a nature found in the world, but *the universality which attaches* to the nature is a logical relation established by the human mind, not a real relation obtaining among things independently of their being known by us. Is a category something real?

A category is a supreme genus and a genus is a kind of universal so the answer is clear: the nature to which the logical relation of universality attaches is real, e.g., substance, but for it to be something one said of many is a consequence of its being known.

To be predicated belongs to the genus *per se*, since it is part of its definition, and predication is something which is completed by the act of the intellect composing and dividing, having as its foundation in reality of the unity of those things of which one is said of the other. Thus the note of predicability can be contained in the notion of this intention which is genus which is similarly completed by an act of intellect. Nonetheless, that to which intellect attaches the intention of predicability, composing it with another, is not itself the intention of genus, but rather that to which the intellect attributes the intention of genus, the sort of thing signified by "animal."[39]

St. Thomas accepts Aristotle's view of the origin of the Platonic Ideas, a view which regards the realm of the Forms as the product of an elementary confusion of the logical and real orders. Platonism, for Thomas, consists in the failure to distinguish between the way things are and the way we think of them. In order to say anything of the way things are, we must of course be thinking of them, but what we say of them is not what happens to them as they are known by us, but what they are independent of our knowledge. The distinction then is not one between things as known and things as unknown. A sort of parlor game idealism can be generated from such swift and slippery

39. Cf. *De ente et essentia*, ed. cit., cap. III, ll. 133–146.

inferences as: we only know things as we know them, therefore we cannot know them as they are. What this draws attention to is the truth that the distinction between how things are in themselves and how they are as known by us, is one we make in knowing them.

But parlor game idealism would in effect conflate what Thomas calls first and second intentions and make any claim about reality the witting or unwitting projection outside the mind of the mental. Thomas sees Platonism as such a conflation but one that sees the logical as a further description of the way things are, rather than the way things are as a projection of the logical into the real order.

The question as to whether logic is a part of philosophy or only its instrument arises in the course of Thomas's exposition of Chapter 2 of Boethius's *De trinitate*—not, however, with reference to the discussion in Boethius's commentary on Porphyry, but in terms of St. Augustine. Augustine, in the eighth book of *The City of God*, included logic or rational philosophy under speculative or contemplative philosophy and, since Boethius does not include it in his division of the speculative, the Boethian division is defective. In response Thomas writes:

It should be noted that speculative sciences, as is evident from the beginning of the *Metaphysics*, are concerned with things knowledge of which is sought for its own sake. But the things with which logic is concerned are not sought to be known for their own sake, but as a kind of help to the other sciences. Therefore logic is not contained under speculative philosophy as a principal part but as something that reduces to speculative philosophy, as providing instruments, for example, syllogisms and definitions and the like, which we need in the speculative sciences. Hence according to Boethius in his *Commentary on Porphyry*, it is not so much a science as the instrument of science.[40]

40. ". . . dicendum quod scientiae speculativae, ut patet in principio *Metaphysicae*, sunt de illis, quorum cognitio quaeritur propter seipsa. Res autem de quibus logica, non quaeruntur ad cognoscendum propter seipsas, sed ut adminiculum quoddam ad alias scientias. Et ideo logica non continetur sub speculativa philosophia quasi principalis pars, sed sicut quoddam reductum ad philosophiam speculativam, prout ministrat speculationi sua instrumenta, scilicet syllogismos et definitiones et alia huiusmodi, quibus in scientiis speculativis indige-

The order of learning the sciences that Thomas sets down in a number of places[41] puts logic first because it teaches the mode of the science. It does not come first because it is easiest; far from it.[42] Because it deals with second intentions it is most difficult.

---

mus. Unde secundum Boethium in *Comm. super Porphyrium* non tam est scientia, quam scientiae instrumentum." In *Boethii de trinitate*, q. 5, a. 1, ad 2m.

41. Cf. for example the prologue to his exposition of the *Liber de causis*. In the exposition of the *De trinitate*, q. 5, a. 1, ad 9m, Thomas gives a most comprehensive picture of the arts and sciences, which fall under philosophy as being either necessary to or useful for the acquisition of wisdom which is knowledge of the divine.

42. ". . . in addiscendo a logica [oportet] incipere, non quia ipsa sit facilior ceteris scientiis, habet enim maximam difficultatem, cum sit de secundo intellectis, sed quia aliae scientiae ab ipsa dependent, in quantum ipsa docet modum procedendi in omnibus scientiis. Oportet enim primo scire modum scientiae quam scientiam ipsam, ut dicitur in II *Metaphysicorum*." In *Boethii de trinitate*, q. 6, a. 1, ad 3m.

PART TWO

*De trinitate*

# CHAPTER 3

# Thomas Comments on Boethius

Boethius wrote five theological tractates or *opuscula sacra* and St. Thomas commented on two of them. In this chapter, after several preliminary considerations, we will take a close look at St. Thomas's commentary on *De trinitate*. Among the preliminary things we must consider are, first of all, the nature of the tractates and their place in the Boethian literary production. We must also notice that Thomas did not write the same kind of commentary on the two Boethian tractates on which he did comment; that on *De trinitate* is far freer and more extensive in its plan—we remember that Thomas did not finish it—than that on *De hebdomadibus*. Given the almost uniform denigration of the latter as a commentary, I shall say a few things about what St. Thomas set out to do in the various kinds of commentary he wrote.

## THE *OPUSCULA SACRA*

To turn from Boethius's logical works, where one is likely to come upon such an ejaculation as *mihercule!*, or from *The Consolation of Philosophy*, where the ambience seems pagan though monotheistic, can produce a shock. There is little in his other writings that suggests what a fervent Catholic Boethius was, but in the tractates he is unequivocally a Christian theologian seeking to apply close analysis to the dogmas of the faith and to refute heresies.

The order in which the tractates are printed in Migne's *Patrologia Latina*, Tome 64, and in the Stewart, Rand and Tester edition and translation is, to use the titles of the latter, this:

[1] *The Trinity is One God and Not Three Gods*

[2] *Whether Father, Son and Holy Spirit are substantially Predicated of the Divinity*

[3] *How Substances are Good in virtue of their Existence without being Substantial Goods*

[4] *On the Catholic Faith*

[5] *A Treatise Against Euthyches and Nestorius*[1]

The fifth tractate, in length the equal of the other four combined, is thought to have been written first. The other four are thought to fall to the same period, but Schurr holds that [2] was written before [1]. That all these treatises can be called theological is clear enough, but whether the adjective distinguishes the third from what pagan philosophers might do is another question. In the next chapter, we will be discussing what Boethius meant by "theology" and will propose an answer to that question on the basis of the different sort of *regulae* which govern [3] as opposed to the other tractates.[2]

The two Christological heresies Boethius refutes are that which holds that Christ has two natures and is two persons (Nestorius) and the Monophysite opposite (for which Euthyches stands), that Christ is a single person with one nature. In order to handle the opposed heresies of Eutyches and Nestorius with respect to Christ, Boethius in the fifth tractate seeks to get clear as to what is meant by nature, what by person, and what the relation between the two is, since it is from confusion about

1. Migne prints the commentaries of Gilbert of Poitiers along with the tractates which are given these titles: [1] *De unitate trinitatis*, [2] *Utrum Pater et Filius et Spiritus Sanctus de divinitate substantialiter praedicentur*, [3] *Quomodo substantiae bonae sint*, [4] *Brevis fidei Christianae complexio*, [5] *Liber de persona et de duabus naturis*. Thomas refers to [2] by its incipit, *Quaero, an pater*, and to [5] as the *De duabus naturis* and [3] as *De fide Christiana*. Cf. Bruno Decker, *Sancti Thomae de Aquino Expositio super librum Boethii De Trinitate* (Leiden, 1959), p. 47. Luca Obertello, in his Italian edition, *La Consolazione della Filosofia e gli Opuscoli Teologici* (Milan, 1979) presents the tractates in this order; [5], [2], [1], [3], [4].

2. That is, the contrast between *universalium praecepta regularum* of *De trinitate* 1 (l. 29) and the *terminos regulasque* of the *De hebdomadibus* (l. 16). Chadwick, p. 174, notes that "the third contains nothing specifically Christian."

these that aberrations arise.[3] Among other things, the tractate is a brief Greek-Latin lexicon of key terms employed in discussions of Christ and the Trinity. The difference between nature and person (*natura: ousia* and *persona: hypostasis*) is not unrelated to the controversies over the sense of the famous first axiom of *De hebdomadibus, diversum est esse et id quod est* and to seemingly parallel considerations in *De trinitate*. We will have to ask if we have anything like a unified Boethian vocabulary. To let the tractates comment on one another, to seek *Boethius ex Boethio*, is a commendable practice, but one not without its pitfalls.

The fifth tractate was occasioned by a dispute which arose over a letter from a bishop who wrote the Pope asking for a clarification. Monophysites hold that Christ is formed *from* two natures but does not consist *in* two natures. Some Catholics say that both are true, and the matter is trivially obvious. In his prologue, Boethius recalls a discussion of the letter and it is clear he was not impressed by the speakers. The bishop is right. This is a matter of profound importance and difficulty. Fast and loose talk about nature and person will not do when the central Christian mystery is at stake. Boethius decides that he will attempt a written clarification, since the oral discussion was so dissatisfying.

Boethius begins by noting that the term nature is sometimes restricted to bodies, sometimes to substances, whether bodily or not, and is sometimes used of whatever exists. These facts of usage can be a source of confusion, so the senses of "nature" must first be distinguished. He gives four. First, "*natura est earum rerum quae, cum sint, quoquo modo intellectu capi possunt*: nature belongs to whatever, since it exists, can be grasped by the intellect in some way." The point of the "in some way" is

3. A thorough historical investigation of the setting in which the tractates were written can be found in Father Viktor Schurr's *Die Trinitaetslehre des Boethius im Lichte des "skythischen Kontroversen"* (Paderborn, 1935). See too John Mair, "The Text of the *Opuscula Sacra*," in *Boethius, His Life, Thought and Influence*, ed. Margaret Gibson (Blackwell, 1981). See too Maurice Nedoncelle, "Les variations de Boece sur la personne," *Revue des Sciences Religieuses* (July, 1955), 29.3, pp. 201–238.

that the extremes of reality, God and matter, can only be imperfectly understood, God because of His perfection, matter because of its imperfection; both are grasped by way of negating or removing what is known of other things. Not everything that can be grasped by mind has a nature, of course; that is the point of "since it exists." The term "nothing" has meaning, but what it means is an absence of nature. *Omnis vero natura est*: every nature exists.[4]

"*Natura est vel quod facere vel quod pati potest*: nature is either what can act or what can be acted upon."[5] In this meaning, "nature" can be predicated of bodies and the souls of bodies but also of God and other divine things.[6] In any case, however, it is applicable only to substances.

In a third meaning, the Aristotelian, "nature is the per se as opposed to the accidental principle of motion: *natura est motus principium per se et non per accidens*."[7] The brief discussion of this is reminiscent of Book Two of the *Physics*, using Aristotle's example of a bed to illustrate the difference between the artificial and the natural. (If you planted a bed and growth occurred, it would be the wood, the natural material, not the bed, the artificial form, that would grow.)

The fourth and final meaning is this, "nature is the specific difference which makes the thing what it is: *natura est unam quamque rem informans specifica differentia*."[8]

It is the last sense of the term that is in play when Catholics and Nestorians say that in Christ there are two natures.

Moving on to the meaning of "person," Boethius remarks that person is rightly thought to relate to substance, but to be narrower in range. What is clear is that nature underlies person and

---

4. *De duabus naturis*—it is thus that I shall refer to the fifth tractate—Chapter I, Rand, Stewart, Tester, p. 78, ll. 8–21.

5. *De duabus naturis*, ed. cit., p. 78.25–6.

6. The reference is to angels. In the *De hebdomadibus* as well as in *De trinitate* 2, Boethius seems to restrict the realm of the simple to God alone. Thus, in the latter text, the *sine materia forma* that is God is unique.

7. *Loc. cit.*, p. 80.41–42.

8. *Ibid.*, p. 80, ll. 57–58.

that "person" isn't used apart from nature.[9] Both substances and accidents are natures, but "person" is predicated of substance alone. Substances are bodily or not, some of the bodily are living, others not, and of the living some have sensation, other don't, and some sensitive substances are rational and others irrational. Having arrived at rational substances, Boethius brings back the incorporeal, namely God and the angels. Men and angels and God are persons because they are rational substances. But substance is also divided by universal and particular, the former being predicated of other things, the latter not. That persons are singular and unique is suggested by the fact that they are named. What then is the definition of person? An individual substance of a rational nature: *naturae rationabilis individua substantia.*[10]

It is at this point that Boethius begins to make correlations between Latin and Greek usage. What he has just given as the definition of *persona* answers to the Greek *hypostasis*. The Greeks have another word, *prosopon*, derived from the masks actors wear before their face and applied to all since a human is recognized as this particular one by his face. The Latin *persona* has the same etymology: *personare* is to sound through, because the actor's mask amplified his voice. Nonetheless, the Greeks use *hypostasis* to speak of an individual rational subsistent, where the Latins with their impoverished vocabulary use *persona*. Boethius then lapses into Greek, to exhibit the greater clarity of that tongue, then translates himself into Latin. *"Essentiae in universalibus quidem esse possunt, in solis vero individuis et particularibus substant*: essences can indeed be in universals, but they subsist only in particulars and individuals."[11]

Knowledge of universals is had from knowledge of particulars and Boethius now speaks of subsistences (*subsistentiae*) as being in universals, but having the status of substance only in partic-

9. "Nam illud quidem manifestum est personae subiectam esse naturam nec praeter naturam personam posse praedicari." *Ibid.*, p. 82.9–12.
10. *Ibid.*, p. 64.4–5.
11. *Ibid.*, p. 86.33–35.

ulars, and it is such individual subsistences that the Greeks call *hypostaseis*. Subsistence and substance differ, as any perceptive thinker will see.

Let us first set down Boethius's lexical correlations and then see what he makes of them.

| einai | esse | to be |
|-------|------|-------|
| ousia | essentia | essence |
| ousiosis | subsistentia | subsistence |
| ousiosthai | subsistere | to subsist |
| hypostasis | substantia | substance |
| hyphistasthai | substare | to stand under |
| prosopon | persona | person[12] |

Very well, how do subsistence and substance differ? A thing is said to subsist when it does not need accidents in order to be. Something is a substance (*substat*) if it is a subject of accidents, giving being to them. We can say, then, of an individual that it both subsists (*subsistit*) and is a substance (*substat*) insofar as it supports and gives being to its accidents. Boethius puts matters in a surprising way.

Therefore genera and species only subsist, since accidents do not inhere in genera and species. Individuals, however, not only subsist but also stand under (*substant*); they do not need accidents in order to exist, for they are already formed by proper and specific differences and can give being to accidents by serving as subjects.[13]

Is Boethius according real existence to universals? The sequel suggests otherwise. The individual substance is not a subject of accidents in virtue of generic or specific expressions of what it is, its essence. The individual substance is called *hypostasis* because it stands under accidents, being placed under (*subposita*)

---

12. Boethius cites Cicero, *Tusculan Disputations*, ii.15.35, as marveling at the richness of the Greek language, but he seems capable of providing Latin equivalents for Greek terms, precisely the corollaries of our chart.

13. "Itaque genera vel species subsistunt tantum; neque enim accidentia generibus speciebusve contingunt. Individua vero non modo subsistunt verum etiam substant, nam neque ipsa indigent accidentibus ut sint; informata enim sunt iam propriis et specificis differentiis et accidentibus ut esse possint ministrant, dum sunt scilicet subiecta." *Loc. cit.*, p. 88.49–55.

and underlying accidents. In Latin too individuals are called *sub-posita* so we can link *substantia* and *suppositum* and *persona*, though the Latin will call only rational individual substances or supposits persons, whereas in Greek it is *hypostasis* (*substantia, suppositum*) that is restricted to rational animals, though this is not explained by its etymology. A man has essence, subsistence and substance and person, Boethius notes, so we should not see any Platonic realism in this text. In the context, the only reason for going into all these matters is to get clear on the relation between nature (*natura, ousia*) and person (*persona, hypostasis*) in order to talk about Christ, the Incarnate God, a person at once human and divine. We will want to refer to these precisions later in this part and in the next part when we will be trying to grasp Boethius's teaching on the structure of the concrete.

Nature is the specifying difference of any substance and a person is an individual substance of a rational nature. Nestorius says there are two persons in Christ, in this sense of person, and we can now see how absurd that is. What kind of connection can there be between a human person and a divine person? Christ is not two individuals, but one. Christ exists and whatever is is one. We have here Boethius's statement of transcendental unity: *Quod enim non est unum, nec esse omnino potest; esse enim atque unum convertitur et quodcumque unum est est.*[14] Against the Monophysites, Boethius stresses that Christ took human nature from the Virgin Mary and that there is no way in which the divine nature could become human or the human nature divine. His argument relies on the Aristotelian teaching that a common matter is required if one thing is to become another.[15]

Once the heretical interpretations have been dealt with, Boethius turns to a positive account of how the Catholic faith does indeed permit one to say that Christ is *from* two natures and *in* two natures.[16]

If the assumptions of tract [3] differ from those of the others,

14. *Ibid.*, p. 94.36–39.
15. See *ibid.*, p. 112.
16. *Ibid.*, p. 116.25–31.

the treatise *On the Catholic Faith* differs in style and method from all the rest. It lays out in its grand lines the Christian faith: the nature of God, creation, man's fall and need for redemption. Like many catechisms it is at one expository and polemical, so we find Boethius anathematizing Arius, the Sabellians, the Manicheans, Pelagius and, again, Nestorius and Euthyches. There is little of argument or analysis of the doctrines. Its power lies in the truths it conveys and the serene faith of its author. The tractate ends, appropriately, on a threnodic and apocalyptic note.

Believers now have but a single expectation: we believe the end of the world is coming, that all perishable things will pass away, that men will be raised up for the scrutiny of the coming judgment when each will receive what each deserves and abide forever and eternally in the end due him, that contemplation of his Creator is the sufficient prize of bliss—insofar, that is, as creature can gaze on Creator—that the number of fallen angels will be made up, thus filling the heavenly city whose king is the Son of the Virgin and in which there will be joy everlasting, delight, food, work and perpetual praise of the Creator.[17]

We still do not possess critical editions of the *opuscula sacra*, the text first published by E. K. Rand and H. F. Stewart in 1918 remaining the best available.

### THE TRACTATES IN MEDIEVAL TIMES

In the words of Henry Chadwick, "These tractates attracted great interest from medieval commentators from the ninth century onwards, culminating in masterful discussions of the first and the third from the pen of St. Thomas Aquinas."[18] The *Con-*

---

17. "Sola ergo nunc est fidelium exspectatio qua credimus affuturum finem mundi, omnia corruptibilia transitura, resurrecturos homines ad examen futuri iudicii, recepturos pro meritis singulos et in perpetuum atque in aeternum debitis finibus permansuros; solumque esse praemium beatitudinis contemplationem conditoris—tanta dumtaxat, quanta a creatura ad creatorem fieri potest—ut ex eis reparato angelico numero superna illa civitas impleatur, ubi rex est virginis filius eritque gaudium sempiternum, delectatio, cibus, opus, laus perpetua creatoris." Stewart, Rand, Tester, ll. 267–276.

18. Chadwick, *op. laud.*, p. 174.

*solation of Philosophy* was the object of many commentaries throughout the medieval period[19] and indeed was never neglected.

While there seems reason to doubt that Alcuin made much use of the *opuscula sacra*, it was in the Carolingian period that they appear to have become part of the liberal arts tradition and the means whereby theology was taught along with the *logica vetus*. Gottschalk does a good deal of quoting from the tractates, but it was Hincmar, Archbishop of Rheims from 845 to 882, whose patronage was crucial. "It was in these years that the *Opuscula Sacra* became standard texts, available in any good library and used with growing fluency by contemporary scholars." [20] At Corbie, Boethius was read seriously, with Bovo wondering whether the author of the *O qui perpetua* could be a Christian, and Ratramnus defending Boethius against inept use.[21] The influence of John Scotus Eriugena on the Boethian tradition was indirect but forceful, through the school of Auxerre.[22]

In the twelfth century, the tractates make an appearance in Abelard's *Sic et Non*[23] and *Theologia Christiana*, Boethius described in the latter as "the greatest philosopher of the western world." Thierry of Chartres and Clarembald of Arras commented on some of the tractates, and Gilbert of Poitiers commented on all of them.[24]

19. See the list in Obertello, *La Consolazione delle Filosofia*, etc., pp. 125–126. Also Margaret Gibson, "The *Opuscula Sacra* in the Middle Ages," in *Boethius, His Life, Thought and Influence*.
20. Margaret Gibson, *op. cit.*, p. 218.
21. Bovo's commentary, *In Boethium De Consolatione Philosophiae Lib. III, Metr. IX, Commentarius*, is found in PL 64, 1239–46.
22. The Auxerre commentary on tractates (1)–(3) and (5), now thought to be by Remigius, was attributed to John Scotus Eriugena in the modern printing. Cf. E. K. Rand, *Johannes Scottus* (Munich, 1906).
23. See B. Boyer and Richard McKeon, *Peter Abailard* (Chicago, University of Chicago Press, 1976), II, pp. 130–36.
24. Gangolf Schrimpf, *Die Axiomenschrift des Boethius (De Hebdomadibus) als Philosophisches Lehrbuch des Mittelalters* (Leiden, E. J. Brill, 1966), and Pierre Hadot, "Forma Essendi," *Les etudes classiques*, XXXVIII (1970), pp. 143–56, discuss the medieval commentaries on the *De hebdomadibus*. See N. M. Haering, *Life and Works of Clarembald of Arras* (Toronto, Pontifical Institute of Mediaeval Studies, 1965); *The Commentaries on Boethius of Gilbert of Poitiers* (Toronto, Pontifical Institute of Mediaeval Studies, 1966); *Commentaries*

In the thirteenth century, William of Auxerre, in his *Summa Aurea,* and Alexander of Hales and Hugh of Saint-Cher commenting on the *Sentences,* rely on the tractates, but St. Thomas seems to be the last medieval master to comment directly on any of them.[25] But if the *opuscula sacra* did not serve as standard works for Masters of Theology to explicate, they were valuable sources for theology nonetheless. Boethius is often cited in the theological writings of St. Thomas[26] but that does not distinguish him from other theologians. It is his *expositiones* of Boethian tractates that make Thomas unique among the theologians of his time.

### THOMAS'S COMMENTARIES ON BOETHIUS

The commentaries on *De trinitate* and on *De hebdomadibus* are thought to have been written in 1257–1258 and to have had their origin in lectures Thomas gave to his fellow Dominicans in the Convent of St. Jacques in Paris. If *De trinitate* is incomplete because the school year ended before it could be finished, this might be reason for placing the completed *De hebdomadibus* commentary first.[27] The latter is like all other Thomistic *expositiones* whether on Scripture or Aristotle or Pseudo-Dionysius or

---

on Boethius by Thierry of Chartres and His School (Toronto, Pontifical Institute of Mediaeval Studies, 1971).

25. See Margaret Gibson, *op. cit.,* p. 227. Schrimpf describes three unedited manuscript commentaries on the *De hebdomadibus,* one from the late thirteenth and early fourteenth, the others from the fifteenth century.

26. The Leonine editors of the *Summa theologiae* and *Summa contra Gentiles* find 135 citations of Boethius in those works (cf. Tomus XVI, p. 206) and in the Marietti editions of the *Quaestiones disputatae* and *Quaestiones Quodlibitales* a total of 180 citations of Boethius are noted. See *Opuscula theologica,* Vol. II, Marietti, containing Calcaterra's edition of the *Expositio in Boethii de trinitate,* p. 294, n. 2. See too Ceslao Pera, O.P., *Le Fonti del Pensiero di S. Tommaso D'Aquino nella Somma Teologica,* con Presentazione di M. D. Chenu, O.P., et Aggiornamento Bibliografico di C. Vansteenkiste, O.P., Marietti, 1979. The original of this is found in the *Introduzione Generale de La Somma Teologica,* Rome, 1949, pp. 31–153.

27. Cf. Siegfried Neumann, *Geganstande und Methode, der Theoretischen Wissenschaften nach Thomas von Aquin Aufgrund der Expositio super librum*

the *Liber de causis*, that is, a word-for-word, line-for-line, explanation of the intention of the text. That on *De trinitate*, on the other hand, is modeled on Thomas's commentary on the *Sentences*.

Of the three available modern editions of the commentary on *De trinitate*, only the 1959 edition of Bruno Decker is complete. In 1948, Paul Wyser, O.P., published Thomas's comments on Chapter Two of the tractate that covers only lines 1–18, which deal with the threefold distinction of the speculative and the different modes of procedure in each. Calcaterra fails to include the *expositiones* of Boethius's *prooemium* and Chapters One and Two.[28]

Decker's edition enables us to see that the commentary is at once a literal exposition of the Boethian text and the development of questions raised by the text which are divided into articles structured in the manner that becomes canonical with Thomas.[29] The parts of the work are these: [1] *Prologue* of St. Thomas; [2] *Exposition* of the *prooemium* of Boethius; [3] *Question I* on the knowledge of divine things, divided into four articles (1) Whether the human mind needs a new illumination of divine light for knowledge of the truth; (2) Whether the human mind can achieve knowledge of God; (3) Whether God is

---

*Boethii De Trinitate* (Münster, Westf., Aschendorff, 1965), p. 8. Leo Elders, in *Faith and Science* (Rome, Herder, 1974), suggests that Thomas undertook the commentary on the *De trinitate* precisely to develop a theory of the nature and distinction of the sciences and, having accomplished that task, did not go on to comment on the rest of the *opusculum*. The other commentaries Thomas left incomplete do not seem explainable in this way, but Elders's suggestion casts into a different light the tantalizing fact that the Thomistic *expositio* stops precisely at the point where so much latter-day scholarly discussion has begun. One might speculate that, at the time of the *expositio*, Thomas did not know quite what to make of the rest of Chapter Two, and set aside the work never to take it up again.

28. Paul Wyser, O.P., *Thomas von Aquin In librum Boethii de Trinitate Quaestiones Quinta et Sexta* (Fribourg, 1948); Mannes Calcaterra, O.P., *In Boethium De Trinitate et De Hebdomadibus Expositio*, in *Opuscula Theologia*, Vol. II, Turin, Marietti, 1954; Bruno Decker, *Sancti Thomae de Aquino Expositio super librum Boethii De trinitate* (Leiden, E.J. Brill, 1959).

29. See Otto Bird, "How to Read an Article in the *Summa*."

the first thing known by the mind; (4) Whether the human mind suffices to achieve knowledge of the divine Trinity; [4] *Question II* on the manifestation of divine knowledge, in four articles (1) Whether it is licit to investigate divine things; (2) Whether there can be a science of the divine; (3) Whether in the science of faith which is of God it is licit to use authorities and philosophical arguments; (4) Whether divine things should be hidden in obscure and newly minted words; [5] *Exposition* of Chapter One; [6] *Question III* on the things which pertain to the commendation of the faith, in four articles (1) Whether faith is necessary for the human race; (2) How faith relates to religion; (3) Whether the faith is fittingly called Catholic or universal; (4) Whether this is the confession of the true faith that Father, Son and Holy Spirit are each God, that the three are one God without any distance of inequality; [7] *Question IV* on the things causative of plurality, in four articles (1) Whether otherness is the cause of plurality; (2) Whether the variety of accidents causes numerical diversity (3) Whether two bodies can be or be understood to be in the same place; (4) Whether variety of place has anything to do with numerical difference; [8] *Exposition* of Chapter Two; [9] *Question V* on the division of speculative science, in four articles (1) Whether the division of the speculative into natural, mathematical and divine is a good one; (2) Whether natural philosophy is concerned with things which exist in matter and motion; (3) Whether a mathematical consideration is without motion and matter of things which exist in matter; (4) Whether divine science is about things which exist without matter and motion; [10] *Question VI* on the modes Boethius assigns the speculative sciences, in four articles (1) Whether it is necessary to treat rationally of natural things, methodically of mathematicals and intellectually of divine things; (2) Whether imagination must be wholly relinquished in treating divine things; (3) Whether our intellect can gaze on the divine form; (4) Whether it can do this by way of any speculative science.

The final articles are suggested by Boethius's remark that in theology we apprehend that form which is pure form and not an image (*sed potius inspicere formam quae vere forma neque imago est*). Indeed, in what is discussed in the questions, Thomas is always guided by the text but is able to bring to bear on his treatment a vast variety of sources, thus enabling him to make the doctrine of Boethius a component of a wider synthesis.

In the remainder of this chapter, we will be concerned with Thomas's *expositiones* of the text of Boethius itself; in the next two chapters we will be concerned with problems which arise from Questions V and VI.

### Exposition of the Prooemium of Boethius[30]

Boethius opens his tractate with a dedicatory letter addressed to his father-in-law Symmachus in which he makes a number of observations about his treatment of the Trinity. He is anxious to have Symmachus's reactions to what he has written, but because of the difficulty of the topic he has adopted a cryptic style lest sacred matters be laid open to the ridicule of the unwise. In short, he is not addressing whom it might concern, but an elite which includes his father-in-law. His guide, he notes, has been St. Augustine and he hopes that he has profited from the work of his great predecessor.

Thomas, taking the dedication to be a *prooeemium*, sees it as attempting three things. First, in order to render the reader docile, Boethius states briefly the causes of the work; second, he excuses himself for his style, thereby eliciting the benevolence of the reader. Third, he notes that the origin and even teaching of the work are from St. Augustine, and this makes the reader attentive. St. Thomas's exposition swings around these three points.

*The Four Causes of the Tractate.* It may seem unusual to ask after the four causes of a tractate since the doctrine of causes is developed to explain natural things. Nonetheless, St. Thomas does this, and all the more willingly, we may assume, because

---

30. In the Bruno Decker edition, pp. 49–55.

Aristotle does in fact examine the causes of artifacts *before* turning to natural things.[31]

The material cause of the tractate is its subject matter, the Trinity, which also explains its difficulty: the subject requires prolonged and diligent study. Indeed, St. Thomas says, it was this question that particularly vexed the faithful as the Church first developed.[32]

The mind of the author is the proximate and secondary efficient cause of the work (*quantum mentis nostrae igniculum*), but the primary is God (*illustrare lux divina dignata*). Denis tells us that fire is particularly apt to express divine attributes, because of its subtlety, illumination, heat, place and mobility. These answer to the divine simplicity and immateriality, perfect clarity, omnipotence and sublimity, and apply in a lesser way to angels and least of all to the human mind whose bodily condition is an obstacle to a movement toward the highest. Hence the need for divine illumination, particularly in the matter before us.[33]

The discussion of the formal cause immediately subdivides into the tractate's threefold mode of approach: it proceeds by way of argumentation *(formatam rationibus)*, in written not just oral form, and thus is not addressed only to the present generation but to others as well.[34]

31. St. Thomas, in his exposition of Peter Lombard's *prooemium* to the *Sentences*, also develops a causal analysis. Cf. *Scriptum super libros Sententiarum*, ed. Mandonnet (Paris, Sumptibus P. Lethielleux, 1929), pp. 19–24. St. Bonaventure does something similar in his commentary on the *Sentences*.

32. ". . . quia a principio nascentis ecclesiae haec quaestio ingenia fidelium maxime fatigavit." *Ed. cit.*, p. 50.9–10.

33. "Ignis enim, ut dicit Dionysius 15 c. Caelestis hierarchiae, maxime competit ad significandas divinas proprietates, tum ratione subtilitatis, tum ratione luminis, tum ratione virtutis activae per calorem, tum ratione situs et motus. Quae quidem deo maxime competunt, in quo est summa simplicitas et immaterialitas, perfecta claritas, omnipotens virtus et altissima sublimitas, angelis autem mediocriter, sed humanis mentibus infimo modo, quarum propter corpus coniunctum et puritas inquinatur et lux obscuratur et virtus debilitatur et motus in suprema retardatur; unde humanae mentis efficacia recte igniculo comparatur. Unde nec ad huius quaestionis veritatem inquirendam sufficit, nisi divina luce illustrata, et sic divina lux est causa principalis, humana mens causa secundaria." *Op. cit.*, pp. 50.15–51.7.

34. Thomas glosses *formatam* by contrasting it with probable argumentation. "Quaestio namque quamdiu probabilibus rationibus sub dubio exagitatur, quasi

The discussion of the tractate's final cause is dense, with Thomas noting that Boethius seeks the single judgment of his wise addressee rather than public acclaim,[35] although his chief aim is interior, the grasp of divine truth, and then the judgment of Symmachus.

*Boethius's Excuse.* Boethius begs indulgence for both the difficulty and the imperfection of his work. The difficulty is threefold, stemming first from the tractate's brevity, second, its subtle arguments, *ex intimis disciplinis philosophiae sumptae*, third, its neologisms.

To these three he adds a fourth, already touched on, namely the difficulty of the matter, such that the things written in this work are spoken to the wise alone, who can understand them—people like the author himself and the man to whom it is addressed. Others who cannot mentally grasp it are excluded from its readership. They will not gladly read what they do not understand.[36]

The imperfection of the work is excused because one must not demand greater certainty than the human mind can attain in divine things. This is true in lesser matters, like medicine, where sometimes through no fault of the physician the end sought is not reached. "Hence in this work, where the subject is a most difficult one exceeding the grasp of human reason, the author ought all the more be indulged if he does not resolve the question with perfect certainty.[37]

*What Boethius Owes to St. Augustine.* In acknowledging his debt to Augustine, Boethius does not of course mean that he will

---

informis est, nondum ad certitudinem veritatis pertingens, et ideo formata dicitur esse, quando ad eam ratio additur, per quam certitudo de veritate habetur. Et in hoc providit intelligentiae, quia quod credimus, debemus auctoritati. quod intelligimus, rationi. . . ." (p. 51.11–15) On the distinction between oral and written teaching, Thomas contrasts Aristotle's *Physics* which bore the title *De naturalia auditu* with the *De anima*, the former being addressed to those present, the latter, like other exoteric works, to the absent.

35. Decker links Thomas's gloss on *et clamoribus vulgi*, namely, "sicut poetae recitantes carmina in theatris" to the commentary ascribed to John Scotus Eriugena, where the same explication is found. Cf. p. 52, n. 2.

36. *Ibid.*, p. 54.9–14.

37. *Ibid.*, pp. 54.22–55.2.

say only what Augustine already said, but rather that he will take as his starting point his great predecessor's teaching that *in absolutis divinae personae conveniunt et in relativis distinguuntur*. From this as seed, Boethius will try to produce fruit, by establishing its truth by many arguments. In his prologue, Thomas noted that the Trinity can be treated either by appealing to authorities or by argument. Ambrose and Hilary rely on authority alone, Augustine on authority and argument, whereas Boethius uses only arguments.[38]

The *expositio textus* is followed by the first two questions of the commentary.

### Exposition of Chapter One[39]

His *prooeemium* behind him, Boethius begins to treat of the trinity of persons and unity of the divine essence. Thomas observes that the tractate is divided into two parts, [I] in the first of which Boethius pursues what pertains to the unity of the essence, against the Arians, [II] in the second of which what pertains to the trinity of persons, against Sabellius. The incipit of this second part, *Sed hoc interim ad eam*, is found in Chapter Three of the tractate. The first part is subdivided into two sections, [A] in the first of which he sets down the teaching of the Catholic faith on the unity of the divine essence, [B] in the second of which he investigates the truth of the teaching (at the beginning of Chapter Two). The first section is again subdivided, [1] a first part describing the characterization of the faith whose teaching he intends to examine, [2] a second setting forth the teaching of that faith on the matter at hand, at *Cuius haec de trinitate unitate sententia est.* [40]

The faith is characterized as Catholic or universal to distinguish it from heretical sects. These usurp the reverence due the Christian religion. He suggests "reverence" can be understood in two ways, as the reverence owed Christianity—"Haec est vic-

38. Cf. *ed. cit.*, pp. 47–8.
39. In the Decker edition, pp. 101–106.
40. Rand, Stewart, and Tester, p. 6.7.

toria quae vincit mundum, fides nostra"—or as the reverence that faith shows God. Heretics are called Christians by an abuse of the term since they do not accept the doctrine of Christ which is universally and commonly held.

Boethius provides two reasons for calling the faith Catholic, Thomas notes. First, *propter universalium praecepta regularum, quibus eiusdem religionis intelligatur auctoritas*: because of the universal precepts and rules whereby the authority of this same religion is understood; second, because its cult extends to the far corners of the world. Unlike the Law of Moses, which was given to one people, the Catholic faith proposes precepts for all nations. "Or they are called universal rules because no falsehood or iniquity is contained in no matter what article and no matter what case." [41]

[IA2] *The Catholic Teaching.* Boethius sets down the Catholic teaching on this matter, then he gives the reason for it and, finally, he shows the appropriateness of the reason given. The teaching itself is expressed in the form of an argument in which, given the fact that deity is uniformly attributed to each of the persons, it is concluded that the name "God" is predicated in the singular and not in the plural. [42]

The argument works because deity does not differ in the three persons: *ratio est indifferentia.* "This is why the stated conclusion follows from the premises, because undiffering deity is attributed without difference to the three persons." [43] Arians, on the other hand, say the Father is more God than the Son, thus introducing

41. "Vel dicuntur universales regulae, quia eis nihil falsitatis, nihil iniquitatis admiscetur in quocumque articulo sive in quocumque casu." P. 103.8–10.

42. "Proponit autem fidei catholicae sententiam per modum argumenti, eo quod fides 'argumentum non apparentium' dicitur Hebrews 11:1. In quo quidem argumento ex hoc quod deitas singulis personis uniformiter attribuitur, concluditur quod de omnibus non pluraliter, sed singulariter hoc nomen 'deus' praedicatur." P. 103.17–21.

43. "Ex hoc enim est quod ex praemissis praedicta conclusio sequitur, quia indifferens deitas tribus personis non differenter attribuitur." P. 103.26–104.1. The Tester translation of "Cuius coniunctionis ratio est indifferentia" takes the *coniunctio* to refer to the union of the persons. "The cause of this union is absence of difference." (p. 6.10) Thomas sees it as what enables the conjunction of premises to generate the conclusion, surely a better reading of the text.

diversity within the nature of deity itself, which must lead to a plurality of gods. "Catholics by contrast confessing the equality of the persons profess their nondifference and hence unity." [44]

Showing the appropriateness of the argument is a lengthier matter and Thomas sees Boethius dividing it into two parts, in the first of which he demonstrates the necessity of the aforesaid argument, in the second of which he proves something presupposed in his demonstration. The proof of the necessity of the argument involves two steps.

First, he proposes that otherness is the principle of plurality, taking otherness to be the difference whereby something is set off from other things. Boethius prefers *alteritas* (otherness) to *alietas* (otheredness?), Thomas thinks, because it is not only substantial differences that constitute plurality, making another, but accidental ones as well, which make other. *Alietas* follows on *alteritas*, but not vice versa. We have here the root of the Arian deduction: if otherness is the cause of plurality and, given the cause, the effect follows, therefore, given otherness because of increase and decrease, there follows plurality of deity. [45]

Second, he proposes that otherness is the proper principle of plurality, since without it plurality cannot be understood. Hence the root of the Catholic argument (*coniunctionis*). Take away the proper cause and you take away the effect. If then in the three persons there is no otherness of deity, there will be unity, not plurality. [46]

Boethius now undertakes to prove his supposition that otherness is the proper principle of plurality. Here is the argument.

Of all things differing in genus or species or number, some otherness or difference is the cause of the diversity.
Wherever there are many things, three or whatever number, they are generically, specifically or numerically diverse.

44. *Ibid.*, p. 104.9–10.
45. *Ibid.*, p. 104.15–23. See also *Summa Theologiae*, Ia, q.31.
46. "Ex quo habetur ratio catholicae coniunctionis. Remota enim propria causa tollitur effectus. Si ergo in tribus personis non est alteritas aliqua deitatis, non erit pluralitas, sed unitas." P. 104.26–7.

Therefore the principle of all plurality is some otherness.[47]

Boethius then proves the minor premiss in this way. "Diverse" will be said in as many ways as "same" is. But things are said to be the same in three ways, generically, specifically, numerically. And so will things be said to be diverse. The first premiss of *that* argument is taken from the *Topics*, which states the rule that a thing will have as many senses as its opposite does, and from the *Metaphysics* which points out that same and diverse are opposites. The second premiss is manifested by examples of generic, specific and numerical identity.[48]

Next Boethius proves the major of the basic argument, since a doubt can arise about it. That otherness is the cause of diversity of genus and species may seem clear enough, but it is doubtful in the case of things numerically different. Indeed, plurality would seem to be the principle of their diversity. "Therefore, in order to verify the major of his syllogism he shows that this difference too, that whereby some things are said to differ numerically, is caused by some otherness or variety. Which he proves by the fact that in three men who agree in genus and species other accidents are found, as in man and cow another species and in man and rock another genus. Hence just as man and cow are set off from one another by species, so two men are by accidents."[49]

47. "Et est ratio sua talis. Omnium rerum genere vel specie vel numero differentium est aliqua alterias sive differentia causa diversitatis. Sed omnes res plures, sive tres sive quotlibet, sunt diversae vel genere vel species vel numero. Ergo omnium plurium principium est aliqua alteritas." P. 105.2–6.

48. The text on p. 105, line 7, seems defective. Just after the statement of the basic argument, we read, "Circa hanc rationem tria facit. Primo ponit minorem, secundo ibi: *Quotiens enim,* etc. probationem minoris, quae talis est." Decker must take this last sentence to mean "First he sets down the minor, second, namely at 'for as often as same' etc., [he sets forth] the proof of the minor, which is this," making *ponit* function twice though it is rendered idle in its explicit occurrence.

49. "Et ideo ad verificandum maiorem sui syllogismi ostendit quod hanc etiam differentiam, qua aliqua dicuntur differre numero, facit aliqua alteritas sive varietas. Quod probat per hoc quod in tribus hominibus, qui conveniunt genere et specie, inveniuntur altera accidentia, sicut in homine et bove altera species et in homine et lapide genus alterum. Unde sicut homo et bos distant specie, ita duo homines distant accidentibus." P. 105.24–106.2.

Of course one might say that the variety of accidents cannot be the cause of numerical plurality because, accidents having been removed, really in the case of separable ones, mentally in the case of inseparable, the subject remains, accidents being by definition what come and go without the subject as such coming into or passing out of being. To counter this, Thomas notes, Boethius says that while all accidents can be separated, at least mentally, from the subject, nonetheless the diversity of one accident can in no wise, not even mentally, be separated from individuals, namely diversity of place. Two bodies cannot occupy the same place, either really or in a mental fiction, since this can be neither understood nor imagined. So he concludes that men are numerically many because they are many thanks to accidents.

*Exposition of Chapter Two*[50]

Boethius set out to state and defend the teaching of the Catholic faith on the unity of the trinity. He now proceeds to inquire into the matter, but, mindful of Aristotle's teaching that one should first inquire into the proper mode of a science before undertaking the science itself, he first sets forth the mode appropriate to this inquiry and then undertakes the inquiry. The inquiry proper begins just where Thomas's exposition breaks off.[51]

The first part is subdivided into two, since Boethius first states the necessity for showing the mode of inquiry, and then sets forth the mode appropriate to this inquiry. The chapter begins with the exhortation that what has been stated, namely, the Catholic doctrine on the trinity, be looked into carefully so that the deep and hidden truth may be scrutinized, but that this be done in an appropriate way, one that takes into account the way such things can be grasped and understood.

He uses both "grasped" and "understood," because the mode of inquiry must be appropriate both to the things and to us; if it

---

50. Decker edition, pp. 157–160.
51. Namely at "quae vere forma neque imago est et quae esse ipsum est et ex qua esse est," precisely where so much recent discussion begins.

is not congruent to the things they cannot be understood, if it is not congruent to us, we cannot grasp them. Divine things are of their very nature such that they can be known only by intellect: *res divinae ex natura sua habent quod non cognoscantur nisi intellectu.*[52] Thus, were one to follow his imagination in considering them, he would fail to understand them, since they are not intelligible in that way. By the same token, to want to see and comprehend divine things as one may comprehend sensible things and mathematical demonstrations won't do because, while divine things are intelligible, our intellect is defective. Aristotle's authority is invoked by Boethius, Thomas says, to the effect that it is the mark of a wise man to formulate beliefs about things as they actually are.[53] We cannot have equal evidence and certainty about all things.

That being said, Boethius now seeks the mode appropriate to this inquiry by distinguishing it from the modes observed in other sciences. Since the mode should be congruent to the thing being scrutinized, this part is divided into two, in the first of which he will distinguish sciences according to the things with which they deal, in the second of which he will assign appropriate modes to each science.

The first part requires three steps. First, he will show the things natural philosophy deals with; second, the things mathematics deals with; third, the things divine science considers. "It was well said that as each thing is, so should belief of it be formed: *Bene dictum est quod ut unumquodque est, ita debet de eo fides capi.*"[54] Since there are three parts of speculative philosophy—Boethius means to distinguish them from ethics, which is practical—each will have a mode appropriate to its subject matter.

Natural philosophy deals with mobile things which are not

52. *Ibid.,* p. 158.9–10.
53. Rand feels it is Cicero Boethius has in mind (*Tusculan Disputations,* v.7.19), and so did Remigius of Auxerre and Gilbert of Poitiers, who would not have known Aristotle's *Ethics,* I, 1, 1094b23–25. See Decker, p. 158nn.
54. *Ibid.,* p. 159.8.

abstracted from matter—*in motu inabstracta*—and Boethius illustrates the points with examples of fire and earth.

When he says "form conjoined with matter has motion," this should be understood to mean that the composite of matter and form, as such, has motion due to it, or that the form itself existing in matter is the principle of motion; so it is that the consideration of material things and mobile things is the same.[55]

When Boethius says that mathematics is concerned with what is *sine motu inabstracta*, he means it does not consider motion or mobile things, differing in this from natural philosophy, but considers forms which are not as they exist abstracted from matter, and in that it is like natural philosophy. Mathematics considers forms without matter and thus without motion—*speculatur formas sine materia ac per hoc sine motu*—since wherever there is motion there is matter, something proved in the *Metaphysics*.[56] Forms are separated from matter as considered by the mathematician, but that is not how they exist. Thomas underscores the difference: *sic secundum speculationem sunt separabiles, non secundum esse*.[57]

And what now of theology, the third part of speculative philosophy, which is called variously divine science, metaphysics and first philosophy? Boethius says it is *sine motu* and thus it is like mathematics and unlike natural philosophy; he says it is *abstracta*, from matter that is, *atque inseparabilis*, in both of which it differs from mathematics. It will be noted that the text Thomas used had *inseparabilis* rather than *separabilis*, and it is

---

55. "Quod autem dicit: *habetque motum forma materiae coniuncta*, sic intelligendum est: ipsum compositum ex materia et forma, in qunatum huiusmodi, habet motum sibi debitum, vel ipsa forma in materia exsistens est principium motus; et ideo eadem est consideratio de rebus secundum quod sunt materiales et secundum quod sunt mobiles." P. 159.15–20.

56. Thomas refers to Book IX, a text Decker suggests is found in Chapter Eight, 1050b20–22, and notes that in commenting on that text, Thomas expressly states: *quia quod movetur, oportet habere materiam* (lectio 9, n. 1875).

57. *Ed. cit.*, p. 160.3–4. This is no more than what Boethius himself explicitly says: "haec [mathematica] enim formas corporum speculatur sine materia ac per hoc sine motu, quae formae cum in materia sint, ab his separari non possunt." P. 8.11–14.

instructive to see what he makes of this defective reading; the correct reading is precisely *separabilis*.

Divine things as they exist are abstracted from matter and motion but mathematicals are not, but they are separable as considered; but divine things are inseparable, *because nothing is separable unless it is conjoined*. Hence divine things are not separable from matter as considered, but exist abstracted from it; with mathematicals it is just the opposite.[58]

Thomas, faced with the negative of the term Boethius actually wrote, yet manages to find the basic contrast between theology and the other sciences Boethius intended.

Boethius goes on to assign an appropriate mode to each of these sciences and then develops the ultimate mode, the one proper to the present inquiry. Of it he says negatively that it must eschew imagination and positively that it must concentrate on pure form, that is, form without matter and motion. Boethius goes on to describe the nature of pure form, Thomas says, and then his own exposition breaks off.

### SOME CONCLUSIONS

When only the questions Thomas developed on the basis of the text of Boethius were published, the reader was of course unaware of the care with which Thomas read the text itself. His exposition of *De trinitate* is half the length of his exposition of *De hebdomadibus* but is proportional to it. The text of the third tractate is 175 lines in the Rand edition; the text of the first tractate Thomas commented on *qua expositor* amounts to 84 lines. Clearly the commentary on *De trinitate* would have been enormous if the plan had been carried through to completion.

That Thomas is concerned to search out and clarify the mean-

58. "Res enim divinae sunt secundum esse abstractae a materia et motu, sed mathematicae inabstractae, sunt autem consideratione separabiles; sed res divinae inseparabiles, quia nihil est separabile nisi quod est coniunctum. Unde res divinae non sunt secundum considerationem separabiles a materia, sed secundum esse abstractae; res vero mathematicae e converso." P. 160.10–15.

ing and intention of the text of Boethius is manifest. None of the
tools he employs to display the meaning of the text is alien to it.
Rarely if ever was Boethius read with such care. Thomas, alerted
by the *prooemium*, knows that the text will be enigmatic and
inchoate. His task then will be to make explicit what is implicit
in the text. When we consider the *expositio* on *De trinitate*, it
seems clear that Thomas is seeking the truth of the matters under
consideration in the text of Boethius rather than simply using
the text of Boethius as an occasion to develop his own independent doctrine.[59] That the *quaestiones* are not *expositiones* is of
course true, but far from being the typical way Thomas comments, they are, the *Sentences* commentary apart, unique. Thus
to suggest that Thomas's commentaries are works in which he is
chiefly concerned to develop his own doctrines is an extraordinary claim that requires grounding and argument. Nonetheless,
it has regularly been said of Thomas's exposition of *De hebdomadibus* that he is developing in it a doctrine undreamt of by
Boethius and absent from the text of the tractate. No one ever
made an effort to support this baffling claim and, since it quickly
acquired the status of received opinion, it was not thought to
need one. If we use the expositions of the first tractate as a control on what we say of the exposition of the third, we will not
be tempted to make untenable statements about the latter. And
we will feel compelled to subject received opinion to close scrutiny.

59. Cf. M.D. Chenu, O.P., *Introduction a l'étude de Saint Thomas d'Aquin*
(Paris, 1954), pp. 173–196.

# CHAPTER 4

# Tres speculativae partes

The division of the theoretical that Boethius sets down at the outset of Chapter Two of *De trinitate* has obvious roots in Aristotle, as we shall see, but before looking into that we must take into account another and earlier and manifestly different division of the theoretical, that found in Boethius's first commentary on Porphyry. In *De trinitate*, there is a double criterion at work: the way things exist, the way they are considered by us. The earlier division appears to have a much simpler basis: *tot speculatiuae philosophiae species, quot sunt res in quibus iustae speculatio considerationis habetur.*[1] Does the division of sciences simply match ontological differences?

## THE DIALOGUE ON PORPHYRY

The context of this earlier division is one we have already looked at when we were discussing the nature of logic. We also had recourse to it in setting forth Boethius's conception of philosophy. It is just after he defines philosophy as *amor et studium et amicitia quodammodo sapientiae*[2] that Boethius takes up its divisions. Philosophy is a genus which has two species, one theoretical, the other practical. *Theoretica* and *speculativa* and *contemplativa* are synonyms, as are *practica* and *activa*. The theoretical and practical have species of their own; in fact, each is divided into three subtypes.

---

1. *In Isagogen Porphyrii Commentum, editio prima*, ed. Brandt, p. 8.3–4 = *PL* 64,11B.
2. *Ibid.*, p. 7.12–13 = *PL* 64, 10D.

There will be as many species of speculative philosophy as there are things with which appropriate speculative consideration can be concerned, just as there are as many species and varieties of virtue as there are diversities in acts.[3]

What are the things with which the various species of the theoretical are concerned? Intellectibles, intelligibles, naturals. Fabius, with whom Boethius is carrying on the semblance of a dialogue, is struck by the neologism *intellectibile*. Boethius tells him it is his rendering of the Greek *noeta* and even suggests it is his invention, perhaps forgetting that the term is already found in Marius Victorinus.

The intellectible is that which existing always one and the same and itself in its own divinity is grasped by none of the senses but by intellect alone. That which is constituted by the inquiry of true philosophy for speculating on God and considers the incorporeality of the soul is the part the Greeks call theology.[4]

The part of speculative philosophy called theology answers to the highest reality, the divine, the changeless, the incorporeal, with God and soul exemplifying the realm.

The second part of theoretical philosophy is the intelligible and it comprehends the first intellectible by thought and understanding. It is concerned with all the celestial works of the higher divinity, with whatever of the sublunary serves a pure and blessed soul, and finally with human souls. Intelligibles are described as once having been of that prior realm of intellectible substance but to have degenerated from intellectibles to intelli-

3. The continuation of the text cited in n. 1 above. The addendum or parallel, *quotque actuum diversitates, tot species uarietatesque uirtutum*, may suggest the basis of the division of the practical which is given on p. 9.13–22 = *PL* 64,11D–12A. It should be noticed that the order in which Boethius lists the practical sciences is ethics, politics, economics (he does not use these terms). He does not develop the basis for their distinction, but he does add that each practical science can be further subdivided.

4. "est enim intellectibile quod unum atque idem per se in propria semper diuinitate consistens nullis umquam sensibus, sed sola tantum mente capitur. quae res ad speculationem dei atque ad animi incorporalitatem considerationemque uerae philosophiae indagatione componitur: quam partem Graeci *theologian* nominant." P. 8.13–16 = *PL* 64,11B.

gibles because of contact with body, such that "they are not now understood but understand and are blessed by purity of understanding as often as they apply themselves to intellectibles."[5] This second part of theoretical philosophy, then, is concerned with celestial bodies and their movements, with the active principles which presided over the formation of the sublunary world and with incarnate human souls.

A third part, call it physiology, is concerned with the natures and properties of bodies.

The passage suggests an ontological declension from intellectibles, through intelligibles, to physical bodies, with speculative philosophy divided up according as it bears on one or the other of these realms. The second part, the science between theology and physiology, has no name. Efforts have been made to see in it a fusion of psychology and mathematics, but they are unsuccessful.[6] It is common to describe what Boethius is doing in this passage as Neoplatonic, but this does not mean that what Boethius puts before us is commonplace stuff. Even those who hold that Boethius had before him Ammonius's commentary on Porphyry as he wrote acknowledge that where Ammonius gives an Aristotelian account of the intermediate as mathematics, Boethius quite simply does not.[7]

5. "secunda uero est pars intellegibilis, quae prima intellectibilem cogitatione atque intellegentia comprehendit. quae est omnium caelestium supernae diuinitatis operum et quicquid sub lunari globo beatiore animo atque puriore substantia ualet et postremo humanarum animarum. quae omnia cum prioris illius intellectibilibis substantiae fuissent, corporum tactu ab intellectibilibus ad intellegibilia degenerarunt, ut non magis ipsa intellegantur quam intellegant et intellegentiae puritate tunc beatiora sint, quotiens sese intellectibilibus applicarint." P. 8.19–9.6 = *PL* 64, 11C.

6. Philip Merlan, *From Platonism to Neoplatonism*, 2nd rev. ed. (The Hague, M. Nijhoff, 1960), pp. 82–3, finds the intermediate science easy to understand. "It was almost inevitable that somebody should have described the second branch of theoretical philosophy as psychology, instead of mathematics, since soul = mathematicals." The way was prepared by Iamblichus and Proclus. Obertello has questioned this, noting that Boethius makes no mention of mathematics here and nowhere else accepts the identification of soul and mathematics.

7. Cf. Bruno Maioli, *Teoria Dell'Essere E Dell'Esistente E Classificazione Delle Scienze in M. S. Boezio* (Arezzo, 1977), p. 64. The division found in *Physics* II, 7, 198a29–31 seems to answer to Boethius's first division of theoretical

What stands out in this division of the speculative is its criterion: *tot speculativae species . . . quot sunt res.* This is in sharp
contrast to the twofold basis of the division in *De trinitate,* the
mode of being and the mode of consideration.

## THE DIVISION IN *DE TRINITATE*

If the first division descends from the most to the least perfect
reality, the division in *De trinitate* is ascending. More importantly, it is not the ascent of a ladder of reality, as if the division
answers to grades of being. At the end of the previous chapter,
Boethius has noticed the way in which the mind can separate
what is conjoined in reality,[8] and this carries over into the present consideration.

The speculative has three parts: the *natural* considers the forms of bodies with matter, [that is,] in matter and inabstract and unable to be
separated actually from bodies which are in motion (as earth is moved
downward and fire upward); form conjoined with matter has motion;
the *mathematical* considers the inabstract without motion, for it speculates on the forms of bodies without matter and thus without motion,
forms which since they exist in matter cannot be separated from these
[bodies]; the *theological* [considers things] without motion, abstract
and separable, for the substance of God lacks both matter and motion.[9]

Since the text is clear, distinguishing between the way things are
and the way they are considered by us, and avoiding any one-

---

science, to be a division into theology, astronomy and physics, and is presented
in the same order. "Hence there are three branches of study, one of things which
are incapable of motion, the second of things in motion but indestructible, the
third of destructible things."

8. *De trinitate,* p. 6.27. Indeed, this is a commonplace in Boethius. It figures
prominently in the statement of the question in the *De hebdomadibus,* 86–95.

9. "Nam cum tres sint speculativae partes, *naturalis*, in motu inabstracta, an-
upechaireta (considerat enim corporum formas cum materia, quae a corporibus
actu separari non possunt, quae corpora in motu sunt ut cum terra deorsum ignis
sursum fertur, habetque motum forma materiae coniuncta), *mathematica*, sine
motu inabstracta (haec enim formas corporum speculatur sine materia ac per
hoc sine motu, quae formae cum in materia sint, ab his separari non possunt),
*theologica*, sine motu abstracta atque separabilis (nam dei substantia et materia
et motu caret)." P. 8.5–16.

to-one correspondence between objects of science and levels of reality, it is odd to read Merlan's judgment that the text shows complete chaos. His difficulties arise from what he takes to be equivocal uses of the key terms. Given the severity of his judgment, it should be noticed at the outset that Merlan's key terms are not the ones found in the text.

Merlan synopsizes the text in terms of physicals, mathematicals and metaphysicals, and sets down the following correlations.

> Physicals: *in motu, inabstracta* = *considerata cum materia, anupexaireta,* i.e., non-subtracted.
> Mathematicals: *sine motu* = *speculata sine motu, inabstracta* = *speculata sine materia, non separabilia* = necessarily embedded in matter
> Metaphysicals: *sine motu, abstracta, separabilia,* i.e., not embedded in matter.[10]

*Inabstracta* as applied to physicals means, according to his scheme, *considerata cum materia,* but as applied to mathematicals it means *speculata sine materia.* This is wrong. It is not Boethius who defines *inabstracta* to mean "considered with matter." His phrase is *in motu inabstracta* and it is glossed by the parenthetical *considerat enim corporum formas cum materia, quae a corporibus actu separari non possunt.* The forms natural philosophy considers with matter and motion cannot be separated in act from matter and motion. The description of mathematics refers to those same *inabstracta,* the word meaning exactly what it did a few lines earlier, namely, that the forms of bodies cannot be actually separated from them, but mathematics considers them without matter and thus without motion. Why does Merlan think *inabstracta* means *speculata sine materia* in the description of mathematics? Presumably it contrasts with *abstracta* in the description of theology, where *abstracta* is linked with *sine motu.* Merlan says that "[e]pistemonic and ontic points of view are in a hopeless tangle." On the contrary, they are clearly distinguished, with *inabstracta* and *abstracta* referring to what Merlan

10. Merlan, *op. cit.,* p. 77.

calls the ontic and *actu separari* and *separari non possunt* and *separabilis* also referring to the ontic. What Merlan infelicitously calls epistomonic matters are conveyed by *considerat cum materia* and *speculatur sine materia*. Precisely in order to keep things clear, Boethius does not use such phrases as *animo separemus* and *cogitatione separantur*. Maioli shares my misgivings with Merlan's rather cavalier treatment, rejects his understanding of the interrelations among the key terms, and suggests the following correlations.

a) *In motu inabstracta* are both epistemic and ontic qualifications, to use Merlan's language, of the forms which are the object of physics, which considers them precisely as they are, in motion and not abstracted.

b) *Sine motu inabstracta* characterizes the typical status of the objects of mathematics; "without motion" signifies, from an epistemic point of view, forms which, insofar as abstracted from matter and conceived by prescinding from matter, are conceived as immobile, while *inabstracta* signifies the ontic status of forms which are, in fact, immanent in and not separate from matter.

c) *Sine motu abstracta* are first of all ontic notes of the forms which are the object of theology, which being precisely immobile and transcendant, are considered as they are, even if theological considerations require, as we shall see, an *altior intellectus*.[11]

This is a good deal more faithful reading of the text of Boethius.

If the division of the theoretical Boethius gives in his commentary on Porphyry is Neoplatonic in tone, that of *De trinitate* seems obviously Aristotelian. The basis for that judgment is the clear echoes of *Metaphysics*, E, 1 in the text of Boethius. Aristotle wrote, "For physics deals with things which exist separately but are not immovable, and some parts of mathematics deal with things which are immovable but presumably do not exist separately, but as embodied in matter; while the first science deals with things which both exist separately and are immovable."[12]

11. Maioli, *op. cit.*, p. 66, n. 19.
12. *Metaphysics* E, 1, 1026a13–16. Parallel texts are *ibid.*, K, 7, 1064b1–3; *Physics* II, 2, 193b6–19 and *Nicomachean Ethics* VI, 9, 1142a17–18.

We notice, of course, in the description of the things with which physics deals the occurrence of *separately* where Boethius used *inabstracta*. Manuscripts support Boethius's reading, however; it is modern editors who have substituted *Chorista* for the reading Boethius can be presumed to have had, namely, *Achorista*. "Separate" (*Choriston*) sometimes is used by Aristotle to mean enjoying existence *per se* as opposed to being an accident, and thus any substance, including physical substances, would be, redundantly, "separate substances." Sometimes it refers to what is separated in thought. Thus either reading of the text in *Metaphysics* E, 1, is compatible with the Boethius of *De trinitate*, 2. The objects of physics are *Chorista* in the sense of autonomous existents and they are *Achorista* in the sense of not existing separate from matter. Since the whole context of *Metaphysics* E, 1 concerns the way in which objects of science are or are not in matter, the *Chorista* reading seems less relevant.[13] And then we have these parallels:

| | BOETHIUS | ARISTOTLE |
|---|---|---|
| *Phys.* | *in motu inabstracta* | peri achorista all'ouk akineta |
| *Math.* | *sine motu inabstracta* | peri akineta men ou chorista |
| *Theo.* | *sine motu abstracta* | peri chorista kai akineta |

When the first division of the theoretical Boethius gives is called Neoplatonic this is not of course to suggest that it is devoid of Aristotelian content, and we have seen there is a passage in the *Physics* that seems a parallel to the passage in the first commentary on Porphyry. After all, the literary project which guided the efforts of Boethius was Neoplatonic in aim. In the end, he hoped to show the fundamental agreement between Plato and Aristotle. He was aware of previous efforts along the same line and there is good reason to think that his own writings·were influ-

13. See E. De Stryker, "La notion aristotélicienne de séparation dans son application aux Idées de Platon," *Autour d'Aristote* (Louvain, Publications universitaires de Louvain, 1955), p. 131, n. 68, for a judicious consideration of the matter. He prefers the *chorista* reading. See too A. Mansion, *Introduction à la physique aristotélicienne* (Louvain, Editions de l'Institut Supérieur de Philosophie, 1946), pp. 127–186.

enced, sometimes heavily influenced, by earlier Neoplatonic authors. Nonetheless, on crucial matters, Boethius exhibits independence from his sources and mentors.

If then the second division of the theoretical that Boethius gives betrays its Aristotelian origins, its context makes clear that it is not pure Aristotelianism we are confronting. For example, in Chapter 2, Boethius goes on to distinguish between *forma* and *imago*—true form, which exists apart from matter, and derivative form, which exists in matter. Images derive from true forms. "For from those forms which are outside matter come these forms which are in matter and effect a body." [14] The forms in bodies, which are only abusively called forms and should be called images, imitate true forms. The phrase "earthly man" (*homo terrenus*) [15] may seem to suggest another, separate man. In short, the atmosphere of the chapter soon echoes with the doctrine of Forms. In the plural? The chapter, after speaking of forms existing apart from matter in the plural, ends on a singular note and the lack of plurality and self-identity of the divine substance are echoed in the final sentence.

### THE NATURE OF THEOLOGY

Boethius introduced a division of the speculative into his treatise *On the Trinity* in order to find the appropriate science and method for the proposed inquiry. An appeal to Aristotle yields a notion of theology or divine science, certainly, but is it the one appropriate for a discussion of the trinity? Is what Boethius sets out to do in this tractate of a piece with what Plato and Aristotle and other pagans did under the title of theology? We will see how carefully St. Thomas distinguishes the theology of the philosophers from the theology based on Holy Writ. Is there any basis in Boethius for such a distinction? What precisely is meant by calling the tractates theological, *opuscula sacra*?

14. "Ex his enim formis quae praeter materiam sunt, istae formae venerunt quae sunt in materia et corpus efficiunt." P. 12.51–53.
15. *Ibid.*, p. 10.35.

Having recalled St. Augustine's remark that the trinity can be approached either by way of authority or by way of argument, St. Thomas noted that Boethius proceeds by way of argument, *praesupponens hoc quod ab aliis per auctoritates fuerat prosecutum.*[16] The explicit reference to St. Augustine in the *prooemium* to *De trinitate* indicates what Thomas had in mind, but there are many other clues in the tractates that Boethius was consciously engaged in an inquiry quite different from a merely philosophical one.

The axioms set down at the outset of *De hebdomadibus* are called "terms and rules" (*terminos regulasque*) and provide the parameters within which the discussion to follow will remain. The "precepts and rules" (*praecepta regularum*) of the Christian faith referred to at the outset of *De trinitate* would seem to echo that idea, the universally held truths providing both a guide and constraint for reasoning about the trinity. And how should the question addressed by the second tractate be handled? "I think the path for our inquiry can be found in that manifest source of all truths, namely in the basic teachings of the Catholic faith." [17] That the faith provides the guide for the inquiry is restated at the end of the second tractate. "I beg you to tell me if these things are correct and of faith or, if perchance you disagree on anything, that you diligently look into what has been said and if possible conjoin faith and reason." [18] The fourth tractate states explicitly that the authority of the New and Old Testaments announces the Christian faith and that the faith is grounded in the foundations now to be set forth.[19] Indeed, this tractate exhibits the method *per auctoritates* throughout and we are often re-

16. Thomas, *In de trinitate Boethii*, ed. Decker, pp. 47.22–48.1.
17. "Viamque indaginis hinc arbitror esse sumendam, unde rerum omnium manifestum constat exordium, id est ab ipsis catholicae fidei fundamentis." P. 32.3–5.
18. "Haec si se recte et ex fide habent, ut me instruas peto; aut si aliqua re forte diversus es, diligentius intuere quae dicta sunt et fidem si poterit rationemque coniunge." P. 36.68–71.
19. "Haec autem religio nostra, quae vocatur christiana atque catholica, his fundamentis principaliter nititur. . . ." P. 52.8–9.

minded how different it is from the other tractates. The task of the fifth tractate is to show the reasonableness of the Catholic faith in holding as true that Christ is *ex duabus naturis* and *in duabus naturis* and that the heretical alternatives are absurd.

In the previous chapter we suggested that *De hebdomadibus* is not a theological tractate in the same sense as the others. It is now clear why this is so. The other tractates either set forth the authoritative teachings of the Catholic faith (*De fide catholica*) or, accepting those truths as foundations, guides, rules, proceed to frame arguments to show their reasonableness (tractates 1, 2 and 5). *De hebdomadibus* makes no appeal to the Catholic faith. Indeed, it proceeds on the basis of truths which need only be heard to command assent, hardly a description of the trinity or the union of divine and human natures in the person of Christ.

Boethius nowhere makes an explicit distinction between theological considerations which proceed from commonly held truths and those which proceed from the truths of faith, but the seeds of the distinction are in his writings. Thus, while Thomas does not attribute the distinction of two theologies to Boethius in the exposition of the text of *De trinitate*, he develops the distinction in several places in the *quaestiones*.

## THOMAS AND THE TRIPARTITE DIVISION

Discussions of the tripartite division of the speculative in terms of a Neoplatonist version, on the one hand, and an Aristotelian, on the other, are complicated by the claim that Aristotle's division is derivative from Plato.[20] Furthermore, a comparison of Boethius and Thomas Aquinas is complicated by quarrels within the Thomistic school as to whether or not the procedure Thomas adopts in his commentary on *De trinitate* amounts to a rejection of the doctrine of three degrees of formal

---

20. Cf. A. Mansion, *Introduction à la physique aristotélicienne*, pp. 122–195; Obertello, *Boezio*, vol. 1, p. 573, with its references to Zeller and Merlan.

abstraction, a doctrine elegantly developed in the great commentators, notably Cardinal Cajetan. This dispute is not precisely the same as the dispute over the role of *esse*—Jacques Maritain, second to none in his emphasis on the novelty of the act of existence in Thomas, remained a champion of the three degrees of abstraction. But latent in the dispute is the claim that Thomas adopts a radically different approach to Aristotle's and thus comes up with a conception of metaphysics *toto coelo* different from the Aristotelian.

Our primary concern is the relation between Boethius and St. Thomas Aquinas. As for Boethius himself, while it is difficult to reconcile the division of the theoretical in the commentary on Porphyry with that given in *De trinitate*, the former seeming to rely on a direct correspondence between different sciences and realms of being (*tot/quot*), the latter combining ontological and logical factors, we will take that of *De trinitate* as our point of reference, not least because it provides us with a direct point of contact between Boethius and Aquinas.[21]

In his exposition of the relevant portion of *De trinitate* 2, Thomas sees Boethius looking first for the *res* of each science and then to the *modus* of each. The former is synonymous with *de quibus determinant*, the things with which the sciences deal, also referred to as the matter of the sciences. How do we know that some things belong to one science and others to another? Natural philosophy considers forms which do not exist apart from matter and as conjoined with matter have motion. The mathematical consideration is of forms which cannot exist separate from matter and motion but can be thought of (*speculatur*) without matter and motion. Of Mathematicals generally we can say that *secundum speculationem sunt separabiles, non secundum esse*. In theology we consider things which exist separately

21. Stephen Gersh, *Middle Platonism and Neoplatonism: The Latin Tradition* (Notre Dame, IN, University of Notre Dame Press, 1986), vol. 2, pp. 655–56, describes both Boethian divisions of the theoretical as involving objective and subjective factors. If there is less of a contrast between the two Boethian texts than is commonly asserted, my concentration now on the *De trinitate* account is less partial than it would otherwise be.

from matter and motion and thus do not enjoy this status because of the abstractive activity of the mind. (This was Thomas's way of dealing with his reading of *abstracta atque inseparabilis*.) So much by way of summary of the *expositio capituli secundi*.

One can imagine Thomas, as he glosses the text of Boethius, wanting to discuss the reason that separation from matter and motion plays such a central role here, to take up the question why form is so central, and a dozen allied questions. Given the literary form of his commentary, he postponed such discussions, preferring to take them up in Question 5. The question discusses the division of the speculative posed by the text in four articles.

1. Whether it is fitting to divide the speculative into these three parts: natural, mathematical and divine.

2. Whether natural philosophy is concerned with things which exist in matter and motion.

3. Whether mathematics considers without matter and motion things which exist in matter.

4. Whether divine science is concerned with things which exist without matter and motion.

## The Criteria for the Division

The theoretical use of the mind is distinguished from its practical use by having a different end in view. The former has truth as its end, the latter orders truth to the end of operation.[22] Since the matter has to be proportioned to the end, the concern of practical reasoning is those things subject to our operation, whether doing or making. By contrast, the objects of speculative thinking are things which do not result from our activity. If there are significant differences among such things, we will have a basis for speaking of different speculative or theoretical sciences.

The objects of speculation must be distinguished as such, that is, as objects of speculation, and not on just any basis. The senses

22. Thomas invokes the *De anima*, III, 10, 333a15. Cf. *In Boethii de trinitate*, q. 5, a. 1, ed. B. Decker, p. 164.9. The distinction is not between two faculties, but of two uses of the same faculty. Cf. *ST*, Ia, q. 79, a. 11.

are not distinguished on the basis of the difference between animate and inanimate objects which is accidental to their color or taste. What belongs *per se* or essentially to the object of theoretical thinking, to what Thomas calls the *speculabile* as opposed to the *operabile*, the object of practical thinking? Two things are essential to the speculable, he replies, one deriving from the intellectual faculty, the other from the nature of science which perfects that faculty. The object of speculation must be immaterial, because the intellect itself is, and it must be necessary because science is concerned with necessary truths. The necessary is that which cannot be otherwise, that is, cannot change, but matter is the presupposition of change. It is of the essence of the object of speculative thinking, accordingly, that it be removed from matter and motion. And, insofar as there is an order or hierarchy or, we might say, degrees of such removal, there will be distinct speculative sciences.[23]

Obviously this account relies on the cogency of the proof of the immateriality of the intellect and on the account of science, both Aristotelian doctrines Thomas accepts and argues for elsewhere. To do so here would have taken him so far afield he might never have returned to the question at hand. But we should not imagine that he thinks the immateriality of the intellect self-evident or that the requirements for *scientia* do not have to be painstakingly established.

How are the speculative sciences ordered on the basis of the removal from matter and motion of their objects?

[1] There are some *speculabiles* which depend upon matter in order to be since they can only exist in matter, but these are distinguished:

[a] because some depend upon matter both to be and to be understood, such as those into whose definitions sensible matter is put, so they cannot be understood without sensible matter, e.g., flesh and bone

23. "Sic ergo speculabili quod est obiectum scientiae speculativae, per se competit separatio a materia et motu, vel applicatio ad ea. Et ideo secundum ordinem remotionis a materia et motu scientiae speculativae distinguuntur." *loc. cit.*, p. 165.14–15. Notice the interchangeability here of *separatio* and *remotio*.

must be put into the definition of man. Physics or natural philosophy is concerned with such things.

[b] But there are others which, although they depend on matter in order to be, do not in order to be understood, because sensible matter does not enter into their definitions, e.g., line and number. Mathematics is concerned with such things.

[2] There are some *speculabiles* which do not depend on matter in order to be, because they can exist without matter, either because they are never in matter, like God and angel, or because in some things they exist in matter and in some not, like substance, quality, being, potency and act, one and many, and the like. *Theology* is concerned with all of these, that is divine science, because the chief thing among the things it knows is God, which is also called *Metaphysics*, that is, beyond the physical, because it is learned after physics since we must proceed from the sensible to what is non-sensible. It is also called *First Philosophy* in that all other sciences follow on it and take their principles from it.[24]

It may be asked why different modes of defining, that is, the different ways in which things are defined with reference to matter and motion, are taken as the basis for distinguishing sciences. A science is, constitutively, a syllogism of a definite kind and then the set of such demonstrative syllogisms so related that the subject of the conclusion of one is a genus of which the subjects

---

24. "[1] Quaedam ergo speculabilium sunt, quae dependent a materia secundum esse, quia non nisi in materia esse possunt. Et haec distinguuntur, quia [a] quaedam dependent a materia secundum esse et intellectum, sicut illa, in quorum diffinitione ponitur materia sensibilis; unde sine materia sensibili intelligi non possunt, ut in diffinitione hominis oportet accipere carnem et ossa. Et de his est physica sive scientia naturalis. [b] Quaedam vero sunt, quae quamvis dependeant a materia secundum esse, non tamen secundum intellectum, quia in eorum diffinitionibus non ponitur materia sensibilis, sicut linea et numerus. Et de his est mathematica. [2] Quaedam vero speculabilia sunt, quae non dependent a materia secundum esse, quia sine materia esse possunt, sive numquam sint in materia, sicut deus et angelus, sive in quibusdam sint in materia et in quibusdam non, ut substantia, qualitas, ens, potentia, actus, unum et multa et huiusmodi. De quibus omnibus est theologia, id est scientia divina, quia praecipuum in ea cognitorum est deus, quae alio nomine dicitur metaphysica, id est trans physicam, quia post physicam discenda occurrit nobis, quibus ex sensibilibus oportet in insensibilia devenire. Dicitur etiam philosophia prima, in quantum aliae omnes scientiae ab ea sua principia accipientes eam consequuntur." *Ibid*, q. 5, a. 1, Decker, pp. 165.16–166.6. (I have added numbers to the text.)

of the conclusions of others are species, and so on.[25] The middle term of a demonstration *propter quid* is the definition of the subject.[26] By drawing one of his criteria or essential constituents of the *speculabile* from the demands of *scientia*, Thomas indicates why he is interested in modes of defining.

Taken as a commentary on the Boethian division of the theoretical, what Thomas has done is to spell out the presuppositions of the cryptic and somewhat enigmatic account of *De trinitate*. More than other texts, given the style deliberately adopted by Boethius, *De trinitate* requires and permits such spelling out. The correlations between the members of Boethius's division of the speculative and the account of Thomas seem exact.

Or are they? "St. Thomas seemingly accepts Boethius' tripartition of speculative philosophy. But he changes its meaning considerably." [27] St. Thomas bases the threefold division entirely on cognitive differences or grades of abstraction, Merlan avers, and arrives at a consistent account, but one which gives a different status to physicals than Aristotle does and leaves no place for "special metaphysics." To pursue the sinuous path of Merlan's argument is not to our purpose, but his remark serves to introduce a controversy that has raged over the import of Thomas's commentary on *De trinitate*. Merlan's interpretations of Aristotle seem antic—he wants to show that Aristotle was a Neoplatonist—but on the question of Thomas's commentary, he joins forces with those who see it as a repudiation of the theory of three degrees of formal abstraction. Whether one thinks Aristotle's tripartition of the speculative is a matter of degrees of abstraction (as Merlan does not), those who repudiate it on the basis of the commentary on *De trinitate* do so because they think they find there a view of metaphysics which is novel and serves

25. This is what Thomas calls the *processus in determinando* as opposed to the *processus in demonstrando* of a science. One does not deduce the species of triangle from triangle; one deduces the properties of triangle. Cf. *In I Physic.*, lectio 1, n. 8.

26. *In I Post. Analytic.*, lectio 4.

27. Merlan, *op. cit.*, p. 81.

to set Thomas apart from other metaphysicians. All this should serve to drive a wedge between Boethius and Thomas, and so it is said to do. It is not an easy matter to follow these discussions since they are not always characterized by clarity, but we must make the effort because claims and counterclaims about the nature of the commentary on *De trinitate* provide the current setting within which the relation between Boethius and Aquinas must be established.

### The Nature of Mathematics

We have the commentary on *De trinitate* in an autograph, written in Thomas's distinctive hand, the *littera inintelligibilis*. A feature of this manuscript is that we become privy to Thomas's thinking. We see him start off a passage in one way, cross it out and set off on another tack. Fortunately, passages marked for deletion were preserved along with the final version. Comparing the aborted beginning of Question 5, Article 3 with the final one has led some to see a radical shift in Thomas's thinking, one fraught with significance for the way we understand the speculative sciences, particularly metaphysics. One of the merits of Bruno Decker's edition is that he includes in an appendix the rejected passages which have survived with the autograph.[28]

L.-B. Geiger, O.P., defined the terms of the controversy in an article titled "Abstractio et Separation d'après S. Thomas: In de trinitate, q. 5, a. 3."[29]

Since the controversy swings around Question 5, Article 3, we will take a close look at the text and, in the following chapter, take up the controversy which is far more concerned with claims to the distinctiveness of Thomas's views than with their relation to Boethius.

28. Cf. *op. cit.*, pp. 230–234. Decker discusses the autograph and allied problems in his *Prolegomena*. See especially pp. 1–4 and 12–28.

29. *Revue des sciences philosophiques et théologiques* XXXI (1947), pp. 3–40. J. D. Robert, O.P., writing at the same time and unaware of Geiger's views, argued some of the same points in "La métaphysique, science distincte de toute autre discipline philosophique selon saint Thomas d'Aquin," *Divus Thomas* (Piacenza), L (1947), pp. 206–223.

The third article of Question 5 asks whether mathematics considers without matter and motion what can only exist in matter. In order to answer the question we must know how the intellect is able to abstract (*abstrahere*). Intellect operates in two ways, a first which is called the grasp or understanding of incomplex things, whereby it knows what a thing is, another whereby it composes and divides, forming affirmative and negative enunciations. There are two things in reality which answer to these two operations.

The first operation looks to the very nature of the thing according to which it has a certain rank among beings, whether it is a complete thing, like some whole, or incomplete, like a part or accident. The second operation looks to the very existence of the thing which in composites results from the coming together of the principles of the thing or is concomitant with the simple nature, as in simple substances. So the first operation grasps essence or nature, the second bears on existence.

Because the truth of intellect is the result of its conforming to reality, it is evident that one cannot by means of the second operation truly abstract (*abstrahere*) that which is conjoined in reality, because abstracting (*abstrahendo*) would signify a separation (*separatio*) according to the existence of the thing. Were I to abstract (*abstraho*) man from whiteness by saying "man is not white," I would mean a separation (*separatio*) in reality. And if man and whiteness are not really separate (*separata*) the intellect would be false. Only what is really separate (*separata*) can be truly abstracted (*abstrahere*) by this operation of the intellect, for example, "man is not an ass." In the first article, *abstrahere* and *separare* were used interchangeably; here *abstrahere* seems to be reserved for the activity of intellect and *separatio* for disjunction in reality. But *abstrahere* is also used to speak of the second operation of the intellect, that whereby one says "A is not B." The constraints on abstraction in this sense, the negative judgment, are in the real order. What is not separate in reality cannot be truly judged to be separate.

What constraints are there on abstraction as undertaken by the first operation of the mind? Well, when that through which the notion of a nature is understood is ordered to or dependent on something else, the nature cannot be understood without that other thing, whether (a) they are linked as part is linked to whole, as foot cannot be understood without understanding animal, because that thanks to which a foot is a foot depends on that thanks to which an animal is an animal, or (b) they are linked in the way form is conjoined with matter, part to part or accident to subject, as snub cannot be understood without nose, or (c) even when they are really separate, as father cannot be understood without understanding child, although the relations are found in different things.

Only when a thing does not depend on another in what constitutes its nature can it be abstracted from the other by intellect and understood without it, not only when they are really separate, like man and rock, but even when they are really joined, whether as part to whole, as letter can be understood without syllable, but not conversely, and animal without foot, but not conversely, or conjoined as form is to matter, and accident to subject, as whiteness can be understood without man, and vice versa.

There are then constraints of different kinds on abstracting in the sense of saying A is not B and on abstracting in the sense of understanding a part without its whole or an accident without its subject or vice versa. What is the point of these precisions? Thomas wants to make as clear a statement as he can about the nature of mathematical abstraction. In order to do this, however, he must show how mathematics differs from the other theoretical sciences. That is why we are given this lengthy and complex statement.

So it is then that the intellect distinguishes one thing from another in different ways according to its different operations, because according to the operation whereby it composes and divides, it distinguishes one thing from another by understanding that the one is not in the other, whereas in the operation whereby it understands what a thing is, it distinguishes one from the other, when it understands what this is, not understanding anything about something else, neither that it is with it or separated from it. The latter distinguishing (*distinctio*) is not properly called separation; only the former is. The latter is properly called abstraction but only when the things, one of which is understood without the other, are really together. We don't say animal is abstracted from rock if the animal is understood without thinking of rock. Since abstraction properly speaking bears only on things really conjoined, in either of the two modes of union mentioned, that is, of part to whole, and form to matter, abstraction is of two kinds, one whereby form is abstracted from matter, the other whereby the whole is abstracted from its parts.[30]

Thomas now assigns restricted, technical meanings to terms which had hitherto been interchangeable. As commonly used, the terms are indistinguishable. To abstract is to separate and vice versa and both are ways in which the mind distinguishes one thing from another. Given what he has said of the two operations of the intellect and the constraints on abstraction in the two cases, Thomas now reserves *abstrahere* to that act whereby the mind considers apart what does not exist apart, that is, distinguishes something in consideration from something else with which it exists. In the narrow or proper, as opposed to common or generic, sense of the term, the mind will be said to abstract A from B only if A and B exist together. Thomas reserves *separare*

---

30. "Sic ergo intellectus distinguit unum ab altero aliter et aliter secundum diversas operationes; quia secundum operationem, qua componit et dividit, distinguit unum ab alio per hoc quod intelligit unum alii non inesse. In operatione vero qua intelligit, quid est unumquodque, distinguit unum ab alio, dum intelligit, quid est hoc, nihil intelligendo de alio, neque quod sit cum eo, neque quod sit ab eo separatum. Unde ista distinctio non proprie habet nomen separationis, sed prima tantum. Haec autem distinctio recte dicitur abstractio, sed tunc tantum quando ea, quorum unum sine altero intelligitur, sunt simul secundum rem. Non enim dicitur animal a lapide abstrahi, si animal absque intellectu lapidis intelligatur. Unde cum abstractio non possit esse, proprie loquendo, nisi coniunctorum in esse, secundum duos modos coniunctionis praedictos, scilicet qua pars et totum uniuntur vel forma et materia, duplex est abstractio, una, qua forma abstrahitur a materia, alia, qua totum abstrahitur a partibus." *Ibid.* q. 5, a. 3, Decker, pp. 183.23–184.6.

for that act whereby the mind asserts that A is not B, which can only be true if in fact A does not exist with or in B. The mental distinguishing which is separating in the narrow or proper sense of *separare* will thus be expressed in a negative judgment.[31]

Interesting enough, to be sure, but what does it have do with distinguishing speculative sciences from one another? So far, nothing. Thomas proceeds now to make that application.

A form can be abstracted from a matter only when an understanding of what it is does not depend on that matter. Mind cannot abstract a form from the matter on which the definition of its essence depends. All accidents relate to substance as form to matter and the definition of any accident depends on substance, so it is impossible for any such form to be separated from substance. However, accidents inhere in substance, not randomly, but in a definite order, for quantity first comes to it and then quality and then passions and motion. Thus quantity can be thought about as inhering in substance without thinking about the sensible accidents whose inherence in substance presupposes quantity. The *ratio substantiae* of quantity, that is, the essence of quantity, does not depend on sensible qualities. The only matter on which the understanding of quantity depends is the substance whose form it is and, since substance is accessible only to intellect, it was called "intelligible matter" by Aristotle. We have, then, a way of describing the objects of mathematics. They are abstract things, more precisely, quantities and the properties of quantities in abstraction from sensible qualities. The subject matter of mathematics is the form quantity abstracted from sensible qualities, sensible matter.

The other kind of abstraction in the narrow or proper sense was the abstraction of a whole from its parts. Of course a whole cannot be considered in abstraction from parts which enter into its definition; for example, a syllable cannot be understood apart

---

31. The claim that *duplex fit abstractio per intellectum* recurs often in subsequent works of Thomas. Cf. *ST*, Ia, q. 40, a. 3; *De substantiis separatis*, cap. 1. ed. Marietti, n. 46.

from letters. Such parts are *partes speciei et formae*.[32] Other parts are accidental to the whole as such, as the semicircle is to the circle. That a circle be divided into equal or unequal parts is not of the essence of circle. (Such parts are called *partes materiae*.) On the other hand, that it have three lines is no accident so far as the triangle is concerned. It is noteworthy that Thomas, in discussing this second form of abstraction, should give mathematical examples. The kind of abstraction involved is that of the universal from the particular, and this kind of abstraction, *abstractio totius*, is found in all the sciences, including that whose subject has just been described in terms of *abstractio formae*. Only those things enter into the definition of a species which are essential to the individuals of that species, not what happens to be true of this or that individual of the species. The abstraction involved considers the nature *absolute*, in abstraction from, all accidental parts.[33]

Thus far, Thomas has used all these precisions only in order to describe the subject matter of mathematics which, given the point of the article, is hardly surprising. He ends his discussion with a statement on all the theoretical sciences which takes advantage of the distinctions he has so carefully made.

So it is that a threefold distinction is found in the operation of intellect. One according to the operation of intellect composing and dividing, which is properly called separation; and this characterizes divine science or metaphysics. Another according to the operation whereby the quiddities of things are formed, which is the abstraction of form from sensible matter; and this characterizes mathematics. A third according to the same operation which is the abstraction of the universal from the particular; and this characterizes physics and is common to all sciences, because in science the accidental is set aside and what is per se considered. It was because some did not understand the difference between the last two and the first that they fell into the error of positing mathe-

32. *Ibid.*, p. 184.26–27.
33. *Ibid.*, p. 185.24–25. The language recalls that of the *De ente et essentia*, where the *natura absolute considerata* is distinguished from the nature as subject to the accidents of individuals or those which are true of it because of its existence in the mind. See Bobik, J., *Aquinas on Being and Essence* (Notre Dame, 1965).

matics and universals separate from sensible things, as the Pythagoreans and Platonists did.[34]

Needless to say, the characterization of metaphysics by way of the mental distinguishing called separation in the narrow or proper sense of the term is wholly enigmatic at this point and constitutes a promissory note that will be redeemed in Article 4 where divine science or metaphysics will be taken up *ex professo*. Furthermore, what is here said of natural philosophy is scarcely illuminating, since the abstraction involved is common to all the sciences. But of course in the previous article Thomas treated *ex professo* of natural science and he presupposes here what he established there. The focus of Article 3 remains on mathematics. Only mathematics emerges as clarified by the distinctions made. This is not to say that these precisions are not important for characterizing metaphysics, far from it, only that the application to metaphysics has not yet been made. Of course, if we recall the threefold distinction of Article 1, we will get an intimation of what Thomas means by allocating separation to metaphysics.

## The Nature of Metaphysics

When Thomas in the fourth article turns to the nature of divine science, his discussion will proceed by distinguishing two divine sciences or theologies as well as distinguishing both from mathematics and natural philosophy.

If divine science is a science it must have a subject matter, a *genus subiectum*, whose properties it will study in the light of

---

34. "Sic ergo in operatione intellectus triplex distinctio invenitur. Una secundum operationem intellectus componentis et dividentis, quae separatio dicitur proprie; et haec competit scientiae divinae sive metaphysicae. Alia secundum operationem, qua formantur quidditates rerum, quae est abstractio formae a materia sensibilis; et haec competit mathematicae. Tertia secundum eandem operationem ⟨quae est abstractio⟩ universalis a particulari; et haec competit etiam physicae et est communis omnibus scientiis, quia in scientia praetermittitur quod per accidens est et accipitur quod per se est. Et quia quidam non intellexerunt differentiam duarum ultimarum a prima, inciderunt in errorem, ut ponerent mathematica et universalia a sensibilibus separata, ut Pythagorici et Platonici." *Ibid.*, p. 186.13–24.

principles appropriate to the subject. Such principles are of two kinds. Some principles are in themselves complete natures as well as principles of other things, as the heavenly bodies exercise causality on earthly things and thus are principles of their changes and characteristics. Such principles are not only considered in the science dealing with their effects, physics, but can also be the subject of another separate science, astronomy. Other principles are not natures complete in themselves, but only principles of natures, as unity is the principle of number, point of line, matter and form of physical body. Principles of this kind are only studied in the science concerned with the things of which they are the principles.

Any determinate genus has some common principles which extend to all the principles in that genus. It is also the case that all beings, insofar as they share in being, have certain principles which are the principles of all beings. But such principles can be called common in two ways, in one way, by predication. When I say, "Form is common to all forms," I mean it is predicated of each of them. In another way principles are common through causality, as when we say that numerically one sun is the principle of all generable things. All beings have common principles in both these senses, not only in the first, which is what Aristotle has in mind when he says that all beings have the same principles by analogy, but also in the second, since there are certain numerically distinct existents which are the principles of all things. This causal reduction is illustrated thus. "The principles of accidents are reduced to the principles of substance and the principles of corruptible substances are reduced to incorruptible substances, and thus in an orderly hierarchy all beings are led back to some principles. And since the principle of the being of all things should be the highest being, as is said in II *Metaphysics*, principles of this sort should be most complete and thus most actual, because act is prior to and more powerful than potency, as is said in IX *Metaphysics*. That is why such things must exist without matter, which is in potency, and without motion, which is the act of that which exists in potency. Things of this kind are divine "because if the divine exists anywhere, it exists in such a nature," namely immaterial and immobile, as is said in VI *Metaphysics*."[35]

Divine things of this kind, being complete natures in themselves as well as the principles of all other things, can be treated in two ways, first insofar as they are principles of all beings, second as things in themselves. But first principles of this kind, however intelligible in themselves, cannot be known by us except through their effects; our mind relates to them as the eye of an owl does to the sun. Moreover, St. Paul wrote that the invisible things of God can be known from the things that are made. This is why philosophers treat of them only insofar as they are the principles of things. They are treated in that science which treats of what is common to all beings and whose subject is being as being; this is what philosophers call divine science. But there is another way of knowing such things, not as manifest through their effects, but insofar as they reveal themselves. "The things that are of God, no one knows except through the spirit of God." 1 Cor. 2: 11 ff.

Theology or divine science, then, is of two kinds. [1] One in which divine things are considered, not as the subject of the science, but as principles of the subject, and this is the theology philosophers pursue and that they call metaphysics.

[2] Another which considers the divine things for their own sake as the subject of the science, and this is the theology which is transmitted in Sacred Scripture.

Each of these is concerned with what is separate in existence from

35. "... principia accidentium reducuntur in principia substantiae et principia substantiarum corruptibilium in substantias incorruptibiles, et sic quodam gradu et ordine in quaedam principia omnia entia reducuntur. Et quia id quod est principium essendi omnibus, oportet esse maxime ens, ut dicitur in II Metaphysicae, ideo huiusmodi principia oportet esse completissima, et propter hoc oportet ea esse maxime actu, ut nihil vel minimum habent de potentia, quia actus est prior et potior potentia, ut dicitur in IX Metaphysicae. Et propter hoc oportet ea esse absque materia, quae est in potentia, et absque motu, qui est actus existentis in potentia. Et huiusmodi sunt res divinae, "quia si divinum alicubi existit, in tali natura," immateriali scilicet et immobile, maxime "exsistit," ut dicitur in VI Metaphysicae." Q. 5, a. 4, Decker, p. 194.2–13.

matter and motion, but differently, insofar as there is a twofold way in which something can be separated in existence from matter and motion.

[a] In one way such that it is of the very essence of the things said to be separate that they can in no way exist in matter and motion, as God and angels are said to be separated from matter and motion.

[b] In another way such that it is not of its essence that it exist in matter and motion, but it can exist without matter and motion, although sometimes it is found in matter and motion. Thus being and substance and potency and act are separate from matter and motion, because they do not depend on matter and motion in order to exist, as do mathematicals which can never exist except in matter, although they can be understood without sensible matter.

Philosophical theology, therefore, deals with things separate in the second way as its subject, and with things separate in the first way as with the principles of its subject.

The theology of Sacred Scripture treats of things separate in the first way as its subject, although in it are treated some things which exist in matter and motion insofar as they are needed for the manifestation of divine things.[36]

We thus see the significance of introducing separation as opposed to abstraction. In its proper and narrow sense, separation is a negative judgment and precisely the judgment that being and substance and act and potency and the like do not necessarily

36. "Sic ergo theologia sive scientia divina est duplex. Una in qua considerantur res divinae non tamquam subiectum scientiae, sed tamquam principia subiecti, et talis est theologia, quam philosophi prosequuntur, quae alio nomine metaphysica dicitur. Alia vero, quae ipsas res divinas considerat propter se ipsas ut subiectum scientiae, et haec est theologia, quae in sacra scriptura traditur. Utraque autem est de his quae sunt separari a materia et motu secundum esse, sed diversimode, secundum quod dupliciter potest esse aliquid a materia et motu separatum secundum esse. Uno modo sic, quod de ratione ipsius rei, quae separata dicitur, sit quod nullo modo in materia et motu esse possit, sicut deus et angeli dicuntur a materia et motu separati. Alio modo sic, quod non sit de ratione eius quod sit in materia et motu, sed possit esse sine materia et motu, quamvis quandoque inveniatur in materia et motu. Et sic ens et substantia et potentia et actus sint separata a materia et motu, quia secundum esse a materia et motu non dependent, sicut mathematica dependebant, quae numquam nisi in materia esse possunt, quamvis sine materia sensibili possint intelligi. Theologia ergo philosophica determinat de separatis secundo modo sicut de subiectis, de separatis autem primo modo sicut de principiis subiecti. Theologia vero sacrae scripturae tractat de separatis primo modo sicut de subiectis, quamvis in ea tractentur aliqua quae sunt in materia et motu, secundum quod requirit rerum divinarum manifestatio." Q. 5, a. 4, Decker, p. 195 ll. 6–27.

exist in matter and motion, that a sense of these terms can be fashioned which does not include matter and motion in the account and that these terms have application *as so defined*. They are not, of course, defined in such a way that matter and motion are positively excluded from their meanings, but, as is generally the case with universal terms, leave it open as to whether a substance will or will not be material.[37] In short, in metaphysics as in any science *abstractio totius* will be in play. Nonetheless, we do not want to speak of the constitution of the subject of metaphysics in terms of abstraction. "Substance, however, which is the intelligible matter of quantity, can exist without quantity. Hence to consider substance without quantity belongs rather to separation than to abstraction."[38] When Thomas does use abstraction to speak of the concerns of metaphysics, he makes clear that he is saying the same thing he was saying in the commentary on *De trinitate*.

> There are some things which can be abstracted from common intelligible matter, like being, one, potency and act, and other like things, which can also exist without any matter, as is evident in immaterial substances.[39]

It is no mystery that it became traditional in the Thomistic school to speak of degrees of abstraction and to rank the sciences insofar as their subjects are more distant from sensible matter. The subject of natural philosophy abstracts from individual sensible matter, but not from common sensible matter.

37. Thomas makes this comparison explicitly in q. 5, a. 4, ad 5: ". . . dicendum quod ens et substantia dicuntur separata a materia et motu non per hoc quod de ratione ipsorum sit esse sine materia et motu, sicut de ratione asini est sine ratione esse, sed per hoc quod de ratione eorum non est esse in materia et motu, quamvis quandoque sint in materia et motu, sicut animal abstrahit a ratione, quamvis aliquod animal sit rationale."

38. "Substantia autem, quae est materia intelligibilis quantitatis, potest esse sine quantitate; unde considerare substantiam sine quantitate magis pertinet ad genus separationis quam abstractionis." Q. 5, a. 3, Decker, p. 186.10–12.

39. "Quaedam vero sunt quae possunt abstrahi etiam a materia intelligibili communi, sicut ens, unum, potentia et actus, et alia huiusmodi, quae etiam esse possunt absque omni materia, ut patet in substantiis immaterialibus." *ST*, Ia, q. 85, a. 1, ad 2.

The subject of mathematics abstracts from all sensible matter but not from intelligible matter. The subject of metaphysics abstracts even from intelligible matter. There can scarcely be any dispute about the propriety of speaking in this way and it is an easy matter to supply texts in which Thomas himself did.

But such talk should not lead us to think that metaphysics is simply a more abstract consideration than that of natural philosophy, although it is more abstract. It is not simply a manifestation of our ability to fashion a definition of substance which does not include any sensible matter. Nothing is easier to do. But the great argument with Platonism that Thomas takes on from Aristotle is that we cannot assume that things must exist as we think them. Our ability to formulate a notion of substance which does not include matter and motion is no warrant for asserting there exist immaterial substances. The point of distinguishing separation from abstraction is precisely here. The distinction arises in the context of talking about mathematicals and, like Aristotle, Thomas does not think that our abilility to fashion concepts which do not include sensible matter, as the concepts of line and triangle and circle do not, commits us to the existence of these things in the way they are talked of in mathematics. That commitment would be expressed in a negative judgment: "the number 7 exists apart from matter and motion," which is equivalent to the negative judgment, "7 does not require matter and motion in order to exist." Such a judgment about substance is precisely the foundation of metaphysics as a science.

What is the basis or warrant for such a judgment? In virtue of what we know is it true of substance that it can exist apart from matter and motion?

It is on this point that a dispute has raged in recent years, one which is thought to be appreciably altered by the approach Thomas took in his commentary on *De trinitate* of Boethius. Since this dispute can cast light on our understanding of St. Thomas and Boethius and the relation of the former to the latter, we now turn to it.

# CHAPTER 5

# Metaphysics and Existence

Thomas's commentary on Boethius's *De trinitate* has occasioned claims that the metaphysics of Thomas is fundamentally different from that of Aristotle. The articles that stand at the beginning of this development, those of Robert and Geiger,[1] draw attention to the distinction made in the course of *Question* 5, Article 3, between *abstractio* and *separatio*. Geiger bases his remarks on the holograph as well and is thus able to show that the approach taken in the final version of the body of the article was one Thomas hit upon only after a certain amount of searching. Not that the two articles, which were written at about the same time, though quite independently of one another, are identical.

Robert, setting out to show that metaphysics is a science distinct from every other discipline for St. Thomas, takes his cue from Van Steenberghen's effort to insulate philosophy from science, an effort that ends by seeing the various philosophical disciplines as forms of metaphysics. There is general metaphysics, which apparently comes first pedagogically as well as otherwise, and then there are many forms of special metaphysics—epistemology, philosophy of nature, psychology, and so on. No wonder Robert is concerned to show how metaphysics is a distinct discipline and not just a synonym for philosophy. What distinguishes it is *separatio*, since metaphysics considers things which are removed or separated from all matter and motion.

Geiger was writing before the appearance of Wyser's edition

1. Geiger, "Abstractio et séparation d'après S. Thomas: in de trinitate, q.5, a.3," *Revue des Sciences Philosophiques et théologiques*, XXXI, 1947, pp. 3–40. Robert, J. D., O. P., "La métaphysique, science distinct de toute autre discipline philosophique selon Saint Thomas d'Aquin," *Divus Thomas* (Piacenza), L 1947, pp. 206–223.

of the fifth and sixth questions of Thomas's commentary on *De trinitate*,[2] but he had access to the holographs which retain earlier versions of the body of the third article of Question 5. The final version moves with such ease that it comes as a surprise to find that Thomas made a number of false starts before he found the approach he wanted.

The first version begins, "It should be said that the operation of intellect is completed insofar as the intellect is conformed with the intelligible." [3] He cites Algazel and Aristotle and continues on the basis of the fact that knowledge involves an assimilation. He cites the Boethius of *De hebdomadibus* to the effect that many things which are not separated in reality can be separated in thought[4] and then discusses things not amenable to this kind of separating. Why is it that some things which exist together have to be thought together? Well, sometimes the one is part of the notion of the other, as rational is of man. On the other hand, as in the case of father and son, some things which exist separately must nonetheless be thought together. It is when one thing is prior to another that the former can be understood without the latter. But whenever the connection is essential, separation is impossible. "For essence is the principle of being. Hence insofar as one thing can or cannot exist without another, it will be or not be dependent on it in its essence and thus in its understanding." [5] But then, after nearly fifty lines, Thomas stops and begins again.

"It should be said that in order to make this question clear, we must see the diverse modes of abstraction whereby the intellect is said to abstract, and the reasons for them." [6] Now he cites

2. Paul Wyser, O.P., *Thomas von Aquin In librum Boethii De trinitate Quaestiones Quinta et Sexta* (Fribourg, 1948).

3. "Dicendum quod operatio intellectus completur secundum hoc quod intellectus conformatur intelligibili." In Bruno Decker, *Sancti Thomae de Aquino Expositio super librum Boethii De trinitate* (Leiden, E. J. Brill, 1959), p. 231.

4. *De hebdomadibus*, ed. Stewart, Rand, Tester, p. 44.86–91.

5. "Essentia autem est principium essendi. Unde secundum quod aliquid sine altero esse potest vel non potest, sic secundum suam essentiam et per consequens secundum intellectum dependet ab illo vel non dependet." *Ibid.*, p. 232.24–27.

6. "Dicendum quod ad evidentiam huius quaestionis oportet [scire] videre diversos modos abstractionis, qua intellectus abstrahere dicitur, et rationes eorum." *Ibid.*, p. 232.31–33.

the twofold act of intellect noted in *De anima*. One act considers the simple quiddity of the thing, the other is that whereby the mind composes and divides. It is with reference to the mind's grasp of quiddity that Thomas first speaks of abstraction. Once more he asks when a quiddity can and when it cannot be understood without thinking of something else. Out of this emerges the following observation. "But when two things are not ordered to one another and although what the one is can be understood without thinking of the other, this is not called abstraction; for example, when I understand stone without understanding animal. Abstraction is properly said to come about through understanding when the things are ordered to one another and conjoined in reality."[7] He goes on for several more lines but then stops and begins over again. "It ought to be said that to make this question clear it is necessary to distinguish the ways in which the intellect is said to abstract."[8] But this beginning too is discarded and Thomas begins what will be the final form of the body of the article.

Not that he doesn't correct himself again in the body of the article, but at last he has found his path and the discussion moves along easily, not least because many of the distinctions and clarifications have already been made in the aborted versions. In short, the final version is not *toto coelo* different from the earlier ones. Many of the elements of the argument are already at hand, but Thomas now finds a way to gather those elements into a unity and the final version of the article makes the previous ones seem almost random.

7. "Sed quando duae res non habent aliquem ordinem ad invicem, quamvis de una earum intelligatur quid est sine intellectu alterius, non tamen dicitur abstractio, sicut si intelligam lapidem sine intellectu animalis. Tunc enim proprie dicitur abstractio per intellectum fieri, quando ad invicem ordinatae sunt et coniunctae in rerum natura." *Ibid.*, p. 233.9–14.

8. "Dicendum quod ad evidentiam huius quaestionis distinguere oportet modos, quibus intellectus abstrahere dicitur." *Ibid.*, p. 233.17–18.

### THE DISTINCTIVENESS OF METAPHYSICS

Those who praise this article do not mean to say that Thomas has hit upon an ingenious way to display the nature of metaphysics as it was commonly understood. On the contrary. The discussion in Article 3 is taken to exhibit the distinctiveness of Thomistic metaphysics, the way in which it differs from other understandings of this science. The passage to which interpreters are drawn moth-like is this: *secunda vero operatio respicit ipsum esse rei*: the second operation looks to the very existence of the thing.[9] Separation is linked to the second operation of the mind and metaphysics is characterized by separation.

The claim that Thomas has a fundamentally different conception of metaphysics than, say, Aristotle has become familiar. The fact that the claim is associated with the commentary on *De trinitate* is appropriate since the whole of the fifth question is concerned with the way in which sciences are distinguished. Presumably, when it is said that the metaphysics of Thomas is fundamentally different, the difference can be expressed in terms of the formal criteria for distinguishing sciences.

Indeed, we have in the text itself a model for such a distinction. I have in mind not the way Thomas distinguishes divine science from mathematics and natural philosophy but the way in which he distinguishes two formally different divine sciences. One who wants to speak of formally different sciences of metaphysics need only follow Thomas's procedure here.

Let us recall that procedure and then go on to see why those who have spoken of a fundamentally different Thomistic metaphysics rarely refer to the formal requirements for the unity and plurality of sciences which presumably must be met to speak of a plurality of metaphysics. Etienne Gilson is one of the few who has seen what the claim of a distinctive Thomistic metaphysics requires and said straightforwardly what others only hint at.

What governs the fifth question of Thomas's commentary on

9. *Ibid.*, p. 182.9–10.

*De trinitate* is the Aristotelian conception of science. Science is the apodictic or demonstrative syllogism; science in the strongest sense is had when something is shown to belong *per se* to a subject because of what that subject is. That is, the link between the subject and predicate of the conclusion is a middle term which is the definition of the subject. It is because of the crucial role of definition in the scientific proof that Thomas sought in formally different definitions the formal distinction of the theoretical sciences. Those definitions are of the subjects of scientific syllogisms—the *genus subiectum* as well as the grammatical subject of the conclusion. It is a genus first of all because it is the subject of and generator of its properties, but it is a genus also in the sense that scientific syllogisms whose subjects relate to one another as species to genus form a plurality of connected arguments. It is usually of this plurality of connected proofs that we speak when we speak of a science. When plane figure is the subject of a proof, it can relate to proofs about triangles and squares, and the proof which has triangle as the subject of its conclusion relates to others which have scalene and isosceles triangles as the subjects of theirs.

## Metaphysics as a Science

It is notorious that construing metaphysics as a science in this sense constitutes one of the chief problems for Aristotle when he goes in search of a theoretical science beyond natural philosophy and mathematics. "The science we are seeking" is a reiterated phrase in the *Metaphysics*. If those other theoretical sciences cut off a part of being and study it, the science we are seeking will study being as being.[10]

The suggestion that there is a science which studies all the things that are sounded as strange to Aristotle as it does to us.

10. "There is a science which investigates being as being and the attributes which belong to this in virtue of its own nature. Now this is not the same as any of the so-called special sciences; for none of these others treats universally of being as being. They cut off a part of being and investigate the attribute of this part. . . ." *Metaphysics*, IV, 1.

Indeed, it will be remembered how he chided the Platonist for speaking of Being and Good as if they named some one thing or some one kind of thing. But being isn't a kind, a type. What sense of being does the Platonist have in mind, then? Which of the various senses of good is meant when one speaks of the Good? G. E. L. Owen, in a famous article,[11] discussed the way in which Aristotle's metaphysics amounts to a triumphing over those earlier taunting questions.

The "things that are" do not constitute a kind or genus of reality because the things that are fall immediately into various kinds and the term "being" is not said of them all univocally, in the same sense, but only by a kind of equivocation. Aristotle found his way out, we remember, when he saw that "being" as predicated of the kinds of being is a *pros hen* equivocal. Just as "healthy" and "medical" and the like have not only a plurality of uses but a plurality of meanings with one controlling meaning, so too does "being." "Being is said in many ways," but one of its meanings is primary; moreover, the thing primarily meant by "being" is also what is first in reality, namely, substance. Thanks to this, the science of being as being becomes all but identified with the science of substance, the primary being. Any being other than substance enters into this science to the degree that it relates to substance.

Of course, that "being" is thus equivocally predicable of all the things that are is not yet grounds for any claim that there is a science beyond natural science and mathematics. If all the things that are were physical objects, things that have come to be as the result of a change, bringing them all under the compass of "being" is simply to speak of them in a more general and less informative manner. For Aristotle, such common and general knowledge is a sign of imperfection rather than perfection and

11. G. E. L. Owen, "Logic and Metaphysics in some Earlier Works of Aristotle," in *Aristotle and Plato in the Mid-Fourth Century*, ed. I. Duering and G. E. L. Owen, Goteborg, 1960, pp. 163–190. This can now be found in *Logic, Science and Dialectic: Collected Papers on Greek Philosophy* (Ithaca, NY, Cornell University Press, 1986), pp. 180–199.

scarcely seems an apt way to describe wisdom, first philosophy, the divine science, the culminating effort of the philosopher. From the very outset we are able to speak of all the things that are in this way. It is only by going on to speak of what is peculiar to this or that kind of thing that knowledge is perfected. Surely Aristotle does not mean to put a premium on confused and general knowledge.

It was because Aristotle became aware, in the course of doing natural philosophy, that not everything that exists exists in the same way as the objects of natural philosophy that the possibility of another science beyond it opened up. If every substance were material, natural philosophy would be wisdom; there would be no science of substance apart from it.[12] The project of metaphysics is for Aristotle precisely the effort to achieve some further knowledge of these immaterial substances—e.g., of God and the soul, the Prime Mover and the human substantial form whose activity is such that it cannot corrupt. But how to go about it?

If Aristotle's aim is what was just suggested, why doesn't he fashion a science of the divine or changeless rather than waste time establishing a science of being as being? Aristotelian studies through much of this century turned on two conceptions of metaphysics, ontology and theology, which so far as Aristotle is concerned constitutes a false option. The notion that Aristotle could ever have seriously intended to formulate a science whose subject matter is divine substance, immaterial substance, makes no Aristotelian sense. Such things simply are not accessible to the human mind in the way required by the four questions of the *Posterior Analytics*.[13]

12. See Thomas, *In Metaphysicorum Aristotelis*, ed. Cathala and Spiazzi (Turin, Marietti, 1964), nn. 395, 1170 and 2267.

13. Furthermore, in *Metaphysics* Z.17, Aristotle explicitly rejects the possibility of a science whose subject would be the simple. Werner Jaeger's dramatic portrait of Aristotle vacillating between a theology so understood and an ontology is wholly imaginary. On the basis of this unintelligible option, Jaeger and an army of others imagined they saw layers and submerged versions and ultimately incoherence in Aristotle's *Metaphysics*. But the fault is in their theory, not in the

In the *Metaphysics*, we see Aristotle trying to fashion a meaning of "substance" that will be applicable to immaterial things as well as to substances in the usual sense, i.e., physical substances, the things that have come to be as the result of a change. He concentrates first on physical substance—how could he not? But now he interrogates it with a view to arriving at more knowledge of the divine. (More, that is, in the sense of beyond negative and relative to quidditative knowledge.) So he will ask, "What in physical substance is most substance?" The thing that has come to be as the result of a change is composite, a union of matter and form. This composite is substance, but its components can be called substance derivatively. Does form or matter deserve the appellation more? It is when he concludes that form is more substance than matter that Aristotle has a means of speaking of separate substances as forms.

## Theology as Science

These few reminders of the difficulties Aristotle faces in applying his conception of science to a theoretical science beyond natural philosophy and mathematics are meant to serve two purposes. First, they make it clear that when Thomas attempts to show that there are two theologies, it should not be thought that theology in the first sense is unproblematically plain and only the second sort of theology presents problems. In different ways, they both pose all but insurmountable methodological problems. Second, we see that the option Jaeger mistakenly thought open to Aristotle is indeed open to Thomas as a believer. Not only is there a theology that has as its subject being as being, and says whatever can be said of the divine by reference to material being, there is also a theology which has the self-revealing God as its subject matter.

The important thing to notice here is that any claim to a diversity of sciences is a claim to a diversity of subject matters. In

---

text. No one seems to have questioned the idea of a putative science of theology with the divine and simple substance as its subject in the light of Aristotle's conception of science.

the case of the threefold division of theoretical science, the mode
of defining, that is, the degree of separation or abstraction from
matter and motion, was the basis for asserting that there are
three formally different subject matters. How can Thomas maintain that there are two theologies?

The mode of defining in the two theologies is the same: both
define the objects of their concern without matter and motion.
They both employ *separatio*. How then can they be formally distinct sciences? If they have different subject matters, being as
being and God, respectively, they do not employ a different mode
of defining. Or do they? What Thomas does, we remember, is to
note two senses of "defined without matter and motion." There
are some things of which this can be said, for example, being,
substance, act, and so forth, which are not necessarily found in
matter and motion: sometimes they are, sometimes they are not.
But there are other things which are defined without matter and
motion because they never exist in matter and motion, for example, God and the angels.

### THE DISTINCTIVENESS OF THOMISTIC METAPHYSICS

We now have criteria which must be met if the claim that
metaphysics as St. Thomas understands it is fundamentally different from anyone else's, notably from Aristotle's, is to be sustained.

Admittedly this claim is often made in ways which do not
promise any precise account of what is meant. For example, it is
often said that since metaphysics is the science of being as being,
and Thomas has a different conception of being than Aristotle
had, Thomistic metaphysics differs from the Aristotelian. How
does Thomas's conception of being differ from Aristotle's? In
answer, reference will be made to article three of the fifth question of Thomas's commentary on *De trinitate*, so we have come
full circle.

When Thomas links the second operation of the intellect,

"which looks to the very existence of the thing," with separation and then metaphysics, this is taken to provide a basis for asserting that Thomas's conception of metaphysics is formally different from Aristotle's. Leroy[14] intimates that what this means is that metaphysics becomes a possibility as soon as a real distinction between essence and existence is recognized. What he means is left tantalizingly obscure, however. One suspects that there is a connection between seeing the text just cited as referring to the real distinction and what has unfortunately become the familiar claim that Aristotle was unaware of this distinction. From this it is taken to follow that Thomas has a new and different conception of metaphysics. The suggestion as to the uniqueness and novelty of Thomistic metaphysics, in short, is linked to the real distinction between essence and existence.

The question must therefore be asked: What role if any does the real distinction between essence and existence play in the constitution of metaphysics? This question can be asked even while conceding for purposes of simplicity the claim that Aristotle was unaware of this distinction. Is the recognition of the real distinction a prerequisite of metaphysics? Is it a conclusion reached in the course of doing metaphysics? Or is it, as Thomas regards it in *De hebdomadibus*, a *per se nota* principle and thus not a conclusion at all, whether prior to or within metaphysics?

One longs to have the claim made straightforwardly rather than by implication and indirection. What is implied is that the separation which is characteristic of metaphysics is tied to distinguishing or separating essence from existence. Is it the subject of metaphysics that is then separated out? And what is the subject? Essence? Existence? Clarification about the nature of this claim comes, quite unsurpisingly, from Etienne Gilson in *Being and Some Philosophers*. With his customary precision Gilson lays out for us the basic claim of existential Thomism.

The subject of metaphysics is existence or *esse*. That this is Gilson's understanding is clear from what he says about the angels. Does the consideration of angels fall to metaphysics? Not

14. "Le savoir spéculatif," *Revue thomiste*, Maritain Volume, p. 335.

for St. Thomas, according to Gilson.[15] Angels have essences and any concern with essence falls to the philosophy of nature. The study of the angels is thus a concern of natural philosophy! Gilson seriously contends that this is the teaching of St. Thomas Aquinas. What then is the concern of metaphysics? What else could it be but existence?

One expects such forthrightness from Gilson. Where others are coy or obscure, or both, he states the matter flatly. There is a distinction between essence and existence and this is effectively the basis for the distinction between natural philosophy and metaphysics. Essence is the subject of natural philosophy, existence is the subject of metaphysics. Here at last we have what is meant by the claim that there is a distinctive Thomistic metaphysics.

Unfortunately, this interpretation of Thomas has no justification in his writings, for the very good reason that it makes no sense.

15. "Such is the way the world of Aristotle can enter the Christian world of Thomas Aquinas, but there remains now for us to see that, while it enters it whole, it also becomes wholly different. The world of Aristotle is there whole in so far as reality is substance. It is the world of science, eternal, self-subsistent and such that no problem concerning existence needs nor can be asked about it. It is one and the same thing for a man in it to be man, to be one and to be. But, while keeping whole the world of Aristotle, Thomas Aquinas realizes that such a world cannot possibly be metaphysical. Quite the reverse, it is the straight physical world of natural science, in which natures necessarily entail their own existence; and, even though such natures may happen to be gods, or even the supreme God, they still remain natures. Physics is that very order of substantial reality in which existence is taken for granted. As soon as existence no longer is taken for granted, metaphysics begins. In other words, Thomas Aquinas is here moving the whole body of metaphysics to an entirely new ground. In the philosophy of Aristotle, physics was in charge of dealing with all natures, that is, with those beings that have in themselves the principle of their own change and of their own operations; as to those true beings which are unchangeable, they make up the order of metaphysics, in virtue of their own unchangeability. In the new philosophy of Thomas Aquinas, even unchangeable beings still remain natures, so that their handling falls within the scope of the philosophy of nature. Some of his readers sometimes wonder at the constant readiness of the Angelic Doctor to thrust angels in the very middle of his discussions concerning man or any other natural beings. Then they say that, of course, it helps him, because angels provide such convenient examples and means of comparison. In point of fact, if Thomas Aquinas is so familiar with angels, it is because to him they are just as natural beings as men themselves are, only they are better natural beings." *Being and Some Philosophers*, second edition (Toronto, 1952), pp. 166–167.

# PART THREE
## *De hebdomadibus*

CHAPTER 6

# Survey of Interpretations

This part is devoted to three things. First, a rapid survey of scholarly opinion on the third Boethian tractate which the medievals called *De hebdomadibus*. Second, a look at the tractate through the eyes of St. Thomas Aquinas. Third, a brief indication of discussions of the good by Boethius and St. Thomas in other places. The deficiencies of the other interpretations will become clear and we will see that better than anyone else St. Thomas enables us (a) to understand the Boethian tractate in itself and (b) to place the solution the tractate reaches in a broader context, as an element of the comprehensive view Thomas constructs from Boethian and other sources.

## INTERPRETATIONS OF THE TRACTATE

There can be no question of surveying *all* interpretations that have been made of *De hebdomadibus* from medieval times to the present. Various partial surveys and appraisals are available.[1] That of Pierre Duhem[2] has been extremely influential in appraisals of the medieval interpretations of the Boethian tractates, in

1. Cf. Gangolf Schrimpf, *Die Axiomenschrift des Boethius (De Hebdomadibus) als Philosophisches Lehrbuch des Mittelalters* (Leiden, E. J. Brill, 1966). Volume II of the magisterial *Severino Boezio* of Luca Obertello (Genova, Academia ligure di scienze e lettere, 1974), is over 300 pages of Boethian bibliography, which is supplemented by that in his edition of *La Consolazione della Filosofia e Gli Opuscoli Teologici* (Milan, 1979). The introduction and notes of this volume add to its usefulness. It is amazing that the Toronto dissertation of Peter O'Reilly, *Sancti Thomae de Aquino, Expositio super librum Boetii "De Hebdomadibus"*, an edition and a study, 1960, shows up on none of the standard bibliographies and seems to have been completely ignored. Since I regard it as easily among the very best ever done on the tractate and the commentary, I am happy to draw attention to it.

2. *Le système du monde*, tome 5, Paris, 1917, pp. 285–316.

particular that of Thomas Aquinas. Since Duhem's point is that the medieval commentators, including St. Thomas, largely missed the point of Boethius's pithy remarks, it will be important for our purposes to look at the reaction of Thomists to such estimates of their master's exposition. Since one of the features of the appraisal by Thomists of the text of Boethius is that it is Aristotelian in its doctrine,[3] it should be noted that in recent years a good deal of emphasis has been put on the Neoplatonic origins of Boethius's teaching and we are told that enigmatic remarks in the tractates deliver up their meaning more easily when this is recognized. With the crescendoing of Existential Thomism, there has been an increasing urgency in the effort to show that Boethius did not teach what Thomas takes him to teach on *esse*. Peter O'Reilly is one of the few who has spelled out what such Thomists are saying and the relevance of his criticism is not confined to Thomists.

> But once a man sets out to expound the text as of that author, he is committing himself to the job of saying what the text as belonging to that author means; and therefore to the extent that he does anything other than that, he is wrong, dead wrong; and he is (knowingly or not) lying about that author's text and consequently about that author. And no amount of saying it gently or obscurely will lessen the fact.[4]

Among those to whom this refreshingly frank judgment is taken to apply are Duhem, Roland-Gosselin, Fabro and Geiger.

This enables us to see the stakes of the present chapter. It is no small matter if there should be more or less common scholarly opinion that the meaning of the Boethian tractate is significantly different from what Thomas takes it to be. If Boethius means one thing and Thomas takes him to mean another, not on minor points such as the meaning of *hebdomad*, but in the main

---

3. "Boece est resté en cette doctrine entièrement fidèle au point de vue d'Aristote." M.-D. Roland-Gosselin, O.P., *Le De Ente et Essentia de S. Thomas d'Aquin* (Paris, first edition 1926, second 1948), p. 145. If one holds that there is a chasm between Aristotle and Thomas, linking Boethius to Aristotle has predictable results.

4. O'Reilly, *op. cit.*, p. 327.

moves of the argument, we will have to make a judgment as severe as O'Reilly suggests. There is an amazing tendency among Thomists of late to commend St. Thomas for his inability to read the text he is purporting to expose. Indeed, Thomists seem in the forefront of those insisting on the distance between the text and its interpreter. To echo Kierkegaard in another connection, "Poor Thomas, to have such disciples." [5]

We shall look first at Duhem, go on to Roland-Gosselin and then to other Thomists, look at the suggestions of Pierre Hadot and end with the interpretation of Peter O'Reilly. What we find is not unanimity, but a cacophony of voices. While there are many points of agreement among recent interpreters, it is clear that the disagreements are fundamental. As for the Thomists, while they are in verbal agreement that Thomas's "existential" metaphysics is light-years distant from the thought of Boethius, fundamental disagreement breaks out among them when they set forth the teaching of Thomas on *esse*. What I hope to provide is a representative sampling rather than exhaustive survey, but the authors invoked, given their influence and credentials, provide an adequate picture of the current situation.

### Pierre Duhem

The section that interests us in the fifth volume of Duhem's monumental work *Le systeme du monde* is titled "Digression au sujet d'un axiome de Boece: l'*esse*, le *quod est*, le *quo est*." The key to Boethius is to be found in the proposition, *Diversum est esse et id quod est*. What is the sense of this claim? Duhem says it is identical to the distinction Themistius makes between a particular instance and its essential nature, this water, on the one hand, and that thanks to which it is water, on the other. The opposition is expressed in the Greek by a noun, water, *hydor*,

---

5. "Heraclitus the obscure said, 'One cannot pass twice through the same stream.' Heraclitus the obscure had a disciple who did not stop with that, he went further and added, 'One cannot do it even once.' Poor Heraclitus, to have such a disciple!" *Fear and Trembling*, trans. W. Lowrie (Princeton, Princeton University Press, 1941), p. 132.

and a phrase made up of a definite article, the dative of the noun and the infinitive to be: *to hydati einai*. The phrase expresses what the Greeks call *ousia* and St. Augustine calls *essentia*. The diversity indicated by the proposition, then, is that between a concrete thing and its essence.

That this is what Boethius means is taken to be clear from what he says of God. *Divina substantia sine materia forma est, atque ideo unum, et est id quod est. Reliqua enim non sunt id quod sunt.*[6] The meaning of this, we are told, is that only in God is there identity of the concrete being and its essence, in all other things they differ. And that is the clear meaning of *omne simplex esse suum, et id quod est, unum habet; omni composito aliud est esse, aliud id quod est.*[7] Duhem now skips back to the second chapter of *De trinitate*, for corroboration of his interpretation. How does Boethius illustrate what he has said of the divine substance as opposed to the rest (*reliqua*)?[8] A colored thing is not the same thing as its color, nor generally a substance the same as any of its accidents. God, being pure form, is not subject to accidents, and that is why in him there is identity of *esse* and *quod est*. The *id quod est*, we are assured, is "the concrete and really existing thing which the union of matter and form produces" and *esse* is its essence, the form common to individual things of the same species.[9] Duhem now careens back to *De trinitate*, to a passage earlier than the one he began by discussing, and cites as proof of his interpretation of what is being identified in God and held to differ in creatures the following: *quae vere*

6. Boethius, *De trinitate*, 2, ll. 29–31. Duhem cites Boethius, not by the text in Migne, but according to the 1570 Basel edition which apparently combines several *opuscula* under the single title *De trinitate*. On p. 286, note 2, Duhem informs us that the *De hebdomadibus* is the same work as the *De trinitate*. This explains his confidence that the passage he cites will provide a gloss on *diversum est esse*. . . .

7. *De hebdomadibus*, ll. 45–48.

8. He seems to be citing *De hebdomadibus.*, ll. 100–117.

9. "Le *id quod est*, c'est la chose concrète et réellement existante que produit l'union de la matière et de la forme; l'*esse*, l'essence, c'est la forme commune à toutes les choses individuelles de même espèce, telle la gravitè, forme spécifique commune à tous les corps graves." Duhem, *loc cit.*, p. 289. In short, Boethius is in agreement with Themistius.

*forma neque imago est et quae esse ipsum est et ex qua esse est.*
*Omne namque esse ex forma est.*[10] He continues the quotation
which takes him to the passage with which he began, namely,
*Sed divina substantia. . . .* What follows is an explanation by
Boethius of what he meant by saying that all *esse* is derived from
form. Something is a statue because of its shape or form, not
because of its matter, bronze, and bronze is bronze not because
of the earth that is its matter but because of the form of bronze,
and earth is earth not because of prime matter but because of
the dryness and gravity which are its forms.

What is to be made thus far of Duhem's interpretation of Boethius? His main concern seems to be to establish the agreement
of Boethius with Themistius. At this point he repeats it as a kind
of Q.E.D.[11] The problem we face, however, is one of trying to
read the passages of Boethius in the way Duhem suggests.

Even assuming that the passages he quotes are from the same
work, it is difficult to see how Duhem can say of them what he
does. We are asked to accept the identification of *esse* and essence or specific nature, on the one hand, and of *id quod est* and
concrete thing, on the other. On this basis, *reliqua enim non sunt
id quod sunt* does not mean what Duhem takes it to mean. He
interprets it as saying that things other than God are not the
same as their essence. But this requires that *id quod sunt* mean
essence and not concrete thing. One can understand why Duhem
did not want to read it as saying that concrete things are not the
concrete things they are. But it is unsettling that he does not even
allude to the inconsistencies of his own interpretation. A passage
that should have made him wonder about the identifications of
*esse* and *id quod est* with essence and concrete thing is invoked
as if it illustrates rather than undermines what he is saying.[12]

10. *De trinitate*, 2, ll. 19–21.
11. Cf. *loc. cit.*, p. 289: "Être de l'eau, avait dit Themistius, c'est posséder la
forme de l'eau; être du bronze, répète Boece, c'est posséder la forme du bronze.
Les pensées de ces deux auteurs s'identifient. Lors donc que Boece écrit *diversum
est esse et id quod est*, nous devons entendre: L'essence (*esse*), qui est la forme,
ne se confond pas avec la chose concrète et réellement existante (*id quod est*)."
12. Many pages later, on p. 297, in speaking of Robert of Lincoln and later
sinuous developments at the hands of medieval divines, Duhem will note that *id*

Nor is he given pause by *omne namque esse ex forma est*, cited in the course of assuring us that *esse = forma*. But the remark that all *esse* is from form simply is not an identification of *esse* and form. Is *esse* perhaps the existence of the concrete thing that results from the combination of form and matter? Since true form, in the context, is the divine substance, one might have thought that *omne esse ex forma est* refers to the *esse* of *imagines*, but the examples of statue and bronze and so forth would not encourage that, since they are said to have forms, not images.

Duhem might have tried this route: *esse* means essence and in compound things the form is the principal component of essence. Then he could have identified *esse* and *essence* and *id quod est* but would have no word left to talk of that of which the essence is the essence. In fact, appealing again to Themistius, Duhem assures us that Boethius identifies essence and form. *Omne namque forma ex forma est*?

One thing is clear. Duhem's suggestions about the relation between some texts taken from *De hebdomadibus* and *De trinitate* simply collapse under scrutiny and the fact that we know, as he apparently did not, that these are different *opuscula* does not seem a sufficiently exculpating circumstance.

Waiving these difficulties, what does Duhem make of St. Thomas's interpretation of Boethius? He likes it. He praises Thomas for seeing, as no one else had, that the distinction between *quo est* and *quod est* cannot be attributed as such to Boethius, whose distinction is rather between *esse* and *quod est*. And indeed he thinks Thomas is getting it just right at the outset of his exposition of *De hebdomadibus*, mainly because he makes no mention of any real distinction between essence and existence.[13] Indeed,

---

*quod est*, taken as an answer to the question *quid est*, is understood as the form or essence and not the determined thing: hence the Scholastic term *quidditas*. On that basis, *diversum est esse et id quod est* takes on a very different valence than it has in Boethius. But, if Duhem applied his own interpretation consistently, he would see that he attributed to Boethius the identification of essence and *id quod est*.

13. "Dans tout ce que nous venons de lire, l'existence (*esse*), le principe de l'existence actuelle (*principium actus essendi*), l'essence (*essentia*) et la forme

Duhem attributes to Thomas the view that *esse* and *principium essendi* and *forma* are synonyms, which Duhem thinks is what Boethius thought. But, alas, a cloud appears. Thomas's fidelity to Boethius weakens when he thinks of simple things, in the plural, whose complexity cannot be explained in terms of matter and form. Thomas, under the influence of Avicenna, we are told, writes, "Quaelibet forma est determinativa ipsius esse; nulla earum est ipsum esse, sed est habens esse: each form makes existence finite; none is existence as such, but something having existence." And thus Thomas departs from the meaning of the text.

Up to this point, for Boethius and his commentator, *esse* signified existence understood in a general and abstract, not a concrete and particular, way; but it signified at once the essence, which was not distinguished from existence; it designated the substantial form which constituted the essence and which at the same time is the principle of existence in act. Now, in the commentary of St. Thomas, all that changes; for an Intelligence, *esse* becomes the existence it has from the supreme being, while the *id quod est* is the form by which this Intelligence is specifically distinct from every other, by which it is of one species and not another, that is, the essence or quiddity of Avicenna.[14]

Duhem goes on to discuss Thomas's teaching on essence and existence in other texts, but we can leave him now. This much

---

substantielle (*forma*) sont constamment regardés comme des expressions équivalentes d'une même notion. Cette notion s'oppose à celle de la chose qui existe (*id quod est*) à la façon dont l'abstrait s'oppose au concret. C'est bien, croyons-nous, ce qu'entendait Boèce. De la distinction entre l'essence et l'existence, à laquelle Thomas d'Aquin attachera, plus tard, tant d'importance, nous ne trouvons encore aucune trace." *Loc. cit.*, p. 306.

14. Duhem, *loc. cit.*, p. 307. "Pour Boèce comme, jusqu'ici, pour son commentateur, l'*esse* signifiait l'existence, prise d'une façon abstraite et générale, non d'une façon concrète et particulière; mais il signifiait en même temps l'essence, qu'on ne distinguait pas de l'existence; il désignait la forme substantielle qui constitue l'essence et qui est, en même temps, le principe de l'existence en acte. Maintenant, dans le commentaire de Saint Thomas, tout cela change; pour une intelligence, l'*esse* devient l'existence qu'elle tient de l'Être supreme, tandis que le *id quod est*, c'est la forme par laquelle cette intelligence est spécifiquement distincte de toute autre intelligence, par laquelle elle est de telle espèce et non point de telle autre, c'est-à-dire l'essence ou quiddité d'Avicenne."

can be said. On the basis of his exegesis here, Duhem is simply an unsure guide to the text of Boethius itself and this must affect what we think of his appraisals of other interpretations. For example, in the passage just quoted, is it the case that Thomas, let alone Boethius, considered *esse* and *essentia* and *forma substantialis* synonyms before taking up the distinction between simple and composite? That neither man so thought will be made clear in the following section.

## Roland-Gosselin

To his critical edition of St. Thomas's *De ente et essentia*, Father Roland-Gosselin appended two studies, one devoted to the principle of individuality, the other to the real distinction between essence and existence. Each study is divided into two parts, the first recounting views of philosophers, the second views of theologians. In discussing essence and existence, Roland-Gosselin puts Boethius second among the philosophers, immediately after Aristotle.[15] When he discusses St. Thomas later, he will say a few things about the Angelic Doctor's interpretation of the Boethian tractates.

The first thing to notice about Boethius's language, we are told, is his use of the Aristotelian formula of a noun in the dative plus the infinitive "to be" to express the form of a thing.[16] Despite appearances, this is the sense *esse* has earlier in *De trinitate*, where we read that it is the task of theology to "inspicere formam quae vere forma nec imago est, et quae *esse* ipsum est, et ex qua *esse* est; omne namque *esse* ex forma est: apprehend that form which truly is form, not an image, which is existence itself,

15. The chapter on Boethius runs pp. 142–145 of his edition of the *De ente et essentia* (Paris, 1948).

16. Roland-Gosselin cites the text in Migne, *PL* 64,1252B. extracting "Idem est *esse* Deo quod justo" and "idem est enim *esse Deo* quod *magno*" from the following passage: "Nam cum dicimus 'deus,' substantiam quidem significare videmur, sed eam quae sit ultra substantiam; cum vero 'iustus,' qualitatem quidem sed non accidentem, sed eam quae sit substantia sed ultra substantiam. Neque enim aliud est quod est, aliud est quod iustus est, sed idem est esse deo quod iusto. Item cum dicitur 'magnus vel maximus,' quantitatem quidem significare videmur, sed eam quae sit ipsa substantia, talis qualem esse diximus ultra substantiam; idem est enim esse deo quod magno."

for all existence is from form." (Chap. 2, ll. 19–21) We might be tempted, Roland-Gosselin cautions, to glide past the identification of what is truly form with *esse* itself and understand the passage in terms of the *ex* which is repeated in *ex qua esse est* and *esse ex forma est*. After all, haven't we learned from Aristotle that form is the principle of existence? But the immediate sequel cuts us off from that interpretation.

What follows, we remember, is the progression from statue to bronze to earth, where in each case we are told that the thing is the thing it is because of form rather than matter. "Nihil igitur secundum materiam esse dicitur sed secundum propriam formam: nothing is said to be according to its matter but according to its proper form." (ll. 28–29) "Here it is quite clear that in Boethius's intention *esse* designates the shape as such, the bronze as such, the earth as such, and in no way signifies their existence." [17]

Roland-Gosselin takes Boethius to be saying that *esse* equals *forma*, no matter that he says that *esse ex forma est*. Moreover, he takes Boethius to mean that the statue is identical with the shape, the bronze with its form, and earth with its forms. This will shortly lead him into trouble since he now quotes the sequel to the lines he has been interpreting. "Sed divina substantia sine materia forma est, atque ideo unum est, et id quod est. Reliqua enim non sunt id quod sunt: unumquodque enim habet *esse* suum ex his ex quibus est, id est ex partibus suis; et est hoc atque hoc, id est partes suae conjunctae, sed non hoc vel hoc singulariter: But the divine substance is form without matter and therefore is one and is what it is. For the rest of things are not what they are, for each of them has its *esse* from those things from which it is, that is, from its parts, and is this and that, that is, its parts conjoined, but not this or that alone." (*PL* 64,1250B; Loeb, p.10, ll. 29–35) What now will Roland-Gosselin take this to mean?

What does this passage mean? Evidently this: the divine substance being pure form without matter is perfectly one, "it is what it is," that

17. *Op. cit.*, p. 143.

is, it is the form that makes it be what is and it is nothing else. Creatures on the contrary "are not what they are," for their *esse* is composed "of this and that," man for example is composed of body and soul; so man is not one or the other of his parts, neither body, nor soul. *In parte igitur non est id quod est.*[18]

That is, the passage evidently means something other than what we were led to expect. Roland-Gosselin just told us that *esse* is equivalent to form alone; now we confront in the immediate sequel of his assertion talk of things whose *esse* is made up of parts and which cannot be equated with one of them alone. Things like statues, things like bronze, which cannot be equated with their forms. Roland-Gosselin suggests that the dialectic is obscure, "but nonetheless it is clear that existence in no way enters into the composition of the creature: it is a matter of his very essence, composed in the case of man of soul and body, and it is a matter of the distinction that this composition entails between the total essence (*id quod est homo*) and any one of the parts which constitute it." This mention of existence is purely diversionary, of course, although it suggests the author's agenda; but what lifts from the page is that this interpretation of Boethius is at cross-purposes with itself. We want to know what the text says, not what it does not say, the latter being infinite.

To give to the thought of Boethius all its precision it would suffice to comment on it thus: the creature is not what it is, in this sense that it is not identified with its form (which makes it what it is); and it is not identified with its form, because it is also matter.[19]

In short and precisely, Boethius does not say what he was said to have said. Nor is he simply making the point that a compound

18. "Que veut dire ce passage? Évidemment ceci: la substance divine étant pure forme, sans matière, est parfaitement une; 'elle est ce qu'elle est,' c'est-à-dire elle est la forme qui la fait être ce qu'elle est, et elle n'est pas autre chose. Les créatures au contraire 'ne sont pas ce qu'elles sont'; car leur *esse* est composé 'de ceci et de cela,' l'homme par exemple, est composé de corps et d'âme; l'homme n'est donc pas l'une ou l'autre de ses parties; il n'est pas corps, il n'est pas âme; 'En partie donc il n'est pas ce qu'il est, *in parte igitur non est id quod est.*' *Op. cit.*, p. 143. The final Latin phrase with which this quotation ends will not be found in the Loeb edition, which punctuates the relevant sentence thus: ". . . non vel corpus vel anima in partem; igitur non est id quod est."

19. *Ibid*, p. 143.

is not identical with one of its components. Both components are necessary to the compound, but that which is as form, not that which is as matter, will set the thing off from other kinds of thing. To be a statue, the thing needs bronze to receive the shape, but it is from the shape that we call the thing a statue rather than a lump of bronze. It is of course a brazen statue. Why did not Roland-Gosselin see this as the explanation of the earlier remarks to the effect that the form is that *ex qua esse est* and that *omne namque esse ex forma est*? By identifying *esse* and *forma* he created a barrier between himself and the text.

But it is clear that he has a hidden agenda in reading Boethius. Quite gratuitously when his misreading prompts him to attribute obscurity to the Boethian dialectic he proclaims that existence is not a component of essence. So too, when he notes that things whose *esse* is composed of form and matter can have attributes which are not theirs thanks to the form, he finds it important to say, "Nor is existence mentioned among these accidents." [20]

It is not too much to say that Roland-Gosselin's is a completely unhelpful account of *De trinitate*. Who reading it would know what Boethius's doctrine is? And doctrine about what? But Roland-Gosselin wants to know if we will find a different doctrine in *De hebdomadibus*. To which he quickly turns.

Here he gives us a resume of the tractate, working up the impasse to which the disjunction "either whatever is is good by substance or by participation" leads Boethius. The solution is to find a third way.

The goodness in creatures is neither accidental nor substantial in the sense just given; creatures are good in what they are, in their *esse*, because their *esse* comes from God and tends to God. Suppress this relation to God and the goodness of creatures can only be an accident like any other or else, as it is objected, the creature is God. [21]

Roland-Gosselin is interested in the question of the tractate only with a view to determining the exact meaning of the principles

20. "L'existence n'est pas non plus mentionnée parmi les accidents." *Op. cit.*, p. 144.20.
21. *Op. cit.*, p. 144.

of the solution enumerated by Boethius. He has no doubt about what that exact meaning is. "In the course of the discussion the term *esse* is always used to mean either the substantial essence or the essence of the accident. The difficulty itself only makes sense if, to explain the substantial goodness of the creature, one thinks he has to identify its substantial essence with the essence of the good." [22] So, Roland-Gosselin suggests, it is normal to take *esse* in the axioms in the same sense. In what sense? As essence. In this way, they represent a firm and explicit restatement of the thought already expressed in *De trinitate*.

How these hurried and confusing pages can ground the certainty Roland-Gosselin has that Boethius never speaks of existence distinct from essence it would be difficult to say, unless one notices that, at the very outset of the discussion, Roland-Gosselin cites Pierre Duhem. But this is indeed to build on sand. The brief chapter concludes with the remark that Boethius has remained faithful to the point of view of Aristotle.

Chapter IX of Part Two of Roland-Gosselin's study of the real distinction of essence and existence is devoted to St. Thomas Aquinas.[23] It interests us only insofar as it relates to Boethius and Thomas's interpretation of Boethius. We already know that, so far as Roland-Gosselin is concerned, there is no recognition on Boethius's part of a real distinction between essence and existence. In Boethius *esse* always means form in the sense of essence. St. Thomas, on the other hand, clearly and definitively expresses his thought on the distinction of essence and *esse* from his earliest writings, including, it appears, in his exposition of the *De hebdomadibus* of Boethius. In telling us what Boethius means by *esse* Thomas will "understand the *esse* of which Boethius speaks in the sense of existing, despite the difficulties to which this interpretation exposes him, and the rather subtle procedures to which he is obliged to have recourse in order to surmount them." [24]

22. *Ibid.*, pp. 144–145.
23. *Op. cit.*, pp. 185–199.
24. ". . . et lorsque, quelques années plus tard, saint Thomas commente le *De hebdomadibus* il prend l'*esse* dont parle Boece au sens d'exister, malgré les diffi-

This is an extraordinary remark, apparently meant as a kind of praise of Thomas. O'Reilly's suggestion that one might just as well say that Thomas is lying may seem excessive only because we have become used to this sort of doubletalk in the Thomistic school. If Roland-Gosselin had provided us with an analysis of Boethius less incoherent than he has, we might be able to take more seriously what he says of Thomas's exposition. But if we were led to his conclusion by way of careful study it would hardly seem to form the basis of any commendation of Thomas. We have seen the caliber of Roland-Gosselin's analysis of the Boethian tractates. His analysis of Thomas's exposition of *De hebdomadibus*, of whose meaning he is so strangely certain, is confined to a long footnote. Somehow this strikes one as extraordinarily casual. I suspect that Roland-Gosselin was cowed by the erudition of Pierre Duhem and was trying to make the best of a bad, if unanalyzed, situation.

But what does he say of the exposition? He notes that this passage will tell us the sense Thomas gives *esse* in his commentary: "Circa ens autem consideratur ipsum esse quasi quiddam commune et indeterminatum: With respect to being however, to be itself is considered as something common and undetermined." The passage is simply quoted. Roland-Gosselin moves on to tell his reader that Thomas interprets the Boethian phrase *sed id quod est, accepta essendi forma* by adding *scilicet suscipiendo ipsum actum essendi* and the Boethian claim that whatever is participates in that which is *esse* in order to be, as meaning that in order for the subject to be simply speaking it must participate in *ipsum esse*. Apparently, all this is taken to speak for itself. Thomas, it is clear to Roland-Gosselin, "has in view the distinction of essence and existence" and here are the passages where one best sees the difficulties of Thomas's interpretation:

[1] When Thomas writes "Secundam differentiam ponit . . ." Roland-Gosselin cites this from the Vives edition of the *Opera*

---

cultés auxquelles cette interprétation l'expose, et les procédés assez subtils auxquels il est obligé d'avoir recours pour les surmonter." *Op. cit.*, p. 186.

*omnia,* t. 28, 471b = Marietti, lectio 2, n. 29. Thomas explains the Boethian remark that *omne quod est, participat eo quod est esse ut sit; alio vero participat ut aliquid sit* as meaning that "in order for something to be a subject simply speaking, it participates in *ipsum esse*; but in order to be such-and-such, it must participate in something other, as a man in order that he might be white participates not only in substantial existence but also in whiteness."

What is the difficulty? ". . . [w]hereas Boethius in this work always takes the term "participate" in the sense of accidental participation, as St. Thomas himself recognizes . . ." (475b = lectio 3, n. 44).

This is confused. As the passage from Boethius on which Thomas is commenting makes clear, Boethius is not there confining participation to participating in an accidental quality. Thomas notes that participation is understood as accidental participation when Boethius is working up the problem of the tractate: if whatever is is good, must this not be either because of its substance or by participation, the latter there being contrasted with "by substance." But this has nothing to do with the clear sense of the axiom.

[2] The next difficulty Roland-Gosselin cites is Vives p. 475b = Marietti, lectio 2, n. 34. Here St. Thomas restricts to God the application of the axiom *omne simplex esse suum et id quod est unum habet* "alors qu'en fait il admet à ce moment, avec Boece, que dans les anges il n'y a pas de distinction entre le sujet et l'essence: even when in fact at this moment he admits, with Boethius, that there is no distinction in the angels between subject and essence."

What is the difficulty? That Thomas says that only in God there is no distinction between subject and essence while asserting (with Boethius?) that there is no such distinction in angels either?

This is confused. Boethius in this tractate does not take *omne simplex esse suum et id quod est unum habet* to refer to a class of things, or if he does it is a class with a single member, God. What Thomas in the passage referred to argues is that an existent substance can be simple, in the sense of lacking matter, can be, in short, a subsistent form, and for all that not exhaust the possibilities of being, can be, in short, one form of being among many. God who is wholly simple is in the fullest sense of the term and is thus *ipsum esse subsistens*. Thomas thus introduces, as Boethius did not, a kind of simple entity between complex beings and the wholly simple being God is.

> [3] Roland-Gosselin refers to Vives, tome 28, p. 476a = Marietti, lectio 3, n. 48 ff. and remarks, "St. Thomas adroitly converts the propositions of Boethius to give a sense to his argumentation."

What we actually have in Thomas is an elegant piece of discourse:

(1) It is necessary that those things whose substance is good be good as to what they are (whatever is required in order for it to be belongs to the substance of a thing).

(2) But things are from that which is *esse*: it was said above that something is when it receives *esse*.

(3) So it follows that the very *esse* of things which are good according to substance is good.

(4) Therefore if all things are good according to their substance, it follows that the very *esse* of all things is good.

St. Thomas then notes that, since Boethius is arguing from premises which are convertible, he can proceed in reverse order.

(5) If the *esse* of all things is good, the things that are, insofar as they are, are good.

(6) So it will be the same for anything to be and to be good.

(7) Therefore it follows that they are substantial goods and not good by participation.

This argumentation is the development of the second possible interpretation of *omne quod est bonum est* and is taken to lead to the identification of creatures with God.

What is the difficulty? There is no way to tell. Is Roland-Gosselin suggesting that Thomas could instruct Boethius on the conversion of propositions? Does he think converting propositions requires adroitness? Is he objecting to converting (4) to (5)? We will never know. What we are given is innuendo, not interpretation.

[4] Roland-Gosselin's final point is taken from Vives 478b = Marietti, lectio 4, n. 62 in medio, which shows that "St. Thomas has to agree that Boethius, by the *esse bonum* refused to creatures, means to signify their essence" and the same at Vives 80b = Marietti, lectio 5, n. 71: "Primo quidem, quia hoc quod est bonum significat naturam quandam sive essentiam."

What is the difficulty? Roland-Gosselin sees Thomas as here forced to admit that when Boethius says that the creature is not the essence of goodness, he is denying something of their essence. Thomas is quite ready to admit this. It is thanks to their existence that creatures are called good because the First Good who wills them to exist is at once Goodness and Being.

The second passage deals with the second of two difficulties Boethius raises against his solution. If the identity of Goodness and Existence in God explains that the existence of creatures is good and thus that what they are as receiving that existence is good, why not say that since Justice and Being are one in God that creatures are also just insofar as they are? The response is that to be good looks to essence and to be just to action (*Nam bonum esse essentiam, iustum vero esse actum respicit* ll. 165–166).

I do not know what difficulty Roland-Gosselin sees here. He takes it to be too obvious to require explanation.

But then he sees little need to buttress his extraordinary remarks about the exposition of St. Thomas with detailed analysis of the work. In half a page of text and a footnote twenty-one lines in length, Roland-Gosselin has dismissed as a work of incredible ineptitude what any reader of it will find the most careful and illuminating reading that *De hebdomadibus* ever received.

*Herman Josef Brosch*

In his monograph on the concept of being in Boethius, Brosch gives us a systematic, not to say pedantic, survey of Boethius's use of *esse* in all his writings.[25] This research leads him to conclude that the term *esse* usually has the meaning of existence (*dasein*) in Boethius's second commentary on the *Isagoge* of Porphyry, whereas in the *Consolation* it usually means essence (*Sosein*) and when it means existence this is made clear by the addition of *subsistere* or *existere*. In *De trinitate*, Brosch maintains, Boethius always uses *esse* in the sense of essence. Brosch lays out these results for us in the first three chapters of Part One of his monograph. Chapter Four deals with *esse* in *De hebdomadibus*.

In what, given his approach, amounts to real daring, Brosch decides to examine the body of the tractate before looking at the axioms as such. His conclusions are unequivocal. We are told that *esse* never, not once, is used in the tractate as a substantival infinitive meaning existence (*dasein*); it *always* means essence, though sometimes the essence of substance, sometimes that of accidents.[26]

Throughout his analysis runs a muted polemical note. Brosch's intention is to prevent any reader from finding anything like the distinction between essence and *esse* in what he imagines is its Thomistic sense in the text of Boethius. "Wie kann man da also noch von der Beziehung zur Existenz sprechen?" is a not untypical aside.[27] Who the target of this rhetorical question might be at the time Brosch is writing would be interesting to know. Historically, of course, it is St. Thomas Aquinas. But it would seem not to be Thomists contemporary with the author. Indeed, when he goes on to look at the axioms, he can enlist their aid. Roland-Gosselin is no foe of the interpretation Brosch

25. Dr. Hermann Josef Brosch, *Der Seinsbegriff bei Boethius, Mit besonderer Beruecksichtigung der Beziehung von Sosein und Dasein* (Innsbruck, F. Rauch, 1931).
26. *Ibid.*, p. 58.
27. *Ibid.*, p. 57.

puts forward, and he solemnly cites the French Dominican's authority for a commonplace. It is normal to assume that *esse* has in the axioms the same meaning as in the sequel. His interpretation of the axioms is thus predestined, a corollary. If *esse* never means anything other than essence in the body of the tractate, it can only mean essence in the axioms.

So sweeping a conclusion requires only a single counterexample to be destroyed. But first a word on the commonplace he takes from Roland-Gosselin. One use of *esse* that does not occur in the axioms and is crucial for the sequel is *esse* as meaning *primum esse* as opposed to *esse omnium*. But Brosch can reply that it means divine essence and essence as predicably common to creatures. Nonetheless, this suggests a certain caution.

What does *ipsum esse nondum est* mean? That essence is not found without accidents. The existent thing must have specific essence as well as qualities. We are struck more and more that Brosch is determined not to permit any interpretation of *diversum est esse et id quod est* that will give textual support to Thomas's interpretation which, following Duhem and Roland-Gosselin, he sees as stemming from the earlier scholastic tradition rather than from Boethius himself.

Imagine trying to maintain Brosch's view when confronted with *Non potest ESSE ipsum esse rerum nisi a primo esse defluxerit*. (ll. 131–133) How is that capitalized (by me) *esse* to be taken? Surely, it is existential. And what of *sunt* in *Qua quoniam non SUNT simplicia, nec ESSE omnino poterant, nisi id quod solum bonum est ESSE voluisset*? (ll. 118–119) Surely God wants creatures to exist and to exist in a certain way. You can't have one without the other. Does this make them identical?

Brosch was careful to say that *esse* as a substantival infinitive never means existence in *De hebdomadibus*. But presumably there is a correlation between the finite and infinitive forms of the verb *esse*. *Fit enim participatio cum aliquid iam est; est autem aliquid, cum esse susceperit*. (ll. 32–34) How are we to understand "now or already is" (*iam est*) if not something as resulting from the reception of *esse*. Whatever else we may understand by *esse* it is clear that it plays an indispensable role in understanding what is meant by saying that a thing exists. We have been told that something exists when it receives a form of being (*forma essendi*). There is no way to speak of the existence of concrete things apart from form, but does it then follow that existence is identical with form?

That Brosch's judgment of *De hebdomadibus* is excessive was pointed out by Schurr.[28] He rejects Brosch's view that there is some kind of evolution in Boethius's use of *esse* from the logical to the theological writings. He rejects Roland-Gosselin's view that in *De hebdomadibus* Boethius always and only uses *esse* in the sense of *esse essentiae*, that is the *esse* that is essence.[29] Schurr thinks it likely that Boethius did not hold a real distinction between essence and existence. But he concludes with two observations. First, the term *esse* throughout the works of Boethius changes, sometimes meaning essence, sometimes existence, and, second, Boethius's thought is predominantly essential in emphasis such that *esse* in *De hebdomadibus* retains its twofold meaning but more often refers to essence rather than to existence.[30]

### Cornelio Fabro

"Recent critical research conducted by both defenders and adversaries of the real distinction arrives at the same result, that the most correct interpretation of the Boethian texts does not suggest, *at least directly*, a real distinction between essence and existence, since it is completely absent from it."[31] The first in-

28. Cf. Viktor Schurr, C.Ss.R., *Die Trinitaetslehre des Boethius im Lichte der 'skythischen' Kontroversen* (Paderborn, 1935), pp. 32–35, 42–44.

29. *Ibid.*, p. 34, n. 61. The note is extensive, as many of Schurr's are, and is replete with textual bases for his criticism of Brosch and Roland-Gosselin.

30. *Ibid.*, p. 44, the end of the lengthy note 77 which begins on p. 42.

31. Cornelio Fabro, *La nozione metafisica di partecipazione*, third edition (Turin, 1963), p. 102: "Ricerche critiche recenti, condotte sia da difensori, come da avversari della distinzione reale, portarono al risultato concorde, che l'interpretazione più corretta dei testi boeziani non suggerisce, *almeno direttamente*, una distinzione reale fra essenza, poiche esse n'é completamente assente."

stance of such critical research Father Fabro refers to is that of
Roland-Gosselin, but he also cites Brosch and Schurr.[32] What
does Fabro himself think?

He characterizes *De hebdomadibus* as a work of limpid logic
which, despite the Neoplatonic character of the Boethian literary
project, expresses in Platonic-sounding formulae Aristotelian
doctrine. (He suggests that the title of the work recalls the *Enneads* of Plotinus, which is interesting whether or not Boethius
used *hebdomads* as a title of the *opusculum*.)[33] Calling the work
logical is meant to distinguish it from Thomas's commentary
on it.

St. Thomas in the youthful commentary that he wrote on *De hebdomadibus* (1257 or 1258?) reads its terms in their metaphysical meaning
and taking off from the notion of participation elevates on its abstruse
propositions the cardinal principles of his own metaphysics, arriving as
the ultimate conclusion at the *real* distinction between essence and existence in creatures, which St. Thomas often likes to express in the terms
of Boethius as a distinction between *quod est* and *esse*.[34]

Everything depends on the meaning of the terms in the axioms
of Boethius. What does *he* mean by *ipsum esse* and *quod est*?
For St. Thomas, Fabro says, *ipsum esse* is the *actus essendi*, and
the *id quod est* the concrete substance. The fact is that Fabro
does not think Boethius meant by these terms what Thomas
understood him to mean, though he does not put it quite that

32. Fabro, p. 102, n. 3, finds tendentious Brosch's use of a phrase dear to
Father Pelster that the Boethius of St. Thomas is a *falsch verstandene Boethius*,
and appeals to Schurr for a more balanced basis for judging St. Thomas. Fabro
offers this somewhat oblique defense. "Invero come é certo che il Tomismo ha
fatto realmente progredire le dottrine che si trovavano nelle fonti precedenti secondo una maggio chiarezza concettuale, cosi é inopportuno e anacronistico
voler trovare esattamente dottrine antithomistiche, prima dell'apparizione stessa
del Tomismo."

33. *Op. cit.*, p. 99.

34. "S. Tommaso nel Comm. giovanile che fece al *De hebdomadibus* (a.
1257–1258?), prese i termini nel loro significato metafisico, e partendo dalla
nozione di partecipazione elaboro su queste astruse propozioni i principi cardi-
nali della sua metafisica, arrivando alla conclusione ultima, della distinzione *reale* fra essenza ed esistenza nelle creature, che S. Tommaso spesso ama enunciare
con i termini di Boezio, come distinzione fra *quod est et esse*." *Op. cit.*, p. 100.

way. A particular merit of Fabro's discussion is that he reminds us that the first anti-Thomist polemics bore precisely on Thomas's interpretation of Boethius, with Henry of Ghent and Peter Olivi insisting that by *esse* Boethius means form. Fabro does not underscore the fact that he is conceding that these early critics were as right as such recent researchers as Roland-Gosselin.[35]

The above remarks occur well along in Fabro's first work on participation, but there is an earlier discussion of participation as notional and as real composition in which the Thomistic commentary on *De hebdomadibus* features prominently.

Fabro is chiefly interested in some of the Boethian axioms because they called forth from St. Thomas a complete exposition of his conception of the structure of the concrete.[36] This suggests that the Boethian tractate is an occasion for Thomas to do his own metaphysical stuff. What Fabro takes Thomistic metaphysics to be about we will put off until we look at what he has to say about the axioms of *De hebdomadibus* and Thomas's comments on them.[37]

Noting the distinction Thomas makes between discussing the diversity of *quod est* and *esse* on the level of meanings (*secundum intentiones*) and then *realiter*, Fabro nonetheless speaks of a metaphysical demonstration of *diversum est esse et id quod est* by way of the three subaxioms. He remarks that Thomas takes *ipsum esse* to mean the *actus essendi*, and it soon becomes clear that he thinks something very different is going on in the commentary than in the text commented upon.[38]

35. *Ibid.*, p. 101. In neither of his major works on participation does Fabro take Pierre Duhem into account, although he quotes the French scholar to the effect that Thomism is not so much a synthesis as a desire for a synthesis. It is a mishmash of incompatible doctrines. To the degree that Duhem's remark is historical, which it is, Fabro and other Thomists seem to concede its truth.

36. *Ibid.*, p. 24.

37. There is such an analysis in *La nozione metafisica*, pp. 24–35, and in *Partecipazione e Causalità* (Turin, 1960), pp. 204–213.

38. "Le preoccupazioni di ordine logico che sentiva Boezio nel porre il problema della bontà delle creature sono diventate per S. Tommaso di ordine metafisico et lo inditizzano verso una serie di considerazioni che toccano la struttura intima dell'essere finito, come essere." *La nozione*, p. 26. Boethius, no mean logician, is not the one who characterizes these opening axioms as manifesting a

In discussing Thomas's threefold division of participation, Fabro says this was unnecessary to understand Boethius and is done to facilitate Thomas' independent aims in his exposition.[39] We are told that it is essential to notice that Thomas introduces a new use of the notion of participation, that between abstractions, that is, of whiteness in color and man in animal, which is not only extraneous to the text of Boethius, but repugnant to his spirit, since for him the abstract is what is participated and the concrete what participates. It should be said that Boethius overcomes his supposed repugnance on a significant number of occasions.[40] When Thomas is discussing the third Boethian illustration of the diversity of *quod est* and *esse*, namely that the former can and the latter cannot be the subject of accidents, he observes that this is why the essence abstractly considered is predicated as a part of the concrete whole. Fabro takes this as occasion to speak of Thomas's vacillation between remaining faithful to the text and taking it to its fundamental metaphysical implications, "as Thomas himself understands them, and which certainly could not have been the object of Boethius's preoccupations." [41] We are given little justification for this condescending attitude toward Boethius, which is certainly not shared by St. Thomas.

In discussing the axioms dealing with the difference between being a substance and being an accident, Fabro indicates what he is reading into the text. In commenting on the Boethian doctrine, Thomas speaks of a twofold existence (*duplex esse*) fol-

---

diversity of meanings (*intentiones*) between *quod est* and *esse*. It seems odd to describe Thomas's commentary as metaphysical and suggest that the text is logical, since it is Thomas who characterizes his and Boethius's procedure as *secundum intentiones*. More alarming, of course, is the insouciance with which it is suggested that Thomas is not commenting on Boethius but engaged in some independent metaphysical activity, presumably of the kind he engaged in in the *De ente et essentia*. But surely Thomas knew the difference between writing a tractate of his own and commenting on someone else's.

39. *Ibid.*, p. 27.

40. "Esse igitur ipsorum bonum est" (ll. 71, 126, and *passim*), not to mention "Omnis diversitas discors." (l. 49).

41. *Ibid.*, p. 29.

lowing on two kinds of form, substantial and accidental.[42] Fabro portrays Thomas as being put into an embarrassing position by Boethius's axiom: *diversum tamen est esse aliquid in eo quod est, et esse aliquid, illic enim accidens hic substantia significatur.*

[The axiom] puts St. Thomas in the embarrassing but for him logical situation of distinguishing in the concrete participant a twofold *esse*: one that is not *praeter essentiam* and another which instead remains *praeter essentiam*: the first makes [something] be *simpliciter*, the second *secundum quid*. In the subtle explanation that follows is found the observation that there is first participation in *esse* as such, whence the subject is constituted in itself and is capable of participating in other (accidental) formalities. Evidently Boethius can speak here only of formal (substantial) *esse* and not of the *actus essendi*, although the commentator for a moment recognizes it without renouncing his own meaning of *esse* as *actus essendi*, and making of the one difference (much easier to understand) three, passes gradually from the first to the third to conclude his intention: *Est autem haec differentia quod primo oportet ut intelligatur aliquid esse simpliciter, et postea quod sit aliquid. . .*[43]

What Fabro seems to be suggesting is that over and above the *duplex esse* of which St. Thomas and Boethius here speak, there is a third, namely, the *actus essendi*. It is easy to agree that this is not to be found in Boethius. But neither is it a doctrine of St. Thomas, in or out of commentaries.[44]

42. *In de Hebdomadibus Boethii*, lectio 2, n. 27.

43. ". . . pone S. Tommaso nel'imbarazzante ma logica per lui situazione di distinguere nel concreto partecipante un duplice *esse*: uno che non e *praeter essentiam* ed uno invece che resta *praeter essentiam*: il primo fa essere *simpliciter*, il secondo *secundum quid*. Nella sottile speigazione che seque si ribatte l'osservazione che prima si da la partecipazione all'*esse* come tale, onde il soggetto si costituisce in se ed e capace di partecipare alle altre formalita (accidentali). Evidentemente Boezio qui non puo parlare che dell'*esse* formale (*sostanziale*) e non dell'*actus essendi*, tanto che il Commentatore per un istante lo riconosce, ma senza rinunciare al suo significato di *esse* come *actus essendi*, e facendo dell'unica differenza (molto facile a comprehendersi) tre, passa gradualmente dalla prima alla terza per concludere il suo intento. . . ." *Op. cit.*, p. 30.

44. Fabro's *Partecipazione e Causalità* enforces the impression that he wants to understand Thomas as teaching that over and above *esse substantiale* and *esse accidentale* there is some third *esse* which is the *actus essendi*. On p. 198 ff. of the later work, Fabro distinguishes between *esse* when it is a synonym for essence

In *The Metaphysical Notion of Participation*, Fabro ends his treatment of the axioms with the statement of two problems. The first has to do with Thomas's extension of the concrete/abstract distinction to essence/*actus essendi*. This is not in Boethius. Surprisingly, Fabro says there is no need for this distinction in dealing with the problem of the tractate! "Di fatti nella soluzione che Boezio presentera, l'estensione introdotta dall'Angelico, non presenta alcuna applicazione: In fact the extension introduced by the Angelic Doctor has no application in the solution Boethius will give." [45] This stands out, even against a frieze of extraordinary remarks.

The second problem concerns the introduction of a real as well as notional participation. This too is idle so far as the Boethian tractate is concerned. "Anche questa precisazione restava fuori delle esigenze del problema boeziano, che e risolto facendo

---

(*esse essentiae*) and *esse* which is the act of essence (*actus essentiae*). "Una conferma ed un'applicazione dell'*esse essentiae* (l'essenza metafisica), è la divisione dell'*esse* in *esse substantiale* ed *esse accidentale* che non può riguardare direttamente l'*esse* come *actus essendi*, il quale è l'atto propria della sostanza completa (*substantia prima*)." (p. 199) "Possiamo quindi concludere che l'*esse in actu* corrisponde all'*esse essentiae*: come all'essenza sostanziale corrisponde un *esse* sostanziale, così all'essenza accidentale (la quantità, la qualità, la relazione . . .) corrisponde l'*esse accidentale*. Ma l'*esse ut actus essendi* è il *principium subsistendi* della sostanza, grazie al quale tanto l'essenza della sostanza come anche quella degli accidenti sono in atto et operano nella realtà: l'*esse* degli accidenti e l'*esse in actu* nel tutto ch'è la sostanza prima, è quindi un'esistenza secondaria derivata dalla sostanza reale come un tutto in atto." (p. 201) And here is the explicit statement of Fabro's doctrine of *triplex esse*. "Se sostituiamo *quo est* con *esse*, come si trova in Boezio e al quale ritorna San Tommaso, abbiamo non uno ma ben tre *esse*: l'*actus essendi*, l'essenza e la 'forma partis,' ch'è la forma come parte attuale dell essenza, rispetto alla materia prima ch'è pura potenza, la quale confersisce l'*esse* alla matera. Nulla di più aristotelico di questo *forma dat esse materiae*—come vedremo—e tuttavia San Tommaso ha già trasformato la terminologia aristotelica grazie all'introduzione dell'*actus essendi* il quale si presenta espressamente come il 'mediatore formale' di attualità fra la forma immanente alle realtà singole e la causa estrinseca dell'ente. L'*esse e non l'essenza esprime nelle cose il quid assoluto di realta et il costituitivo della supreme realtà . . .*" (p. 202). Clearly, it is Fabro's interpretation of St. Thomas that is getting in the way of his appreciating the nature of the Angelic Doctor's exposition of the *De hebdomadibus*. For another study by Fabro of this text, see pp. 173–190 of his "Intorno al Fondamento della Metafisica Tomistica" first published in 1960 and included in *Tomismo e Pensiero Moderno* (Rome, Libreria editrice della Pontificia Universita Lateranense, 1969).

45. *La nozione . . .*, p. 32.

appello ad altri principi, molto più piani: This precision too is beyond the needs of the Boethian problem, which is resolved by appeal to other and much more obvious principles." [46]

The two most touted features of the commentary are thus held to be irrelevant to what the tractate is about.[47]

Needless to say, Fabro's interpetation of St. Thomas is a vast story in itself, but whatever is made of that, his remarks on the exposition of *De hebdomadibus* are difficult to take as praise of St. Thomas. In a nutshell, Fabro agrees with those who hold that Thomas as commentator assigns to the key terms of the tractate meanings other than those intended by Boethius. He is unique in suggesting that the additions Thomas makes are irrelevant to the problem of the tractate.

## Pierre Hadot

In two studies, one devoted to Boethius's distinction between *quod est* and *esse*, the other to the phrase *forma essendi* as it occurs in axiom 1a (p. 203 below), Pierre Hadot attempts to show what Boethius himself might have meant as opposed to what medieval commentators took him to mean.[48]

Hadot conveniently lines up the way in which Boethius pays off on his claim that *diversum est esse et id quod est.*

| ESSE | ID QUOD EST |
|------|-------------|
| nondum est | accepit formam essendi |
| | suscipit esse |
| | participat eo quod est esse |
| | est atque consistit |

46. *Ibid.*, p. 32. Fabro cites Thomas's remark about the *De hebdomadibus* in *Q.D. de veritate*, q. 21, a. 5. in fine, as meaning that the real distinction between essence and existence is not required to solve the problem of the *De hebdomadibus*.

47. In *Partecipazione e Causalità*, p. 209, we are invited limpidly to see the embarrassment of St. Thomas who having introduced a notion of intensive *esse* must deal with the *esse essentiae* of Boethius.

48. Pierre Hadot, "La distinction de l'être et de l'étant dans le De Hebdomadibus de Boèce," *Die Metaphysik im Mittelalter*, Miscellanea Mediaevalia, 2 (Berlin, De Gruyter, 1963), pp. 147–153, and "Forma Essendi: Interprétation philologique et interprétation philosophique d'une formule de Boece," *Les études classiques*, XXXVIII (1970), pp. 143–156.

| | |
|---|---|
| nullo modo aliquo participat | participare aliquo potest |
| nihil aliud praeter se habet | potest habere aliquid |
| admixtum | praeterquam quod ipsum est |

It is noteworthy that Boethius tells us what *esse* is not rather than what it is. We get a better picture of *quod est*. "Il participe donc à la fois a l'être, dans la mesure où il est, et à quelque chose d'autre que l'être, dans la mesure où il est selon une certaine forme, ou il est-quelque-chose: It participates then both in being, insofar as it is, and in something other than being, insofar as it is according to a certain form and is some thing." (p. 147) Hadot also points out that Boethius speaks not only of the *esse* that is common to all the things that are, and are thanks to having received *esse*, but also of the *esse primum* who is God.[49]

Hadot accepts the view of V. Schurr that in order to understand Boethius we have to find the Greek source from which he borrowed this distinction. The distinction in Greek is that between *to einai* and *to on*. There is a Latin precedent for borrowing these terms in Marius Victorinus who speaks of the first and second Neoplatonic hypostases as *Esse* (l'Être) and the thing that is (l'étant). *Esse* is neither subject nor predicate, it has no attributes and is not in a subject. That which is is determined by its proper form and there begins with it a distinction between subject and object.

Far from being original with Marius Victorinus, Hadot goes on, we find the same thing in Porphyry. The One which is identical with Being is featureless and unknowable; the next participates in Being, not in all its indefinite amplitude, but according to a form. "Autrement dit, à partir de l'Étant, l'être n'est plus pur, il devient l'être d'un étant, et il devient l'être-quelque-chose: Put differently, with the thing that is, being is no longer pure since it has become the being of something that is and becomes to-be-some-thing." (p. 149) A further note is that Being (*Esse*) is

---

49. References for Boethius's talk of *esse omnium rerum* are lines 71, 72, 120, 124, 131 and 132 of the *De hebdomadibus*. The *esse primum* references are lines 133 and 150.

spoken of as pure acting, that is, as Existence. *Esse* is not a substance or an act, it is pure action. The infinitive is thus taken to signify an action rather than a state. It is an Idea, a force, a power, an action which produces form.

Another way of understanding the opposition of *esse* and *quod est* is by way of the traditional distinction between substance and existence.[50] By existence they mean being as such, being without addition, being which is neither subject nor predicate; by substance they mean some qualified being, the subject, taken with the accidents inherent in the substance. The tendency is to reserve Existence to God.

So we find in the Neoplatonic tradition, and especially in Porphyry, a doctrine which distinguishes *esse (l'Être)* and *quod est (l'Étant)*, identifying them with the first and second hypostase. According to this doctrine, *esse (l'Être)* is anterior to *quod est (l'Etant)*, because it is simple whereas *quod est* necessarily implies composition.[51] A feature of this teaching is that as indetermination increases so too does activity, so that as one rises from individuals through the genera and beyond forms one reaches pure activity, being itself, existence as such. The key to derived being is always form.

This, Hadot concludes, is the doctrine we find in Boethius. *Esse* is the First Being, and can be thought of as pure act (*agir pur*), transcending all forms. It is not yet, that is, it is not substance, because it is anterior to it and to all formed things and is their cause. *Id quod est* is the thing that is. It is and subsists, that is, it becomes a substance as soon as it receives its form of being.

50. "Nous retrouvons la même opposition entre esse et quod est dans la distinction, également traditionnelle, entre existence et substance, *hyparchis* et *ousia*, et nous retrouvons ici encore, Marius Victorinus et son correspondant, l'Arien Candidus." *loc. cit.*, p. 150.

51. "Ainsi nous trouvons, dans la tradition néoplatonicienne, et spécialement autour de Porphyre, une doctrine qui distingue l'Être et l'Étant, en les identifiant à la première et à la seconde hypostase. Selon cette doctrine, l'Être est antérieur à l'Étant, parce qu'il est plus simple et que l'Étant implique nécessairement une composition." *Op. cit.*, p. 151.

That is how I understand *forma essendi*. I don't in fact think Boethius would have used this formula if he wanted to say that the thing that is receives this form that is *esse*. The being indeed receives *esse*. But it does not receive it as a form.[52]

The whole argument of the tractate makes clear, in Hadot's view, that the *esse* of the things that are is not a form but is rather anterior to all form. To be a substance, the thing must first of all exist, that is receive *esse*, then receive the form which determines the thing in the way proper to a subject; the *esse* of a thing then will be the *esse* of a man, of an animal, of a rock. In other words, the *esse* of the thing that is always of a certain form. "Ce n'est donc pas l'être qui est forme, c'est la forme qui s'ajoute à l'être: Being is not form, then, it is form that is added to being." [53] The opposition of *esse* and *quod est* is then one between pure being without determination and a being determined by a form. The great difference is that, for Boethius, *quod est* is not the second hypostase, but every substance, every thing, produced by Being.

Nonetheless, Hadot sees *De hebdomadibus* as in the main-stream of Neoplatonism and even wonders if it may not be a Latin translation of a Greek work!

We have here a very different picture than we have been given by other interpreters, even those who allude to the influence of Neoplatonism on Boethius. From the perspective made possible by Hadot's essay, the attempt to identify *esse* and form seems fantastic. Perhaps as important as anything else in Hadot's article is his almost throwaway observation that the description of *quod est* by Boethius is not of a putative second entity but renders it a predicably universal phrase applicable to all the things that are.

In the article he devoted explicitly to the phrase *forma essendi* as it occurs in the axioms, Hadot surveys all the medieval inter-

52. "C'est ainsi que j'entends forma essendi. Je ne pense pas en effet que Boece aurait employé cette formule, s'il avait voulu dire que l'étant reçoit cette forme qui serait l'être. L'étant reçoit bien l'être. Mais il ne le reçoit pas comme une forme." *Loc. cit.*, p. 152.
53. *Ibid.*, p. 152.

pretations and then most of the modern.[54] Of these latter, none tries to place Boethius in his exact historical situation, in the precise philosophical tradition in which he lived and worked. Only when this philological task is done can there be a sound philosophical interpretation. We are familiar from his earlier article with what Hadot takes this historical setting to have been. He reminds us of the way Porphyry among the Greeks and Marius Victorinus among the Latins distinguished *on* and *einai*, identifying the latter with the first and the former with the second hypostase. Boethius differs from them in this, but Hadot maintains that the same structure of relations between *esse* and *quod est* is found in Boethius and his predecessors.

(1) For Boethius *esse* is transcendent to *quod est*: the relation between them is one of participation.

(2) Participation explains the possibility of attribution. "Is" is the first predicate of that which is.

(3) It follows that there are two modes of *einai*: one which is anterior and superior to that which is, another which is a derived mode received by the thing and which is coupled with it like a predicate. "Id quod est ( = derived *esse*) participat eo quod est esse ( = absolute *esse*) ut sit ( = derived *esse*)."

After tracking these matters through Plotinus and Porphyry, Hadot makes this extremely important remark.

The error of most modern interpreters, it seems to me, has been to understand *id quod est* as designating the individual thing. But the in-

54. He mentions Bruder, Brosch, Duhem, Manser, Gilson and De Raeymaeker and summarizes their positions thus. "On constate donc ici les variations des interprètes concernant la notion de *forma essendi*. Tous, sauf G. M. Manser, identifient *forma* et *esse*, sans préciser d'ailleurs la signification exacte qu'ils attribuent à *essendi*. Il leur suffit de reconnaître dans la *forma* l'*esse ipsum* dont parle Boèce. Mais ils se séparèrent les unes des autres lorsqu'il s'agit de définir l'*esse*. Pour K. Bruder et E. Gilson, l'*esse*, c'est l'exister, mais E. Gilson précise que cet *esse* est Dieu même. Pour H. J. Brosch, P. Duhem et De Raeymaeker, l'*esse* est l'essence spécifique, grâce à laquelle la chose concrète peut être. G. M. Manser, pour sa part, qui comprend l'*esse* comme être transcendantal, entend la *forma essendi* comme la forme ou essence qui délimite l'existence." "*Forma essendi*: Interprétation philologique et interprétation philosophique d'une formule de Boèce," *Les études classiques*, XXXVIII (1970), p. 147.

dividual thing implies a composition of substance and accidents of which Boethius does not speak. On the contrary, the notion of the thing that is (*l'étant, on*) implies only the duality of a subject (the *id quod*) and a predicate (the *est*). To explain the attribution of this predicate to this subject, it is enough, on Platonic principles, to suppose the preexistence of the predicate (*est*) in an absolute mode, that is to say, the preexistence of pure being. So *esse* is that pure being, that being in itself, which is not a pure abstraction but, as we see in Porphyry, an activity all the more efficacious because it is undetermined. As for the *est* in *id quod est*, it is no longer being in itself, it is being related to a subject, the being of some thing. It is no longer absolute and undetermined being, but a determined and limited being.[55]

Hadot does not of course mean that *id quod est* signifies some existing thing like the second hypostase. It is something predicably common to all the things that are.[56] His point has to do with the content of that concept.

What does *forma essendi* mean? The form that is *esse*? The *id quod est* is constituted when it receives *esse*, but this cannot be the pure and first *esse* who is God. Is then the form identical with the received *esse*? "The *forma essendi* would then correspond to the first predicate the subject receives. Afterward other predicates would come to be added, to constitute *esse aliquid*, for example, animality, rationality, etc. Predicates would be assimilated to forms. *Forma* would have a sense close to *proprietas* or to *qualitas*."[57] *Forma essendi* would then mean the property of being, essentiality. Hadot thinks this interpretation is a possible one. Boethius would then be saying that the thing that is is and consists when it receives the property of being, essentiality.

Another possible interpretation, suggested by the English translation in Loeb, would see *essendi*, not as the definition of form, but the result of form's action. Form gives being to the thing; it makes it be. Hadot does not like this interpretation because it makes *est*, which is the first predicate, depend for its

55. *Ibid.*, pp. 151–52.
56. *Ibid.*, p. 152, "Il correspond plutôt au concept général d'étant, commun à tous les ètants."
57. *Ibid.*, p. 153.

meaning on predicates due to later forms. "To have a substantial form intervene as the principle of the being of the thing would therefore be, for him [Boethius], to introduce an alien element into a relation he wants to be immediate. He would lose what is essential to his doctrine." [58]

The Italian translation of the passage is this: *Ciò che é, é e sussiste dopo aver ricevuto la sua forma d'essere*. The thing that is exists and subsists after having received its proper mode of being. This captures the distinction between pure and undetermined being and that which is. For being to be received introduces a difference between that which receives it and pure and undetermined being. This difference becomes more and more particularized, by generic, by specific, by individual forms, but at the outset is simply the otherness of *id quod est* and pure and undetermined *esse*. Thus it avoids the difficulties Hadot saw in the English translation.

Of the different ways of translating *forma essendi*, I would in the end keep only two as possibles. Either the being (*l'étant*) is when it receives the property of being or the being is when it takes on its proper way of exercising the act of being. This second interpretation seems to me most conformable to the whole of the exegesis I have proposed. [59]

Among the medieval exegetes, Hadot finds Remigius of Auxerre and Thomas Aquinas the most interesting. "The first because he was closer to the universe of thought of Boethius, Thomas Aquinas because his philosophical genius guided him and enabled him to sound the depths of Boethius's formulae by intuition." [60] How different this appraisal of Thomas from that of Thomists over the past sixty years and more! Thomas intuitively gets to the real meaning of the Boethian axioms despite a limited acquaintance with the philosophical milieu in which Boethius worked. That is as different as can be from the odd claim that Thomas uses Boethian formulas to set forth a doctrine alien to the tractate.

58. *Ibid.*, p. 153.
59. *Ibid.*, p. 154.
60. *Ibid.*, pp. 154–55.

*Luca Obertello*

One of the most comprehensive works on Boethius to appear in recent years is the two-volume study by Luca Obertello. In it, Obertello touches on every facet of Boethius's teaching and of the centuries of scholarship devoted to it.[61]

As others had before him, Obertello begins his study of Boethius's doctrine of being with the second chapter of *De trinitate.* Does the formula *esse ex forma est* mean that in the creature *esse* is different from form? "Such an interpretation is evidently wrong. In fact Boethius means to say that to be a statue is to have received a form; the being [*esse*] of the statue consists in the actual possession of that form and not in something distinct from it."[62] If to be a statue is actually to have a certain form, does not this suggest a difference between the form and the actual having of that form? In any case, Obertello seems to accept the identification of *esse* and *forma.* He summarizes the metaphysical structure of created and uncreated being in this way.

In God, form and being are identical; in creatures there is instead a composition of form and matter, with the result that form is only a part of the whole the concrete individual constitutes. The structure thus delineated is an essential one and does not seem to include or exclude actual existence.[63]

Obertello takes an extensive detour through Aristotle in the course of which he says that the error of the Eleatics was to identify essence and being (p. 624) and that for Aristotle being "coincides with" essence, but this means that ontology must begin with essence, not that it must reduce everything to it.(p. 626) For Aristotle, there are two kinds of being: those that are first,

---

61. Luca Obertello, *Severino Boezio*, 2 vols., *Op. cit.* The relevant chapter for our purposes is in vol. 1, pp. 619–656. Obertello has also edited and translated Boethius's *De Hypotheticis Syllogismis* (Brescia, Paideia, 1969), and *La Consolazione della Filosofia e Gli Opuscoli Teologici* (Milan, 1979).

62. *Loc. cit.*, p. 620.

63. *Loc. cit.*, p. 622.

immobile and simple, identical with their essence, and those
whose essence is complex and which are not their quiddity. (p.
627) These Aristotelian reminders are said to be indispensable
to a correct and objective understanding of Boethius. Whatever
his debt to Neoplatonism, Obertello says, Boethius is radically
Aristotelian. But what of *De hebdomadibus?*

The expression *id quod est* means the entire reality of the concretely existing being; it includes matter and form and *esse*
and the collection of accidents which constitute the individual
being.[64] And *esse?* "It would thus seem to be used primarily in
the sense of *forma*; it is the form of being in virtue of which the
whole exists and is what it is. *Esse* is everything that constitutes
a thing in its particular being (*id quod est*); it is the nature of the
thing considered absolutely in itself, prescinding from the individuating principles of the supposit."[65] Yet *esse* is said to be received by the subject according to a determinate form (*forma
essendi*). He speaks of a twofold participation of the subject, in
*esse* in order that it might be, and in a determinate form to be
what it is.

It is difficult to find coherence in this account thus far. Obertello now turns to the interpretation of Hadot despite his earlier
claim that it is the Aristotelian influence that will enable us
to understand Boethius. Thus far that has not led to a crisp
account. The appeals to Hadot are simply added on to what
has gone before, with the result that no Obertellian account
emerges.

What about Thomas's interpretation of *De hebdomadibus?*
Obertello once more makes a pastiche of previous accounts with
the result that it is difficult to know where he stands. He takes
Thomas to be understanding *esse* in Fabro's sense of intensive
actuality and, like Fabro, speaks of *esse* being received first,

---

64. "*Id quod est* é preso come il soggetto dell'essere. . . . Esso indica l'intera
realtà di un essere concretamente esistente: include la materia, la forma e l'essere,
e la collezione di accidenti che costituisce l'essere individuale." *Op. cit.*, p. 638.
65. *Ibid.*, p. 638.

prior to other determinations. (p. 654) In the end, Obertello accepts the common opinion that Thomas finds in the text something that is not there, the real distinction of *quod est* and *esse*.

### Bruno Maioli

In a small work devoted exclusively to *De trinitate* and *De hebdomadibus*, Bruno Maioli gives us the most recent interpretation of the matters that interest us.[66] *De hebdomadibus* begins by establishing the ontological difference between God and finite being, founding it on the ontological dependence of the finite on the First Being and on the simple nature of God as opposed to the composite nature of finite being. The finite being is composed of *esse* and *quod est*. Thus the analysis begins with *diversum est esse et id quod est*. To understand this we must understand what *esse* and *id quod est* mean and what the reason for their diversity is. Maioli's reader knows from the outset that this book has the same kind of precision as the texts it would interpret.

Writing when he is, Maioli can scarcely discuss these matters without taking into account the variety of modern interpretations, most of which were undertaken with an eye to appraising Thomas's exposition. Maioli notes the claim of Duhem and Roland-Gosselin, but mentions as well a caveat of Vanni-Rovighi.[67] Fortunately, Maioli does not accept the received opinion unquestioningly. Nor does he leave the views of Hadot uncriticized.

Of the latter, he says that, however sound the historical and

---

66. Bruno Maioli, *Teoria dell'Essere e dell'Esistente e Classificazione delle Scienze in M. S. Boezio* (Arezzo, 1977).

67. "Non si può quindi interpretare *esse* nel senso di *actus essendi*, atto contingente de essere e di esistere, contrapposto al *quod est*, intenso a sua volta come essenza possibile: ma riconosciuta come storicamente non fondata tale lettura, non si deve cadere—avverte giustamente la Vanni-Rovighi—nell'altra inesattezza di interpretare, sempre in senso scolastico, l'*esse* boeziano come l'essenza in quanto distinta e contrapposta all'esistenza (quod est)." *Op. cit.*, p. 19. The reference to Silvia Vanni Rovighi, "La filosofia di Gilberto Porretano," in *Miscellanea del Centro studi medievali* (Milan, 1955), pp. 8–18. Notice the use of "possible essence" as the complement of *esse*.

philological research of Hadot, his interpretation falsifies something essential to the Boethian position. He has in mind Hadot's suggestion that there is first the reception of *esse* and then of a series of determinations following the genera and species relevant to the thing. "In this sense *esse* is seen as the first perfection, almost as matter with respect to the successive forms which one after the other are added to it." [68] Maioli finds this quite alien to the true Boethian position.

The axioms of *De hebdomadibus*, like the ontological theses of *De trinitate*, are an original impasto of Platonism and Aristotelianism in the spirit of the typical and banal Boethian eclecticism, in which elements and borrowings are so fused that any attempt to reduce them back to the original theses of this or that author (Porphyry, Victorinus, Aristotle himself), besides being very difficult to document, inevitably runs the risk of forcing or betraying—out of love of proof—the unmistakable Boethian savor.[69]

He finds the path laid out by Duhem and Roland-Gosselin more helpful. But against them he brings the objections that, first, it does not seem enough to say that the diversity stated by Boethius between *esse* and *quod est* is simply a logical distinction. As for Brosch, Maioli feels such a noncontextual tracing of a word through the writings of Boethius is unhelpful. Moreover, Brosch's research is governed by a rigid opposition, the essentialistic meaning of *esse* and the existentialistic meaning of *esse*. But "it is more exact to speak of the constitutive co-presence in the Boethian *esse* of this twofold meaning. It is our conviction that the basic meaning of *esse*, substantially constant in the tractates, is that of "the structure that makes be": the *forma essendi*. The basic postulate of the entire Boethian metaphysics is the thesis of *De trinitate*: *omne esse ex forma est*."[70] This is not the identification of *esse* and *forma*, although *esse* is always the being of a form which is precisely a *forma essendi*. Each form makes something be in a particular mode, substantial form in

68. *Ibid.*, p. 21.
69. *Ibid.*, p. 21.
70. *Ibid.*, p. 24.

the strongest sense, accidental forms in a lesser way. As the correlative of form, *esse* is not abstract, universal, undetermined and undifferentiated. Still less is it a form distinct from other generic or specific or differential or proper or accidental forms. "L'*esse* delle realtà finite é un *esse* partecipato in una forma, attraverso una forma e da una forma: é un essere correlato struturalmente ad una forma, che per questo é anche *forma essendi*: The *esse* of finite realities is an *esse* participated in a form, by way of a form and from a form: it is a being structurally correlated to a form which is thus also a *forma essendi*."[71] To be is always to be something or other, to be this or that, not on the level of pure numerical individuality, but on the level of essence, nature.

Maioli sums it up in the following deduction:

(1) *omne esse ex forma est.*

(2) Every form is in its own way a determined and determining form (*forma essendi*), although only substantial forms make something be and be such in the strong sense.

(3) The form gives simultaneously being and being such: it is at once the structural and existential ontological principle.[72]

We have from Maioli a careful interpretation of the axioms which does not see any need to choose between the stark extremes that governed the research of Brosch and the negations of Duhem and Roland-Gosselin and so many of the Thomistic school. Form determines and informs matter, thus constituting *id quod est*; it is thanks to its form that the concrete both is and is a determinate kind of thing existing in the world: *est atque consistit*.[73] The form thus is the reason things exist as the things they are; finite things *id quod sunt habent ex eo quod est esse*. (l. 70)

It is natural that Boethius, with his characteristic Aristotelianized Platonism, favors *esse* in its formal-structural rather than in its existential

71. *Ibid.*, p. 25.
72. *Ibid.*, p. 25.
73. *Ibid.*, p. 26.

aspect; he considers *esse* from a predominantly essentialistic viewpoint, but it would be to impoverish its rich significance to reduce it to the role of pure possible essence which awaits its act of existence. This would be to fall back into the mistake of reading Boethius in the light of the Scholastic distinction between possible essence and act of existence. For its part *esse* is not only the act of existence of a possible essence. The typical trait of the Boethian *esse* is to involve structurally essence and act of existence since for Boethius—more than ever faithful here to the ontological formalism of his masters Plato and Aristotle—the act of existence can only derive from form.[74]

Maioli's interpretation seems clear, but when he notes, with respect to *De trinitate*, that the object of theology is a form which is *esse*, and asks whether this identification is general, he seems to say it is.[75] He insists that for the statue "to be and to be a statue are the same thing and derive from the same form: the being of the statue consists in actual possession of this certain form and is not something distinct or distinguishable from it. The act of existence of subsistence derives from the form."[76] But if being derives from form how can it be indistinct and indistinguishable from it? I think Maioli is here making certain that his position is seen to be distinct both from that of Hadot—with existence the first of many constitutive forms of the concrete—and what he takes to be the Scholastic position.

## Summary

Our survey establishes one point beyond any doubt. There is no scholarly consensus on the meaning of the Boethian tractate taken in itself. Throughout the modern period, most interpretations of *De hebdomadibus* seem intent on relating what is said of Boethius to what Thomas said, or is thought to have said,

74. *Ibid.*, p. 27.
75. "Inoltre: non solo l'*esse* deriva dalla forma, ma si identifica ontologicamente con esse: la forma è l'*esse* dell'ente, anche se—come vedremo—non è tutto l'ente. Se Boezio intendesse dire che l'*esse* di un ente finito si distingue in qualche modo dalla sua propria forma specifica, l'esempio dovrebbe essere interpretato in questo modo: la forma per cui una statua è tale e distinta dall'*esse* della statua. Tale lettura risulta palesemente erronea. . . ." *Op. cit.*, p. 43.
76. *Ibid.*

about Boethius. However diverse the interpretations of *diversum est esse et id quod est* there is an odd unanimity: the Boethian axiom cannot mean what St. Thomas takes it to mean. There has been oddly little examination of the Thomistic exposition itself. When the text of Thomas is studied it is under the assumption that it contains a metaphysical doctrine quite unrelated to that of the text on which it comments. Oppositions of "essentialistic" and "existentialistic" meanings of *esse* are meant to oppose the true essentialistic meaning of Boethius to the existentialistic meaning of St. Thomas. It does not seem too much to say that the Thomistic interpretation haunts modern scholarship. Some scholars seek to save Boethius from the Thomistic real distinction between essence and existence. Most Thomists seek to drive a wedge between their master and the doctrine of Boethius. This survey should dispel any assumption that scholars are agreed on the meaning of the Boethian axioms and their import for *De hebdomadibus*. It would seem to be equally unwise to assume that the exposition of Thomas has received a single interpretation. In the next section we will look closely at Thomas's interpretation.

CHAPTER 7

# The Exposition of St. Thomas

Boethius will address the question how it is that substances are good insofar as they exist without being, for all that, substantial goods: *modum quo substantiae in eo quod sint bonae sint, cum non sint substantialia bona.* (ll. 2–4)[1] His method will be that employed in mathematical and other disciplines; he will first set down certain rules and terms (*terminos regulasque*) and develop a solution in accord with them.

What he means by "rules and terms" is quickly made clear. They are instances of those common conceptions of the mind which, when expressed, gain immediate assent. *Communis animi conceptio est enuntiatio quam quisque probat auditam.* (ll. 18–19) Approval is swiftly given because such statements are seen to be true *per se* and do not come to be understood *per alia.* (lectio 1, n. 15) St. Thomas observes that they are called common because they are commonly conceived, known by any intellect. Why? Because in such statements the predicate enters into the account or definition of the subject: *quia praedicatum est de ratione subiecti.* So it is that so soon as the subject is named and it is understood what it is, it is immediately clear that the predicate is in it: *et ideo statim nominato subiecto, et intellecto quid sit, statim manifestum est praedicatum ei inesse.* (n. 15)[2]

1. The text of Boethius will be cited by lines according to the edition to be found in Stewart and Rand. For the commentary, I use S. Thomas Aquinatis, *Opuscula Theologica*, vol. 2, edited by M. Calcaterra, O.P. (Taurini, Marietti, 1954). Thomas will be cited according to the paragraph numbers of this edition.

2. Thomas is thinking of the notion of *per se* predication, one of the two principles of the demonstrative syllogism according to Aristotle in *Posterior Analytics*, I, 4. See *PL* 64,716D, and Thomas *In I Posteriorum Analyticorum*, lectio 10, as well as *In V Metaphysicorum*, lectio 19, nn. 1054–57. Fittingly, it is the

Immediate assent is thus a function of understanding the meaning of what is said. Insofar as there are some terms whose meaning no one can fail to grasp, common conceptions of the mind employing those are known by everyone. "If equals are taken from equals, the result is equals." [3]

Boethius mentions another kind of self-evident or *per se nota* statement, assent to which is not universal because the meaning of the constituent terms is not universally known but depends on special experience. "Bodiless things have no location." The truth of this is immediately grasped so long as we know that to be circumscriptively in place is a property of bodies. [4]

So now we know what kind of propositions Boethius sets down as regulative of his solution to the question how substances can be good insofar as they exist without being substantial goods. An enunciation is speech which is susceptible of truth or falsity. (*PL* 64,767C) A *communis animi conceptio* is an enunciation whose truth is known as soon as the meaning of its

---

first mode of perseity Thomas cites. Later (lectio 3, n. 47), he introduces the second mode of perseity. One will find *termini* defined as the constituents of propositions in the *De differentiis topicis* (1175), subject and predicate in the case of simple propositions, simple propositions in the case of complex propositions. The same work gives us an important parallel to the description of the axioms. "Propositionum quoque aliae sunt per se notae, et quarum probatio nequeat inveniri, aliae quas, tametsi animus audientis probet eisque consentiat, tamen possunt aliis superioribus approbari. Et illae quidem quarum nulla probatio est, maximae ac principales vocantur, quod his illas necesse est approbari, quae ut demonstrari valeant, non recusant. Est autem maxima propositio ut haec: Si de aequalibus aequalia demas, quae derelinquuntur aequalia sunt. Ita enim hoc per se notum est, ut aliud notius quo approbari valeant, esse non possit. Quae propositiones cum fidem sui natura propriam gerant, non solum alieno ad fidem non egent argumento, verum caeteris quoque probationis solent esse principium. Igitur per se notae propositiones, quibus nihil est notius, indemonstrabiles ac maximae et principales vocantur." *PL* 64,1176.C–D.

3. Of course one can imagine this self-evident truth emerging from discourse: $A = B$; $a = b$; $A > a$; $B > b$; $(A - a) = (B - b)$. But this merely spells out the fact that the statement is understandable when we understand what "equal" and "substract" mean. Since everyone knows that, everyone immediately assents to the statement. Thomas gives as another example "Every whole is greater than its part."

4. Here too a species of proof, a *modus tollens*, could be employed to manifest the self-evident claim: If A then B; not A; then not B. Where A stands for "bod-

constituent terms is known. They are known per se, because there is an immediate, unmediated, relation of predicate to subject. To continue the mathematical analogy Boethius draws, let us call these axioms.

1. *Diversum est esse et id quod est.*

a. Ipsum enim esse nondum est, at vero quod est accepta essendi forma est atque consistit.

b. Quod est participare aliquo potest, sed ipsum esse nullo modo aliquo participat. Fit enim participatio cum aliquid iam est; est autem aliquid cum esse susceperit.

c. Id quod est habere aliquid praeterquam quod ipsum est potest; ipsum vero esse nihil aliud praeter se habet admixtum.

2. *Diversum est tantum esse aliquid et esse aliquid in eo quod est.*

a. Illic enim accidens, hic substantia signficatur.

b. Omne quod est participat eo quod est esse ut sit; alio vero participat ut aliquid sit.

c. Ac per hoc id quod est participat eo quod est esse ut sit; est vero ut participet alio quolibet.

3. *Omne simplex esse suum et id quod est unum habet; omni composito aliud est esse, aliud ipsum est.*

4. *Omnis diversitas discors, similitudo vero appetenda est; et quod appetit aliud, tale ipsum esse naturaliter ostenditur quale est illud hoc ipsum quod appetit.*[5]

---

ies" and B for "are in place." Such enunciations are called immediate, because no middle term is needed to see the connection of predicate and subject.

5. There are several different readings of the axioms in the text Thomas used. Thus for him [2] reads, *Diversum est tamen esse aliquid in eo quod est et esse aliquid.* [1c] for him reads *Id quod est habere aliquid praeterquam quod ipsum esse potest.* [2c] reads *Ac per hoc id quod est participat eo quod est esse ut sit; est vero ut participare alio quolibet possit.* The two parts of [3] are reversed, the statement about the composite coming first, and the wording of the last part of [4] differs: *tale ipsum esse naturaliter ostenditur quale est illud hoc ipsum quod appetit.*

I have enumerated and arranged the axioms according to the suggestions of St. Thomas who saw their connection with the transcendentals. The axioms are such because they use terms which everyone understands. But the most easily understood terms of all are *being, one, good*. Axioms [1] and [2] involve being, [3] unity, since simple and composite are modes of unity, and [4] the good. (lectio 2, n. 20)

*Axioms Bearing on Being*

If we take the infinitive "to be," by definition indeterminate and common, we can see that it is made determinate or finite in one way by the subject of a proposition, that which is (*quod esse habet*, St. Thomas says), and in another way by the predicate, as when of man we say not simply that he is but that he is such-and-such, for example, white or black. The indeterminate actuality expressed by the infinitive thus becomes determined by subject and predicate to definite kinds of actuality.

On this basis, Thomas sees two major axioms involving being, one deriving from a comparison of the infinitive "to be" and the subject that is (*secundum comparationem esse ad id quod est*), the other based on a comparison of that which simply is with that which is in a certain way (*secundum comparationem eius quod est esse simpliciter, ad id quod est esse aliquid*).

[1] *Diversum est esse et id quod est*. To be and that which is are diverse. How diverse? Because they refer to diverse things or because they have diverse meanings and might refer diversely to the same thing? The latter, Thomas suggests. *Esse* has a different meaning than *quod est*. How different? Well, different in the way *to run* and *the one running* differ, different as the abstract way of signifying something differs from the concrete way of signifying it. *Whiteness* and *the white thing* also illustrate the difference of abstract and concrete signification.[6] Boethius manifests this diversity in three ways.

6. "Ad secundum dicendum quod, quia ex creaturis in Dei cognitionem venimus, et ex ipsis eum nominamus, nomina quae Deo attribuimus, hoc modo significant, secundum quod competit creaturis materialibus, quarum cognitio est

[1a] *Ipsum enim esse nondum est, at vero quod est accepta essendi forma est atque consistit.* "To be" doesn't signify a subject of being, something that is, anymore than "to run" means something that runs. We just cannot say "To run runs." "That which is" or "being" on the other hand signifies an existent subject (*subiectum essendi*). We can say that a being is, a runner runs, but we don't say "To be is." "To be" doesn't yet signify actuality in a finite mode, as the subject does.[7] When a subject is said to be, this will be in some manner or other. That is, when we say "A man is," the indeterminate actuality expressed by the infinitive is determined by the form thanks to which a man is a man. That is the sense of *accepta essendi forma est atque consist.* It is thanks to a substantial or accidental form that the subject is said to be.[8] The indefinite actuality expressed by *esse* or "to be"

---

nobis connaturalis. . . . Et quia in huiusmodi creaturis, ea quae sunt perfecta et subsistentia, sunt composita; forma autem in eis non est aliquid completum subsistens, sed magis quo aliquid est: inde est quod omnia nomina a nobis imposita ad significandum aliquid completum subsistens, significant in concretione, prout competit compositis; quae autem imponuntur ad significandas formas simplices, significant aliquid ut non subsistens, sed ut quo aliquid est, sicut albedo significat ut quo aliquid est album." *Summa theologiae,* Ia, q. 13, a. 1, ad 2m. To signify abstractly and concretely are *modi significandi* and it is possible to signify the same *res significata* in different or diverse ways. That is why the different accounts or *rationes* we give of *white* and *whiteness* signify the same *res* in different ways (*modi*)—"that which has whiteness" (*quod*) and "that whereby white things are white" (*quo*).

7. *Ipsum enim esse nondum est* is reminiscent of an Aristotelian remark in the *Perihermeneias* about the verb to be, something Boethius discussed in both his commentaries on that work. Aristotle says that "is" taken alone says nothing, meaning that it does not signify truth or falsity. "Ipsum autem est purum si dictum, inquit, fuerit, neque verum est, neque falsum. . . ." (PL 64,311A) In the second commentary, he puts it this way, "Verba igitur per se dicta significant quidem quiddam, et sunt rei nomina, *sed nondum ita significant, ut vel esse vel non esse aliquid constituant, id est ut affirmationem faciunt aut negationem.* (PL 64,432A) This is a different point than *ipsum enim esse nondum est*—the mode of signification of the infinitive prevents it from being subject of a sentence—but that means it cannot have *est* predicated of it. And the *nondum* is interesting. "Nam quamvis rem designent, nondum tamen subsistendi ejus rei signum est, nec si hoc ipsum est vel ens dixerimus." (PL 64,434A) There is of course a way in which the infinite can function as subject, as in "To be cannot be the subject of a sentence," but for reasons we will not go into here this does not count against the point being made.

8. "*Ipsum esse nondum est*, quia non attribuitur sibi esse sicut subiecto essendi; sed *id quod est, accepta essendi forma*, scilicet suscipiendo ipsum actum

is made finite by form. *Omne namque esse ex forma est,* as Boethius writes in the *De trinitate,* 2 (line 21).

[1b] *Quod est participare aliquo potest, sed ipsum esse nullo modo aliquo participat. Fit enim participatio cum aliquid iam est; est autem aliquid, cum esse susceperit.* That which is can participate in something, whereas "to be," indeterminate actuality, can in no way participate in anything. Participation is possible once a thing is and it is something thanks to receiving existence or "to be." This way of explaining the diversity of *quod est* and *esse* depends on participation, but what is that? Thomas takes the occasion to distinguish three modes of participation after giving the etymology of participate (or partake) as "taking a part of" (which is suggestive as well of "taking part in" and "partaking of").

*First Mode of Participation.* When something receives in a particular or limited way that which pertains to another universally, the former is said to partake of or to participate in the latter. The examples are of the species participating in its genus and the individual participating in its species. "Man is animal" and "Socrates is man" illustrate this.[9] It is as if the extension of the generic term is restricted by the specific subject. Not everything of which "animal" can be said is man, nor is Socrates identical with everything of which "man" is predicated.

*Second Mode of Participation.* A subject or substance is said to participate in accident and matter in form. Form, whether substantial or accidental, is of itself common, but is then determined to this or that subject.

---

essendi, *est atque consistit,* idest in seipso subsistit. Non enim ens dicitur proprie et per se, nisi de substantia, cuius est subsistere. Accidentia enim non dicuntur entia quasi ipsa sint, sed inquantum eis subest aliquid, ut postea [in Axiom 2] dicetur." Lectio 2, n. 23.

9. Boethius seems to speak of the relation of a subject to its accidental predicate as participation. "Sermo hic, quem dicimus est, nullam per se substantiam monstrat, sed semper aliquam conjunctionem vel earum rerum quae sunt, si simpliciter apponatur, vel alterius secundum participationem: nam cum dico, Socrates est, hoc quod dico Socrates aliquid eorum quae sunt, et in rebus iis quae sunt Socratem jungo; si vero dicam, Socrates philosophus est, hic, inquam, Socrates philosophia participat." *PL* 64,433A.

*Third Mode of Participation.* That of effect in cause, particularly when the cause is not of the same genus as its effect. Something heated by the sun is not hot in the way the sun itself is: there is such a disproportion between cause and effect that the effect is said to partake of, to share in, the power of the cause.

Having distinguished these senses of "participate," how are we to understand the term when *quod est* is said to be able to participate whereas *ipsum esse* in no wise can? Thomas suggests that we set aside the third mode for now, but it will emerge as the mode which permits Boethius to solve the problem of the tractate. We are then able to say that *ipsum esse*, to be, indeterminate actuality, is unable to participate in either of the first two modes.

Not in the second, as subject participates in accident or matter in form, because *ipsum esse* is signified as something abstract. Not in the first either, that is, as the particular participates in the universal. What prevents this is not that *ipsum esse* is abstractly signified. Whiteness can participate in color, to run is a kind of activity. What rules out this mode of participation is that there is simply nothing more universal than *ipsum esse*. As such, as the most universal, it is shared in or participated in by everything else, but does not itself participate in something more universal. The term *ens* ("being") is as universal as the infinitive, but because it signifies concretely, it can participate in the abstractly signified actuality, that is, in the second mode.[10]

Now we can understand [1b]. Only that which is signified concretely can participate in anything, that is, only something that already exists (*cum iam est*), and it exists when it has received existence, has become a finite subject of the actuality indeterminately and abstractly signified by the infinitive. *Participatio conveniat alicui cum iam est, Sed ex hoc aliquid est, quod suscipit ipsum esse.* (n. 24) *Participare* and *suscipere* are kept

---

10. "Sed id quod est, sive ens, quamvis sit communissimum, tamen concretive dicitur; et ideo participat ipsum esse, non per modum quo magis commune participatur a minus communi, sed participat ipsum esse per modum quo concretum participat abstractum. Lectio 2, n. 24.

distinct here and, as such, as Axiom 2 will enable us to say, participation has to do with accidental form alone. Later the meaning of the term will be expanded and indeed it has already been so expanded in the list of meanings Thomas gives us, but then that list anticipates the rest of the tractate. Already in discussing [1a] he wrote, "ita possumus dicere quod ens, sive id quod est, sit, inquantum participat actum essendi" (n. 23), a locution yet to be introduced by Boethius.

[1c] *Id quod est habere aliquid praeterquam quod ipsum est potest; ipsum vero esse nihil aliud praeter se habet admixtum.* It is generally true of the abstractly signified that only what is essential to it can be predicated of it. "Humanity" will have attributed to it only what pertains *per se* to the nature, and the same is true of "whiteness." By the same token, when someone is said to be a man, only that is true of him *qua* man which is of the essence of humanity, and so too insofar as he is said to be black. *Qua* black, only what is of the essence of blackness is true of him.[11]

It is otherwise with things concretely signified, like man. Just as *quod est* or *ens* is said to have as its *ratio* "that which has being: *id quod habet esse*," so the account of "man" is "that which has humanity." Of man many things can be truly said which are not true of him just insofar as he is a man, that is, true of him as stemming from humanity as such. This is the reason for saying that "humanity" and "whiteness" are signified as parts (*per modum partis*) and thus are not predicated of the concrete anymore than any other part of its whole. That is, we do not say a part is its whole and we do not say a man is humanity.[12] Thus, what is said of *quod est* and *esse* is taken to be an instance

---

11. "Cuius ratio est, quia humanitas significatur ut quo aliquid est homo, et albedo quo aliquid est album. Non est autem aliquid homo, formaliter loquendo, nisi per id quod ad rationem hominis pertinet; et similiter non est aliquid album formaliter, nisi per id quod pertinet ad rationem albi, et ideo huiusmodi abstracta nihil alienum in se habere possunt." Lectio 2, n. 25.

12. On direct and oblique predication, cf. *In VII Metaphysic.*, lectio 4, nn. 1353–55.

of a familiar truth about things concretely and abstractly signified.

[2] *Diversum est tantum esse aliquid et esse aliquid in eo quod est.* This is the second great axiom based on the notion of being. Not only must we see the diversity of *quod est* and *esse*, we must take into account the distinction between *esse simpliciter* and *esse aliquid.* (n. 21)

[2a] *Illic enim accidens hic substantia significatur.* The first step is to identify the former, *tantum esse aliquid* with accident and the latter *esse aliquid in eo quod est* with substance. In the history of interpretation of this tractate, many commentators have assumed that the reference to former and latter must be mistaken, as if *esse aliquid tantum* must mean substance and that every complicated phrase mean accident, but this is clearly wrong.[13]

[2b] *Omne quod est participat eo quod est esse ut sit; alio vero participat ut aliquid sit.* Here we have the extension of the verb *participat* to cover the reception of *esse* thanks to which that which is is. When it is (*cum iam sit*), it can participate in something else and be such-and-such. This is participation in an accidental form and is the first and dominant, though not the only, sense of *participare* throughout the tractate.

It is because the concretely signified can be the subject of more than pertains to its essence as such that we must consider a two-fold existence (*duplex esse*) in it. But how will the two kinds of existence be distinguished? By the forms which are their principles. "Because form is the principle of being, it is necessary that something is said to be in a certain way because of a form it has." [14]

If then the form is of the essence of the thing having it, if it is constitutive of what it is, the thing is said to be simply as the result of having that form, as a man is, simply speaking, when

---

13. Cf. Chadwick, *op. cit.*, Chap. 4.
14. "Quia enim forma est principium essendi, necesse est quod secundum quamlibet formam habitam, habens aliqualiter esse dicatur." Lectio 2, n. 27.

he has a rational soul. But if the form is extraneous to the essence of the one having it, the recipient will be said to be only something or other, to be in a certain sense, as a result of having that form. Thus a man is not said to be without qualification as the result of having the form whiteness, but to be in a certain way, namely, white.[15] We are now in a far better position to grasp the sense of *accepta essendi forma* in Axiom 1a. In the pithy phrase of the *De trinitate, omne namque esse ex forma est.*[16] It is the form which makes something to be in the one way or the other (*forma quae facit huiusmodi esse*, n. 28), not in the sense of efficient cause, but in the sense of making it a kind or mode of existing.

So in order to be a subject, a concrete thing, the thing must first participate in existence. It does not have existence in some undifferentiated way, it is the kind of thing it is, and thus it exists and exists as the kind of thing it is thanks to form.

[2c] *Ac per hoc id quod est participat eo quod est esse ut sit; est vero ut participet alio quolibet.* This sub-axiom spells out the order of the two participations. The term "participate" may be extended from "having an accidental form" to "having a substantial form," but it is the latter which is ontologically more basic. Unless the substance is constituted in being, by participating in existence according to its substantial form, there is no concrete thing which can participate in accidental form and thus

15. "Si ergo forma illa non sit praeter essentiam habentis, sed constituat eius essentiam, ex eo quod habet talem formam, dicetur habens esse simpliciter, sicut homo ex hoc quod habet animam rationalem. Si vero sit talis forma quae sit extranea ab essentia habentis eam, secundum illam formam non dicetur esse simpliciter, sed esse aliquid." N. 27.

16. Father Fabro, in *La nozione . . .* , p. 30, seems to be flirting with a *triplex esse*, which of course would answer to neither Boethius nor St. Thomas. "Evidentemente Boezio qui non può parlare che dell'*esse* formale (*sostanziale*) e non dell'*actus essendi*, tanto che il Commentatore per un istante lo riconosce, ma senza rinunciare al suo significato di *esse* come *actus essendi*, e facendo dell'unica differenza (molto facile a comprendersi) tre, passa gradualmente dalla prima all terza per concludere il suo intento." Fabro is not the only Thomist who understands Thomas to have a meaning of *esse* (in creatures) which is neither *esse substantiale* nor *esse accidentale*, both of which follow on the possession of a form. There is no basis for this interpretation.

be said to be such-and-such. "Nam aliquid est simpliciter per hoc quod participat ipsum esse; sed quando iam est, scilicet per participationem ipsius esse, restat ut participet quocumque alio, ad hoc scilicet quod sit aliquid." (n. 30)

## Axioms Following on the One

If an axiom is a statement to which assent is given as soon as it is heard, it should not be thought that all axioms are on the same footing. Thomas's arrangement of the axioms makes it clear that some subsidiary ones cast light on the primary ones. Furthermore, insofar as some of the axioms turn on being, others on the one and others on the good, and there is an order among these terms, there will be an order among the axioms themselves.[17] What is the basis of the order between being, one and good?

In laying out this doctrine, the doctrine of the transcendental attributes of being,[18] Thomas draws an analogy between primary judgments and primary concepts. Just as in demonstration it is necessary to arrive at principles which are grasped *per se*, lest we be involved in an infinite regress, so in the order of con-

17. The first principle of all reasoning is given three different expressions in a key passage of Aristotle (*Metaphysics*, IV, 3, 1005b17 ff.) They are (1) the same attribute cannot at the same time belong and not belong to the same subject in the same respect, (2) it is impossible for anyone to believe the same thing to be and not to be; (3) it is impossible for the same thing to be and not to be. How do these relate to one another? "*Ex hoc enim quod impossibile est esse et non esse, sequitur* quod impossibile sit contraria simul inesse eidem. . . . Et ex hoc quod contraria non possunt simul inesse, *sequitur* quod homo non possit habere contrarias opiniones, et *per consequens* quod non possit opinari contradictoria esse vera. . . ." *In IV Metaphysic.* lectio 6, n. 606. The underlined words and phrases indicate the order and dependence. This can be made even clearer as follows: [i] impossibile est esse et non esse; [ii] impossibile sit contraria simul inesse eidem; [iii] homo non possit habere contrarias opiniones; [iv] non possit opinari contradictoria esse vera. [iv] is said to follow from [iii] which follows from [ii] which follows from [i]. The priority here is of the ontological over the psychological and logical. Of course the sequences involved are not *demonstrative*.

18. See Jan Aertsen, *Nature and Creature: Thomas Aquinas's Way of Thought* (Leiden, New York, E.J. Brill, 1987), which gives special prominence to the Thomistic teaching on transcendentals. The key text in Thomas is *Q. D. de veritate*, q. 1, a. 1, c.

cepts there must be something first. Avicenna has said it. Being is the first thing that it occurs to the mind to know. "Illud autem quod primo intellectus concipit quasi notissimum, et in quo omnes conceptiones resolvit, est ens." All other concepts presuppose and add to the concept of being, but how can anything be added to being that is not itself an instance of being? A Parmenidean impasse seems to loom. When Aristotle in the *Metaphysics* denies that being is a genus, he means precisely that there is nothing that could serve as a difference which would not itself be being.[19] The only way in which something could "add" to being is by expressing a mode of being that the term "being" does not itself express. This can come about in two ways. When the modes expressed are special modes of being, as is the case with the categories of being, the additions are like that of "substance" which is being *per se*. But there are other modes which follow generally on being, having the same extension as it does. These are the so-called transcendental properties of being.

St. Thomas divides these general modes of being into two types, the first of which follows on being in itself, the second on its relation to another (Figure 1). Something that can be said of every being in itself affirmatively is what it is, its essence, and the word "thing" (*res*) expresses this, where what negatively can be said of any being in itself is that it is undivided, and that is what "one" (*unum*) expresses. Some general modes of being express its relation to another, as distinct from that other, which is expressed by "something" (*aliquid*), or as something befitting it. What is needed is something to which all being can relate as befitting, and this is the soul, to whose appetitive power all being relates as "good" (*bonum*) and to whose knowing power all being relates as "true" (*verum*).

This explains the way in which "one" and "good" presuppose "being" though not vice versa and thus why the axioms are laid out as they are. Before leaving this *locus classicus* of the doctrine

19. Cf. 998b21 ff. *In III Metaphysic.*, lectio 8, n. 433: "Quod autem ens et unum non possint esse genera, probat tali ratione. . . ."

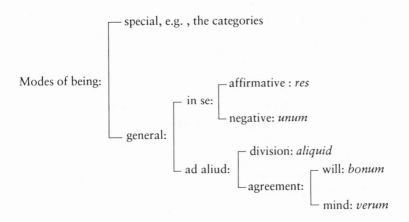

FIGURE I

of transcendental attributes of being, let us note the way *ens* and *res* are contrasted by Avicenna, a way endorsed by Thomas: *ens sumitur ab actu essendi, sed nomen rei exprimit quidditatem sive essentiam entis.* Of course, *ens* and *res* signify the same thing, that which is. Avicenna denied this on the basis of the truth that whatever receives existence from another is such that its existence is other than its essence or substance. Although Thomas, as we shall soon see, accepts the diversity of essence and existence in creatures, he rejects Avicenna's claim that *ens* signifies one thing, *esse*, and *res* signifies another thing, *essentia*. Both terms signify the same thing, but they are imposed to signify from diverse angles.[20]

[3a] *Omni composito aliud est esse, aliud ipsum est.*

[3b] *Omne simplex esse suum et id quod est unum habet.* This is the order in which the axioms turning on the one occur in Thomas and, as we shall see, it is fitting that they should, what-

20. "Sed in primo quidem non videtur dixisse recte. Esse enim rei quamvis sit aliud ab eius essentia, non tamen est intelligendum quod sit aliquid superadditum ad modum accidentis, sed quasi constituitur per principia essentiae. Et ideo hoc nomen Ens quod imponitur ab ipso esse, significat idem cum nomine quod imponitur ab ipsa essentia." *In IV Metaphysic.*, lectio 2, n. 558.

ever the textual situation might be. In any case, it is clear that simple and composed are modes of oneness. Moreover, we are moving from a diversity in the conceptual or intentional order, a diversity in the realm of meanings and accounts of words, to statements about the presence or lack of a corresponding diversity in the things to which the words refer.

Not only is there a difference of account between *ens* or *quod est* and *esse*, in the composite things of this world there is a real difference as well. Here we have a locution that led to talk of the Real Distinction, and the context makes clear what the contrast intended is. "Est autem considerandum, quod ea quae supra dicta sunt de diversitate ipsius esse et eius quod est, est secundum ipsas intentiones; hic autem ostendit quomodo applicetur ad res." (n. 31) Whether we are speaking of simple or composite things, when we use the terms *ens* and *esse* they will have different accounts, different modes of signifying, and certain restraints will follow on those modes. Now this poses a problem when what we are talking about are simple things. We have no choice but to use a language which is suggestive of complexity, and the reason is that our language is fashioned to express what we first know and what we first know are complex, composite, things.[21] "Est ergo considerandum, quod sicut esse et quod est differunt in simplicibus secundum intentiones, ita in compositum differunt realiter." (n. 32)

A question we can put at this point is this. Is it the identification of *esse* and *quod est* in simple things which is taken to be evident and their non-identity in composite things that requires showing, or the reverse? The remark of Thomas we have just recalled makes it clear what his view is. The complexity in our language is a sign of what is most knowable by us, namely, composite things. The major concern then would be to guard against attibuting to the things being spoken of the complexity of our talk about them.

This question would be unintelligible if we had not seen that the status of being an axiom, a *communis animi conceptio*, does

21. This was St. Thomas's point in *Summa theologiae*, q. 13, a. 1, ad 2m.

not exempt a statement from being dependent for its manifestation on another. But, needless to say, the manifestation of an
axiom could scarcely be a matter of demonstration or proof,
since that would require a middle term and axioms are immediate. And what Thomas tells us is that the real diversity of *quod
est* and *esse* in composite things is clear from the foregoing:
*quod quidem manifestum est ex praemissis*. What are the elements of this manifesting?

1. *Dictum est enim supra quod ipsum esse*

   a. *neque participat aliud, ut eius ratio constituatur ex multis;*
   b. *neque habet aliquid extraneum admixtum, ut sit in eo com-
      positio accidentis;*
   c. *et ideo ipsum esse non est compositum.*

2. *Res ergo composita non est suum esse.*[22]

Would it make any sense to speak of this as a proof of the real
distinction between *esse* and *quod est* in composite things?
There is one *ideo* and one *ergo* in the sequence, which might lead
the unwary to think a demonstration is being claimed. But
clearly this is not the case. It seems obvious enough that 1a and
1b mention the kind of complexity not to be found in *ipsum esse*
and thus enable us to know what would be meant by calling it
simple. They could be called a conjunction of *modi tollentes*. If
something participates in another such that its account is composed of many elements, it is composite. But this is not the case
with *ipsum esse*, so it is not composite. And so too with 1b. But
what are we to make of the *ergo* in 2? If *ipsum esse* is simple, as
has just been shown, it follows that a composite thing is not
existence.[23] But 2 says more; the composite thing is not *its* exis-

22. "It was said above that (1) existence itself (a) neither participates in anything, such that its account would be composed of many (b) nor has anything
extraneous mixed with it, such that there is in it a composition with accidents,
(c) therefore existence itself is not composed. (2) Therefore, the composed thing
is not its existence." Lectio 2, n. 32.

23. Whether or not the translation of the *Posterior Analytics* included in *PL*
64 is that made by Boethius, he would have been aware of chapter 7, Book Two

tence. 2 can seem to be merely 1c converted: *Ipsum esse non est compositum* converts to *compositum non est ipsum esse.* The *ergo* then would simply be the sign of the converted form being yielded by the original proposition.[24] But, again, 2 is not just the converted form of 1c. How should we understand this?

The most straightforward way would be this. A composite thing cannot be identified with one of its components, particularly one that has just been shown to be incomplex. But *quod est* is a compound of *what* receives existence and the *existence* received. If this complexity were only in the intentional order, the thing would not be composite, but simple. This enables us to understand the relative swiftness with which Thomas establishes the sense of [3a]. What is being asserted is assented to straight off when we know what is being said.

Anyone who knows what a composite thing is will know that its existence is diverse from what it is. A composite thing is something that has come into being as the result of a change and is thus composed of matter and form. For it to be is for the form to inhere in, to actuate, the matter. But for the form so to inhere in the matter is not what the form is, nor what the matter is, nor what the conjunction of them is. The form explains the kind of existence the composite thing enjoys, but it is not the efficient cause of its own inherence in the matter. For a composite thing to be is for its parts to continue to cohere, for its form to inhere in its matter. For it thus to be in act, to be actual, is what is meant by its existence, *suum esse.*

That nothing more arcane than this is in play is clear when we

---

of that work. "At vero si demonstrabit quid est, et quia est, et qualiter eadem ratione demonstrabit, definito enim unum aliquid, et demonstratio, id autem quod est quid est homo, et esse hominem, aliud est. Postea per demonstrationem dicimus necessarium esse demonstrare omne quia est, nisi substantia sit, esse autem non substantia ulla est, non enim est genus, quod est, demonstratio itaque erit quia est, quod quidem et non faciunt scientiae. . . ." PL 64,748D–749A.

24. Boethius wrote extensively of conversion of propositions as well as of the relation of propositions on the Square of Opposition, and used *sequuntur* and *igitur* lavishly to speak of contradictories, such that *if* the universal affirmative is true, *then* the particular negative is false. See, for example, PL 64,773 ff.

go on to the comment on [3b]. If there are simple things, there can be in them no real diversity of *quod est* and *esse*. If there were, they would be composite and not simple. This is not a proof that there are such simple things. Indeed, so far as the *De hebdomadibus* is concerned, there is only one such simple thing, the First Good, the creator of complex things and the explanation of both their existence and their goodness.

We can thus see the appropriateness of the ordering of the axioms bearing on the composite and the simple as St. Thomas had it. The reverse order might suggest that, while there is no difficulty understanding the identity of *quod est* and *esse* in simple things, problems arise when we try to grasp their diversity in complex things. The fact of the matter is, we have no philosophical warrant for talking of simple thing(s) except on the basis of a proof that they exist. If they exist, there are axiomatic truths about them, such as the one mentioned at the outset, namely, that incorporeal things are not in place. But our knowledge and our language and our certainties commence in the realm of the complex. As we have several times recalled, that is a fundamental reason why our language suggests complexity. The problem is to stretch our knowledge and our language to the incomplex when we have established, on the basis of truths about the complex, that such things exist.

When Thomas turns to [3b], he reminds us of the obvious, namely that our notion of simple things is arrived at by negating composition of them. Since there is composition and composition, there are degrees of simplicity. Something can be called simple because it lacks a certain kind of complexity, yet involve another kind. Typically, Thomas begins with corporeal things that are relatively simple, as the elements are simpler bodies than mixed bodies whose composition involves contraries. Nonetheless, the basic composition in physical bodies is that of matter and form, since this follows on the very fact that they are physical or natural, that is, have come into being as the result of a change. Matter is the subject which persists through the change, and form is the determination it receives as the result of the change.

By comparison with physical substance then, if there were a substance that is form alone, it would be simple. Thomas uses the plural, as Boethius did not, since such subsistent forms admit of variety and plurality. "If then some forms were found not to be in matter, each would be simple insofar as it lacked matter, and thus quantity which is a disposition of matter, but because each form would be determinative of existence, none of them would *be* existence, but all would *have* existence."[25] We see here an application of the Boethian *omne namque esse ex forma est* that he himself did not grasp. In the composite thing, its *esse* can be said to be constituted, as it were, by the principles of its essence (*quasi constituitur per principia essentiae*[26]), but chiefly by its form. Thomas waives the difference between Plato and Aristotle on the Ideas, and cites them as examples. Nor is this unusual. Thomas will always agree with Aristotle's rejection of the Forms or Ideas when taken to be the separate counterpart of common names of sensible things. But he will eagerly embrace the Forms as ways of grasping simple things.[27]

That which is truly, through and through, simple will not be a subsistent form of being, but subsistent existence itself. And here we must say that there can be only one truly simple thing, and this is God.[28]

25. "Si ergo inveniantur aliquae formae non in materia, unaquaeque earum est quidem simplex quantum ad hoc quod caret materia, et per consequens quantitate, quae est dispositio materiae, quia tamen quaelibet forma est determinativa ipsius esse, nulla earum est ipsum esse, sed est habens esse." Lectio 2, n. 34.

26. *In IV Metaphysic.*, lectio 2, n. 558; *In Boethii de trinitate*, q. 5, a. 3, c.: "Secunda operatio respicit ipsum esse rei, quod quidem resultat ex aggregatione principiorum rei in compositis, vel ipsam simplicem naturam rei concomitatur ut in substantiis simplicibus."

27. On this, see the remarkable prologue to St. Thomas's commentary on the *De divinis nominibus* of Pseudo-Dionysius. "Haec igitur Platonicorum ratio fidei non consonat nec veritati, quantum ad hoc quod continet de speciebus naturalibus separatis, sed quantum ad id quod dicebant de primo rerum Principio, verissima est eorum opinio et fidei christiane erit consona." Text as edited by Ceslai Pera, O.P., Marietti, 1950.

28. "Id autem eri solum vere simplex, quod non participat esse, non quidem inhaerens, sed subsistens. Hoc autem non potest esse nisi unum; quia si ipsum

*Axioms Following on the Good*

Now Boethius comes to two axioms which are particularly ordered to the problem of the tractate. In recalling Thomas's elaboration of the general modes of being, we saw the role appetite plays in speaking of the transcendental property of goodness. No wonder then that Thomas observes that the two axioms following on goodness pertain to appetite. After all, the good is that which all things seek. *Bonum est quod omnia appetunt.*[29]

[4a] *Omnis diversitas discors, similitudo vero appetenda est.* What is diverse is repugnant to appetite whereas what is like attracts. Why is this so? A thing is increased and perfected by that which is similar to it. But everything desires its own increase and perfection. So the similar as such is desirable.

Counterexamples flood the mind, and Thomas is quick to take up the objection that something might abhor what is like it and desire what is different, even contrary, to it. When this is true, Thomas suggests, it is true only *per accidens*. What anything desires first and as such is its own perfection or fulfillment, which is its good, and what is perfective is proportioned to the perfectible, and in that sense is similar to it. Any particular thing is chosen or rejected by someone because it does or does not contribute to his proper perfection. Sometimes it does not contribute because of excess or defect. But a thing's proper perfection consists in a certain measure or balance. If then a tradesman, a butcher for example, dislikes his like, another butcher, it

esse nihil aliud habet admixtum praeter id quod est esse, ut dictum est, impossibile est id quod est ipsum esse, multiplicari per aliquid diversificans: et quia nihil aliud praeter se habet admixtum, consequens est quod nullius accidentis sit susceptivum. Hoc autem simplex unum et sublime est ipse Deus." Lectio 2, n. 35.

29. In *Q. D. de veritate*, q. 1, a. 1, it was the human will that provided a reference point for all being and thus a basis for saying goodness is a general mode of being. Here Thomas appeals to the universality of appetite. The good is that which all things seek, and not, there is one kind of appetite with reference to which all things are called good. Of course, it is the divine will with reference to which we have the *per prius secundum rem* of the transcendental term good. But this is an issue which will occupy us when we get to Boethius's solution to the problem of the tractate.

is not because of the similarity that he dislikes him, but because he threatens the desired perfection, namely profit.

[4b] *Et quod appetit aliud, tale ipsum esse naturaliter ostenditur quale est illud hoc ipsum quod appetit.* Thomas says this can be concluded from the foregoing. If a thing naturally desires its like, it exhibits the sort of thing it is by what it desires. Our inclinations are thus revelatory of our nature, whether first or second. For Thomas here distinguishes—and it is not an idle distinction, as we shall see in the sequel—the natural inclination which follows on the essence of the thing from that which follows on the nature of some supervenient form, an acquired habit, that is. Our nature reveals itself in our inclinations, and our moral character in our choices. As we shall shortly see, [4b] is put to immediate work in reformulating the problem Boethius has set out to solve.

For that, let us remind ourselves, is the point of these axioms. Much scholarly work has been devoted to this list without going on to see the use to which the axioms are put in the tractate, which may account for some of the more surprising claims as to what they mean. Thomas's lengthy lectio 2 takes us well beyond the spare statements of Boethius, but as we shall see his understanding of the axioms is guided by the use to which Boethius puts them in working up the problem of the tractate and proposing his solution to it. Boethius himself concludes his listing of the axioms with a reminder of what they are meant to do.

*Sufficiunt igitur quae praemissimus; a prudente vero rationis interprete suis unumquodque aptabitur argumentis.* (ll. 53–55)

## THE QUESTION

The question Boethius addresses bears on the goodness of things. How are we to understand that created substances are good without seeming to identify them with that which alone is substantially good? In order to have the problem, we must first see that it makes sense to say of whatever is that it is good. One way to solve the problem, in the sense of preventing its arising, would be to stop saying that whatever is is good. So Boethius wisely provides us with the basis for the sweeping claim that the things that are are good: *ea quae sunt bona sunt* (ll. 56–57)

The premisses from which it is derived are, first, the common view of the learned that all things seek the good and, second, axiom [4b], that everything tends toward or seeks what is similar to it. Put those together and they yield the desired general claim.[30] Those things which tend toward the good are themselves good.

The question, then, bears precisely on how good can be predicated of all things. This is a *quaestio* in the precise sense Boethius gives the term in his *De differentiis topicis*. Questions bear on propositions which are not *per se notae*, and when these propositions are questioned, the doubt concerns the way the predicate inheres in the subject and then is called a *thesis*. The thesis is the kind of question a philosopher asks, whereas a hypothesis pertains to orators. Boethius goes on to divide *theses* into four kinds.[31] The question of the *De hebdomadibus*, in asking how good is said of all things, is in effect asking what kind of thesis it is.

Are all things said to be good substantially or by participation? The structure of this part of the tractate, which runs from line 56 through line 85, is to quicken our interest in the question by showing that, of the two possible answers to it, *neither* is tenable. But if neither is tenable, we have to abandon the claim that whatever is is good, and the abandonment of that claim is the abandonment of axiom [4b] and the common view of the wise that the good is that which all things seek. Accordingly, we

30. "Ea quae sunt bona sunt; tenet enim communis sententia doctorum omne quod est ad bonum tendere, omne autem tendit ad simile. Quae igitur ad bonum tendunt bona ipsa sunt." (ll. 56–60)

31. Cf. PL 64,1176D–1178C. If the *thesis* is a question dealing with the inherence of the predicate in the subject, it varies depending on whether the predicate is broader than the subject but predicated of it *per se*, broader but predicated of it *per accidens*, equal and predicated of it *per se* or equal but predicated of it *per accidens*. That is they bear either on genus, accident, definition or property.

must be clear on what is meant by the disjuncts in *utrumne participatione an substantia*.

That is said substantially of something which enters into the nature or substance of the subject; that is said by way of participation which does not enter into the nature or substance of the subject. In short, the distinction is equivalent to that between *per se* and *per accidens* predication.

Thomas, who has already distinguished the various senses that *participare* has in the tractate, is in a position to ask which sense of the term is in play when it is said that good is predicated of everything either substantially or by participation. If the disjunct has several senses, the disjunction cannot function as Boethius intends it.[32] Thomas notes the obvious, namely that the question presupposes that to be essentially and to be by way of participation are opposed, but adds that while this is manifestly true if we take participation in its second mode, it is false when participation is taken in the first mode. The second mode of participation is had when form is said of matter or accident of subject and clearly neither is part of the substance of that of which it is said. But what of the first mode, illustrated by a genus being predicated of its species?

Plato might have thought that the generic term names something which is not of the essence of the species and that for the species to participate in the genus does not make the genus of the very substance of the species. The view attributed to Plato is that the genus is one substance, the species is another, and participation is a relation between two substances. But, on the Aristotelian view, according to which man truly is animal and there is no animal existing independently of the differences constitutive of species, something predicated by way of participation is also predicated substantially.[33]

32. Actually both "participation" and "*per se* predication" have several senses. Thomas, in lectio 3, n. 47, will introduce the second mode of perseity. Clearly, if in every sense of the supposed disjuncts, something which is predicated *per se* is at one and the same time being predicated by way of participation, the question of the tractate dissolves.

33. "Sed secundum sententiam Aristotelis, qui posuit quod homo vere est animal, quasi essentia animalis non existente praeter differentiam hominis; nihil

Later Thomas introduces a further precision which is necessary if the disjunction is to be preserved. It is not always the case that what is predicated as an accident excludes predication *per se*. The first mode of perseity is had when the predicate enters into the definition, and thus into the substance or essence, of the subject. But the second mode of perseity is had when it is the subject that enters into the definition of the predicate. This is the case with the properties of the subject.[34]

From such precisions, which is just what we expect from a commentator, Thomas concludes that Boethius, in contrasting *participatione* and *substantia*, intends that we take participation in its second mode, something clear from the examples given in the text. It being established that the disjunction, either by way of participation or by way of substance, is indeed a disjunction, we can ask which of them enables us to understand the claim that whatever is is good.

## By Participation?

If things are called good in this way, the predicate does not express what they are, their substance, but they are called good in the way they might be called white. Those attributes that a thing may or may not have while still remaining the kind of thing it is do not of course enter into the account of the kind of thing it is. But if the things that exist have good predicated of them as an accident, it does not express what they are. However, this means that things do not tend toward the good because of what they are, which is the assumption with which we began.

---

prohibet id quod per participationem dicitur, substantialiter praedicari." Lectio 3, n. 45.

34. "Si vero accipiatur per se secundum alium modum, prout scilicet subiectum ponitur in definitione praedicati, sic esset falsum quod hic dicitur. Nam proprium accidens secundum hunc modum per se inest subiecto, et tamen participative de eo praedicatur." Lectio 3, n. 47. See Boethius, *PL* 64,1178A, and Thomas, *In V Metaphysic.*, lectio 19, n. 1055 and *In I Periherm.*, lectio 10, n. 4: "Cuius quidem ratio est, quia cum *esse* accidentis dependeat a subiecto, oportet etiam quod definitio eius significans *esse* ipsius contineat in se subiectum. Unde secundus modus dicendi *per se* est, quando subiectum ponitur in definitione praedicati, quod est proprium accidens eius."

We established that all things are good by appealing to the truths that the good is that which all things seek and that things seek what is similar to them. So, if whatever is is good, this cannot be understood as predication by way of participation.

### Substantively?

That leaves the other disjunct. When we say that whatever is is good, this must be understood not as predication by way of participation but rather as *per se* predication, such that the predicate expresses the nature or essence or substance of the subject. And of those things whose substance is good we can say that they are good as to what they are, and that they owe to existence that they are what they are. So their very existence is good and for them to be and to be good are the same. But this has the alarming consequence that they seem in every way like the First Good. But nothing else can be like the First Good. Would we wish to say that all good things are God? But this is impious. Thus we seem deprived of the only other possible way of understanding the claim that whatever is is good.

Thomas spells out what Boethius is saying in the following way. Those things whose substance is good must be good with respect to that which they are, for that pertains to the substance of a thing which is required for it to be. That things are of a certain kind they have from existence, since, by [1b], something is when it has received existence.[35] It follows that for those things which are good in their substance to exist is good. Thus if all things are good in their substance, it follows that the existence of all things is good.[36]

If the things that are are good as to what they are then their existence is good and, conversely, if their existence is good they

35. "Illa quorum substantia bona est, necesse est quod bona sint secundum id ipsum quod sunt: hoc enim ad substantiam cuiuscumque rei pertinet quod concurrit ad suum esse. Sed quod aliqua sint, hoc habet ex eo quod est esse: dictum est enim supra quod est aliquid, cum esse susceperit." Lectio 3, n. 48.

36. "Sequitur igitur ut eorum quae sunt bona secundum subiectum, ipsum esse sit bonum. Si igitur omnia sunt bona secundum suam substantiam, sequitur quod omnium rerum ipsum esse sit bonum." Lectio 3, n. 49.

are good in what they are, their substance. We can say that for them it is the same thing to be and to be good.[37]

So we have reached an impasse. The proposition, "Whatever is is good," understood in either of the two possible ways, either entails the falsity of one of the axioms from which it was derived or arrives at the impious conclusion that all things are God. Thus we seem to have to give up a proposition we have no right to give up, since it was derived from self-evident truths. What has gone wrong?

### THE SOLUTION

God is mentioned for the first time in the tractate at line 80 where saying that good is predicated of all things *per se* is taken to confuse all things with the First Good who is God. The problem of the tractate is now revealed explicitly as: How can we predicate good of creatures as well as God? Can it make any sense to say of things other than God that they are good just insofar as they are? Calling God the First Good suggests that there are secondary goods, but in what sense are they good?

As a way to the correct solution, Boethius suggests that we try to speak of the things that are without mentioning God. When we do this and ask ourselves what it could mean to say of them that they are good, we will find ourselves moving toward the same impasse that ended the working up of the question. Once we have seen that, without appeal to God, we cannot say of the things that are that they are good just insofar as they are, we will have our solution.

The way in which Boethius talks of separating God from our

---

37. "Et quia praemissa ex quibus argumentando processit sunt convertibilia, procedit e converso. Sequitur enim e converso quod si esse omnium rerum sit bonum, quod ea quae sunt, inquantum sunt, bona sint; ita scilicet quod idem sit unicuique rei esse, et bonum esse." Nn. 49–50. That is, if (a) that-which-is is such that its substance is good, and whatever is necessary for it to be pertains to its substance, and (b) it is and consists because it receives existence, then (c) its existence is good. And this can be reversed by saying that if (c) the existence of all things is good, then (a) things are good thanks to their substance.

discussion is reminiscent of the distinction of the theoretical in *De trinitate* 2. Things that cannot actually be separated can be separated by mind, as we think of them. We can think of things otherwise than as they exist. The triangle and the like are not actually separated from an underlying matter, but the triangle and its properties can be considered by the mind without attending to its matter. Separation thus has two senses, actual separation (*separari actu*) and mental separation (*cogitatione separantur*). To think apart what does not actually exist apart is not necessarily a distortion.[38] Against this background, Boethius suggests that we absent ourselves from the First Good awhile, making a mental act of separation.

This is a strange invocation of the doctrine of mental separation. When the mind forms the concept of triangle, leaving out sensible matter, we are not committed to the claim that there is something outside the mind which answers just as such to that conceptual content, that is, an existent shape that is not the shape of some physical object. To separate shape from physical matter in thinking of it is to think apart what cannot exist apart. However, if I think of horses without any reference to sunfish, the separation of horses from sunfish is not a consequence of the way I think. Why is not the comparison of God and creature like horses and sunfish rather than figure and material body?

The analogy lies in the fact that we have to make an effort to exclude God from the discussion. This is so because his existence is so manifest that no one, learned or unlearned, even barbarians, are unaware of him. Given the context, it might seem that Boethius is calling "The First Good exists" a *communis animi conceptio* of the most inescapable kind.[39] That would certainly

---

38. "Non enim necesse esse dicimus omnem intellectum qui ex subjecto quidem sit, non tantum ut sese ipsum subjectum habet falsum et vacuum videri." *In Porphyrium commentariorum*, liber 2, *PL* 64,84C–D. In this text, Boethius uses both *abstrahere* and *separari*. For Thomas on the several senses of understanding things other than as they are, see *Summa theologiae*, Ia, q. 85, a. 1, ad 1m.

39. "Deum rerum omnium principem bonum esse communis humanorum conceptio probat animorum." *Consolation*, III, pr. 10, ll. 23–25. He continues with an approach which will have its echoes in Anselm. "Nam cum nihil deo

differ dramatically from St. Thomas's view of the matter. That God exists is a state of affairs which, so to say, possesses objectively all the requirements of the *per se notum*. Not only is the predicate part of the subject, it is in every way identical with the subject. But to say that is to assert something which rests on a vast amount of discourse. The truth is inferred, not self-evident for us: if we knew God's nature we would see that he necessarily exists. So "God exists" is *per se notum in se*, but for not us, *quoad nos*, which is the ordinary meaning of the phrase.[40] In his commentary, Thomas says somewhat the same thing.[41]

If then we remove God from our consideration and posit that everything is good we must ask how they can be good if they do not flow from the First Good.[42] The first thing we would think, according to Boethius, is that then for them to be and to be good would differ. Then if I said of Socrates that he was good, this would be on a par with calling him fat and short and sober. And we would say that the substance of Socrates differs from his goodness and that his goodness differs from his substance and from all his other qualities. If we did not distinguish the substance from its qualities, one result would be that to be fat and short and sober and good would all be the same, on the principle that things identical with something are identical with one an-

---

melius excogitari queat, id quo melius nihil est bonum esse quis dubitet? Ita vero bonum esse deum ratio demonstrat, ut perfectum quoque in eo bonum esse convincat." (ll. 25–29)

40. *Summa theologiae*, Ia, q. 2, a. 1, c.

41. He says that it is possible to separate God from creatures *secundum ordinem cognoscibilium quoad nos*. He goes on, "Quamvis enim secundum naturalem ordinem cognoscendi Deus sit primum cognitum, tamen quoad nos prius sunt cogniti effectus sensibiles eius." Lectio 4, n. 58. But Thomas also holds that custom and good upbringing can make the existence of God seem self-evident to us. "Consuetudo autem, et praecipue quae est a puero, vim naturae obtinet: ex quo contingit ut ea quibus a pueritia animus imbuitur, ita firmiter teneat ac si essent naturaliter et per se nota." *Summa contra gentes*, I, cap. 11.

42. Thomas cannot resist making the point that unless we understand what we mean by calling creatures good we will be unable to grasp the meaning of good as predicated of God. For us, created goodness is a presupposition for knowing and understanding the First Good. "Dicit ergo primo, quod remoto per intellectum primo bono, ponamus quod cetera sint bona: *quia ex bonitate effectuum devenimus in cognitionem boni primi*." Lectio 4, n. 60. We shall see that it is doubtful whether the solution of the tractate permits this distinction.

other. So, in them to be differs from to be good. Thomas notes that here good is read in terms of an accident, namely the habit of virtue, that by which the agent and his activity are called good.[43]

The upshot of all this is that, if we make no appeal to God, the goodness of creatures will be said of them as an accident, and they will not be substantial goods. For them to be and to be good will differ.[44]

If to avoid this result we thought of them as good alone, not heavy or colored or extended in space, having no qualities at all, just goodness, we would be thinking of them not as things but as principles of things, not as concrete beings but as abstract goodness, not as complex but as simple. That is how they would seem. . . . But no. That is how *it* would seem, for there would no longer be grounds for plurality and distinction among them.[45] Furthermore, there is only one thing that is good alone and nothing else.

Thus in a world without God things could not be good just insofar as they are, such that for them to be and to be good would be the same. Goodness could only be a quality they could acquire and lose. If, to overcome this, we try to think of them as good in themselves, as nothing but good, we end by denying their status as complex with the result that they are no longer many and once more are impiously confused with the First Good.

That sounds pretty much like the impasse developed earlier. The import is clear. The only way we can say of creatures that they are good insofar as they are is by bringing God back into the picture. But how precisely does that solve the problem?

---

43. "Intelligitur enim bonitas uniuscuisque rei virtus ipsius, per quam perficit operationem bonam. Nam virtus est quae bonum facit habentem, et opus eius bonum reddit . . ." Lectio 4, n. 60. The definition of virtue is taken from the *Nicomachean Ethics*, 1106a15.

44. Notice how Thomas restates this point. "Sic ergo si aliquo modo essent non a primo bono, et tamen in se essent bona, sequeretur quod non idem esset in eis quod sint talia, et quod sit bona; sed aliud esset in eis esse, et aliud bonum esse." N. 60 *in fine*.

45. Particularly if individuation follows on a cluster of accidents. See *De trinitate*, 1, ll. 24–25.

The thought experiment of a world without God led to trying to think of things as if they were simple.[46] But of course they are not simple, as if they could be goodness alone. Furthermore, in the real world, things only exist because God wills that they do. It is because their existence flows from Him that it is good. The First Good is just as such good, goodness itself; the secondary good, because it derives from that whose very existence is good can also be said to be good. It is the identity of being and goodness in God from whom the being of creatures derives that enables us to speak of a derived link between being and good in creatures. The existence of all things flows from the First Good, Boethius concludes dramatically, and in him to be and to be good are one.[47]

Thomas tells us that Boethius means that God is good *essentialiter* but neither he nor Boethius uses the language of participation to speak of the goodness of creatures. Surely it is the third mode of participation distinguished by St. Thomas that is operative here. Caused or derived goodness, caused or created existence is unlike uncreated goodness and existence. Indeed, for Boethius *participare* bears the restricted sense of accidental predication. (line 138) Here is Thomas's statement of the Boethian solution.

Since then the existence of all things flows from the First Good, it follows that the very existence of created things is good, and that every created thing is good just insofar as it is. Thus created things are good in themselves only because their existence proceeds from the highest good. His solution comes down to this that the existence of the First Good is good in his very definition, because the nature and essence of the First Good is nothing but goodness; the existence of the secondary

46. In *Q. D. de veritate*, q. 21, a. 5, c., Thomas expresses the atheist thought experiment of the *De hebdomadibus* in a striking way, as the denial of the difference of *quod est* and *esse* in creatures. "Dato igitur quod creatura esset ipsum suum esse, sicut et Deus; adhuc tamen esse creaturae non haberet rationem boni, nisi praesupposito ordine ad creatorem; et pro tanto adhuc diceretur bona per participationem, et non absolute in eo quod est. Sed esse divinum, quod habet rationem boni non praesupposito aliquo, habet rationem boni per seipsum; et haec videtur esse intentio Boetii in lib. de Hebd."

47. It is clear from the *ipsum esse omnium* of line 124 that Boethius is thinking of the predicably universal as distinct from the First Good.

good is good indeed, not according to the proper notion of its essence, because its essence is not goodness itself, but either humanity or something else like that, but its existence is good by relation to its cause, the First Good, to which indeed it is related as to a first principle and ultimate end.[48]

He adds, that creatures are called good with reference to God in the way that some things are called healthy by being ordered to the end, health, and other things are called medical with reference to the art of medicine as efficient cause.

Thomas appends to his discussion of Boethius's solution a caveat. To say that goodness can be said of the things that are solely with reference to God cannot be true if we must first understand created goodness and can only then formulate the notion of uncreated goodness. So Thomas says that there is a twofold goodness in created goods, the first the one Boethius speaks of, according to which creatures are called good with reference to the first good. Thanks to that relation of dependence, their existence and anything else in them that is an effect of the first good is good. But there is also, second, a goodness of creatures when they are considered absolutely, insofar as each of them is perfect in being and activity. The latter is not true of creatures because of their substantial existence—which Thomas here calls their *esse essentiae*—but because of something added, namely virtue.[49]

After giving his solution, Boethius underscores the difference

48. "Cum igitur esse omnium rerum fluxerit a primo bono, consequens est quod ipsum esse rerum creatarum sit bonum, et quod unaquaeque res creata, inquantum est, sit bona. Sed sic solum res creatae non essent bonae in eo quod sunt, si esse earum non procederet a summo bono. Redit ergo eius solutio ad hoc quod esse primi boni est secundum propriam rationem bonum, quia natura et essentia primi boni nihil aliud est quam bonitas; esse autem secundi boni est quidem bonum, non secundum rationem propriae essentiae, quia essentia eius non est ipsa bonitas, sed vel humanitas, vel aliquid aliud huiusmodi; sed esse eius habet quod sit bonum ex habitudine ad primum bonum, quod est eius causa: ad quod quidem comparatur sicut ad primum principium et ad ultimum finem." Lectio 4, n. 62.

49. "Alia vero bonitas consideratur in eis absolute, prout scilicet unumquodque dicitur bonum, inquantum est perfectum in esse et operari. Et haec quidem perfectio non competit creatis bonis secundum ipsum esse essentiae eorum, sed secundum aliquid superadditum, quod dicitur virtus eorum. . . ." Lectio 4, n. 63.

between the secondary goods and the First Good. The great difference is that the existence of secondary goods is not good in every way; indeed the existence of things must flow from the first existence, that is from the first good. So their existence is good but not in the same way as that from which it comes. Boethius is calling the creative source of good things Existence as well as Goodness: they come *a primo esse*, from First Existence. (line 132) He is good in every mode and in what he is, since there is nothing extraneous mixed with him. (We notice now how the characteristics of *ipsum esse* laid out in the axioms and there taken to pertain to the existence predicably common to all things are now being associated with a singular entity who is *Ipsum Esse*.) This causal principle is the fullness of goodness, good in every way (*quoquo modo*).

The creature, apart from this dependence on God, might be thought to participate in goodness, but if its existence is not dependent on God, it could not be good insofar as it is. But of course this is an impossible thought experiment. The truth is otherwise.

Things cannot actually exist unless that which is truly good produces them; therefore their existence is good although that which flows from the substantial good is not similar to it.[50]

The cause of secondary goods is wholly simple, but this can be expressed only in the eloquently complex Boethian phrase: *ipsum bonum primum est et ipsum esse sit et ipsum bonum et ipsum esse bonum*: He is the first good and existence itself and he is good and his existence is good. (ll. 149–150)

TWO DIFFICULTIES

(1) If created existence is good, and *quod est* is good because it is thanks to receiving existence from the first good who is existence itself, why don't we argue that since white things owe

50. ". . . et quoniam actu non potuere exsistere, nisi illud ea quod vere bonum est produxisset, idcirco et esse eorum bonum et non est simile substantiali bono id quod ab eo fluxit." (Ll. 143–146)

their whiteness to the fact that they exist and their existence comes from God that whiteness too is in God?[51]

*Ad (1)*. Boethius's answer to this may seem simply voluntaristic. It is the will of God that things should be good insofar as they exist, but not white insofar as they exist. But Thomas makes explicit the basis for the response, namely, the distinction between *esse simpliciter* and *esse secundum quid*. For a thing to be in the primary sense involves receiving existence from God by way of a substantial form. But God's willing it to be substantially is not identical with God's willing it to have some accidental characteristic, since it can lose the latter and continue as an existent substance. If God who is subsistent existence and goodness chooses to create things, their very existence must be good, but since he is not whiteness, if he chooses that they be white, this is not a feature of their existence as such.[52]

(2) But then why is not whatever exists just, since in God there is an identity of existence, goodness and justice?

*Ad (2)*. Boethius replies by noting that when we call something good we are referring to its essence[53] whereas when we call someone just we are referring to action. In God there is an identity of *esse* and *agere*, but of course in us they are distinct. In short, this response is at bottom another appeal to the difference between *esse substantiale* and *esse accidentale*—action being a nonessential characteristic of a thing. We are good simply because we are, but one is just because of what he does. In the first

51. "At non etiam alba in eo quod sunt alba esse oportebit ea quae alba sunt, quoniam ex voluntate dei fluxerunt ut essent, alba minime vero albus. Voluntatem igitur boni comitatum est ut essent bona in eo quod sunt. . . ." (ll.150–157) Thomas states the difficulty in this way: "Dictum est, quod omnia in eo quod sunt, bona sunt, quia ex voluntate primi boni processit ut essent bona. Nunquid ergo omnia alba, in eo quod sunt, alba sunt, quia ex voluntate Dei processit ut alba essent?" Lectio 5, n. 68.

52. "Sic igitur manifestum est quod quia Deus, qui non est albus, voluit aliqua esse alba; potest quidem hoc solum dici de eis quod sunt alba, non autem in eo quod sunt; sed quia Deus qui est bonus, voluit omnia esse bona, ideo sunt bona in eo quod sunt, inquantum scilicet esse eorum habet rationem boni propter hoc quod est a bono." Lectio 6, n. 69.

53. This occurrence of *essentiam* in line 165 is the only use of the term in this tractate.

response the nerve of the argument is the recognition that being white is not an instance of *esse substantiale* with the additional reminder that God is not whiteness. In the second response too the nerve of the argument is the recognition that to be just is not an instance of *esse simpliciter*—in us. That in God there is no distinction between *esse* and *agere* does not alter our situation.[54]

But of course when someone is just that is grounds for saying he is good, and good in a different sense of the term than has been operative in the tractate. Boethius ends with the acknowledgement that to be just is a special case of to be good, and points out that participating (he doesn't use this verb here) in good in general does not entail that one has goodness in all its intensive range. The clarification is not without merit, but it suggests that we are dealing here with a genus and species and thus with a univocal term. Since moral goodness is not a species of substantial goodness, this is an unhelpful suggestion. But there is no need to understand *generale* and *species* here in a univocal fashion.

This has been a presentation of the *De hebdomadibus* as read by St. Thomas Aquinas. We are now in a position to compare the Thomistic interpretations with the cacophony of other claims as to what the text means. We have seen that, despite the total lack of unanimity among interpreters of the text, there is an unexamined negative unanimity: the text cannot mean what Thomas takes it to mean. That the tractate displays an elegant order and cogency in Thomas's reading of it can hardly be denied. The question turns on whether Thomas is reading them into the text or reading them from the text.

Before turning to that task of adjudication, let us first develop Thomas's full teaching on the good, so that it will be clear how the Boethian doctrine contributes a significant element to the whole while not being identical with it.

54. See Thomas, lectio 6, n. 71.

# CHAPTER 8

# More on the Good

If one searched the Boethian tractate for a *ratio boni*, some expression or account that could be substituted for "good," he would come back with his hands empty. Well, not entirely. The Aristotelian account is implicit in the argument developed in the course of stating the problem. *Bonum est quod omnia appetunt.* We might perhaps find intimations of *bonum est diffusivum sui* as well in the tractate. But what are we to understand by "Whatever is is good" let alone "Guinness is good for you?"

Boethius warned us at the outset that he was going to be oblique and elusive. But it leaves one gasping that such a key word is given so little conceptual content. When we are asked to imagine creatures without God and think of something as fat and red and good, "good" was no more explained than fat and red. Is this nitpicking?

We are in effect being told how the term "good" is common to God and creatures. He is the First Good, creatures are secondary goods. Consider this comment of Aquinas.

His solution comes to this that the existence of the First Good is goodness by its very definition, because the nature and essence of the First Good are nothing other than goodness; the existence of the second good is good but not in the very account of its essence, since goodness itself is not its essence, but rather humanity or the like; but its existence is good by relation to the First Good, who is its cause, to whom it is related as to a first principle and an ultimate end, in the way something called healthy is referred to the end health or called medicinal from the effective principle of the art of medicine.[1]

1. Redit ergo eius solutio ad hoc quod esse primi boni est secundum propriam rationem bonum, quia natura et essentia primi boni nihil aliud est quam bonitas; esse autem secundi boni est quidem bonum, non secundum rationem propriae essentiae, quia essentia eius non est ipsa bonitas, sed vel humanitas, vel aliquid

Thomas seems to be spelling out here our worst fears about Boethius's solution. It looks as though the creature is known to be good only with reference to God and thus is denominated good from the goodness of God. But a term is used analogically when it is used to speak of a group of things, some or one of which saves its usual meaning and the others referred to by a secondary meaning dependent on the first or familiar one. To understand what is meant by saying "aspirin is healthy," I have to know what is meant by saying "Joe is healthy." Thus Thomas, in introducing Boethius's thought experiment whereby God is conceptually set aside, says this: "remoto per intellectum primo bono, ponamus quod cetera sint bona: quia ex bonitate effectuum devenimus in cognitionem boni primi: conceptually setting aside the First Good, we posit the other things as good; after all it is from the goodness of its effects that we come to knowledge of the First Good." (n. 60) The Boethian solution, in startling contrast to the account Thomas gives of names common to God and creature, seems to make the divine goodness more knowable to us than created goodness. The introduction of the standard examples of what Thomas calls analogous names,[2] namely, "healthy" and "medical," suggests that God functions as do the quality health and the art of medicine in those examples.

It is just this that Thomas seems to guard against when he introduces the notion of two kinds of goodness in creatures, one consisting of their relation to God, the other absolute, with the latter subdivided into whether the creature is regarded as *perfectum in esse* or *perfectum in operari*. That subdivision recalls the famous contrast of *ST* Ia. 5. 1. 1m between *ens simpliciter/*

---

aliud huiusmodi; sed eius esse habet quod sit bonum ex habitudine ad primum bonum, quod est eius causa: ad quod quidem comparatur sicut ad primum principium et ad ultimum finem; per modum quo aliquid dicitur sanum, quo aliquid ordinatur ad finem sanitatis; ut dicitur medicinale secundum quod est a principio effectivo artis medicinae. (n. 62)

2. In contrast to Aristotle who seems never to have used the Greek *kat'analogian* or *analogia* to speak of the relation between meanings of the same term. Rather Aristotle speaks of equivocation *pros hen* or *pollakos legomena*. Contrast Aristotelian and Thomistic usage in *Metaphysics* IV.1 and lectio 1.

*bonum secundum quid* and *ens secundum quid/bonum simpliciter.*

Thus arises a question that becomes part of Thomas's standard repertoire, *ut ita dicam*, namely: *Utrum omnia sint bona bonitate prima*: Are all things good by the first goodness?[3] This question is very much like another which was fateful for the history of interpreting what Thomas meant by analogous names: *Utrum sit una sola veritas secundum quam omnia sunt vera*: Whether there is only one truth whereby all things are true? If there is numerically one goodness and numerically one truth whereby all creatures are called good and true, this is what is meant by extrinsic denomination. When the question about truth is asked in the *Summa theologiae*, Thomas expresses a universal rule about names analogously common.

In order to see this it should be noted that when something is univocally predicated of many it is found in each of them according to its proper notion, as "animal" in every species of animal. But when something is said analogically of many things, it is found according to its proper notion in only one of them; the others are denominated from it. As "healthy" is said of animal, urine and medicine, though health is found only in the animal and medicine is denominated healthy from the animal's health, as effective of, and urine, as a sign of, that health. And though health is not in the medicine or urine there is in each something through which the former causes and the latter signifies health.[4]

Now if it were the case that every analogous name involves extrinsic denomination from what is first, and if creatures are denominated good and true analogically from God, it looks as if extrinsic denomination is all we have.

3. Cf. *Q.D. de ver.*, q. 21, a. 4; *Summa contra gentiles*, I, cap. 40; *ST* Ia, q. 6, a. 4.

4. Ad cuius evidentiam, sciendum est quod, quando aliquid praedicatur univoce de multis, illud in quolibet eorum secundum propriam rationem invenitur, sicut 'animal' in qualibet specie animalis. Sed quando aliquid dicitur analogice de multis, illud invenitur secundum propriam rationem in uno eorum tantum, a quo alia denominatur. Sicut 'sanum' dicitur de animali et urina et medicina, non quod sanitas sit nisi in animali tantum, sed a sanitate animalis denominatur medicina sana, inquantum est effectiva, et urina, inquantum est illius sanitatis significativa. Et quamvis sanitas non sit in medicina neque in urina, tamen in utroque est aliquid per quod hoc quidem facit, illud autem significat sanitatem. (*Ia*.16.6)

We are not surprised, accordingly, to find Cardinal Cajetan in his commentary on this text deny as universally true of analogous names the rule Thomas gives. Indeed, it is exemplified only in the case of what Cajetan says are misleadingly (*abusive*) called analogous names. Nor are we suprised when Cajetan refers us to his own book on the subject.[5]

Cajetan's *De Nominum Analogia*[6] is easily the most influential interpretation of what St. Thomas means by analogous names, and it is a work based on a misunderstanding of a text parallel to that in *ST* Ia. 16. 6. The text is *I Sent.*, d. 19, q. 5, a. 2, ad 1m. Cajetan took Thomas to be giving a threefold division of analogous names, and that supposed division forms the structure of his opusculum and has haunted discussions of analogy since its appearance in the last decade of the 15th century.[7]

The text on which Cajetan based his opusculum is a reply to an objection and can only be understood with reference to the

5. "Ad secundum vero dubitationem dicitur, quod illa regula de analogo tradita in littera, non est universalis de omni analogiae modo: imo, proprie loquendo, ut patet I Ethic., nulli analogo convenit, sed convenit nominibus 'ad unum' vel 'in uno' aut 'ab uno,' quae nos abusive vocamus analoga. Veritas autem, si comparetur ad res et intellectus, est nomen 'ab uno': quoniam in intellectu solo est veritas, a qua res dicuntur verae. Si vero comparetur ad intellectus inter se, sic est nomen analogum: nam proportionaliter salvatur, formaliter tamen, in quolibet intellectu cognoscente verum. Esse ergo nomen aliquod secundum propriam rationem in uno tantum, est conditio nominum quae sunt 'ad unum' aut 'ab uno,' etc.: et non nominum proportionaliter dictorum. Veritas autem, respectu intellectus divini et aliorum, proportionale nomen est. Et ideo non sequitur quod in solo Deo sit. Iam enim dictum est in solutione primi dubii, quod omni praedicato formaliter de pluribus, convenit plurificari ad plurificationem subiectorum sive illud sit univocum, ut 'animal', sive proportionale, ut 'ens,' etc.—De huiusmodi autem differentia nominum plene scriptum invenies in tractatu 'De Analogia Nominum.'" Cajetan, In Iam, q. 16, a. 6, n. VI.

6. Thomas de Vio Cardinalis Cajetan (1469–1534), *Scripta Philosophica: De Nominum Analogia et De Conceptu Entis*, ed. Zammit and Hering, 1952. The first edition by Zammit alone appeared in 1934.

7. In both *The Logic of Analogy* (The Hague, M. Nijhoff, 1961), and *Studies in Analogy* (The Hague, M. Nijhoff, 1968), as well as in various articles written since the latter appeared, I have contested the Cajetanian interpretation. Nonetheless, it flourishes as if profound difficulties with it have not been pointed out. See, for example, the otherwise excellent book of Avital Wohlman, *Thomas d'Aquin et Maimonide* (Paris, Les Editions de Cerf, 1988). I am currently engaged in rewriting *The Logic of Analogy*, which has been out of print for some years.

problem it sets out to solve. Is there only one truth whereby all things are true?

It seems that all things are true by one truth which is uncreated truth. For as was said in the solution of the preceding article, true is said analogously of things in which there is truth, as health of all healthy things. But there is numerically one health from which the animal is denominated healthy (as its subject) and medicine healthy (as its cause), and urine healthy (as its sign). It seems therefore that there is one truth whereby all are called true.[8]

The argument is clear enough. An animal, medicine, and urine are called healthy analogously and we can see that they are so denominated from the health that is in the animal; there is no need to look for a plurality of healths, one the quality of the animal, another the quality of the medicine, the other the quality of urine. These three are gathered under and share one name because medicine causes and urine shows the quality health in the animal. If this is the case with the analogous term "healthy" and if "true" is said to be analogously common to God and creature, then, so goes the objection, there must be numerically one truth in virtue of which this is so.

The assumption is that a feature of the things called healthy is a necessary condition of their being named analogously, such that wherever there is an analogous name that feature will be present. How does Thomas handle this objection?[9]

8. Videtur quod omnia sint vera una veritate quae est veritas increata. Sicut enim dictum est in solutione praecedentis articuli, verum dicitur analogice de illis in quibus est veritas, sicut sanitas de omnibus sanis. Sed una est sanitas numero a qua denominatur animal sanum, sicut subjectum ejus, et medicina sana, sicut causa ejus, et urina sana, sicut signum ejus. Ergo videtur quod una sit veritas qua omnia dicuntur vera.

9. Ad primum igitur dicendum, quod aliquid dicitur secundum analogiam tripliciter: [1] *vel secundum intentionem tantum, et non secundum esse*; et hoc est quando una intentio refertur ad plura per prius et posterius, quae tamen non habet esse nisi in uno; sicut intentio sanitatis refertur ad animal, urinam et diaetam diversimode, secundum prius et posterius; non tamen secundum diversum esse, quia esse sanitatis non est nisi in animali. [2] *Vel secundum esse et non secundum intentionem*; et hoc contingit quando plura parificantur in intentione alicujus communis, sed illud commune non habet esse unius rationis in omnibus, sicut omnia corpora parificantur in intentione corporeitatis. Unde Logicus, qui

In reply to the first objection it should be noted that something is said according to analogy in three ways: [1] *According to intention alone and not according to being*, as when one intention is referred to many, first to one, later to others, but exists in only one of them, as the intention of health is referred to animal, urine and diet in different ways, according to prior and posterior, but not according to being, because health exists in the animal alone; [2] *According to being and not according to intention*, and this happens when many things are made equal in a common intention which does not exist as such in all, as all bodies are made equal in the intention of corporeity. Hence the dialectician who considers intentions alone says that the word "body" is predicated univocally of all bodies, but this nature does not exist according to the same notion in corruptible and incorruptible bodies. For the metaphysician and the natural philosopher, therefore, who look on things as they exist, neither the term "body" nor any other is said univocally of the corruptible and incorruptible, as Aristotle and Averroes make clear in *Metaphysics* X. [3] *According to intention and being*, as when there is equality neither of common intention nor of being, as "being" is said of substance and accident. In such it is necessary that the common nature enjoy some existence in each of the things of which it is said, but differing according to greater and less perfection. So too I say that truth and goodness and the like are said analogically of God and creature. All these must exist in God and creature according to a notion of greater and less perfection, from which it follows that, since it cannot exist numerically the same in all, there are diverse truths.

On the face of it, it does not seem surprising that Cajetan should have read this response as saying that there are three kinds of analogous name, although this assumption almost immediately gets him into difficulties. The second kind of analogous name is a univocal term! A generic term covers an inequal-

---

considerat intentiones tantum, dicit, hoc nomen, corpus, de omnibus corporibus univoce praedicari: sed esse hujus naturae non est ejusdem rationis in corporibus corruptibilibus et incorruptibilibus, ut patet X Meta., text. 5, ex Philosopho et Commentatore. [3] *Vel secundum intentionem et secundum esse*; et hoc est quando neque parificatur in intentione communi, neque in esse; sicut ens dicitur de substantia et accidente; et de talibus oportet quod natura communis habeat aliquod esse in unoquoque eorum de quibus dicitur, sed differens secundum rationem majoris vel minoris perfectionis. Et similiter dico quod veritas et bonitas et omnia hujusmodi dicuntur analogice de Deo et creaturis. Unde oportet quod secundum suum esse omnia haec in Deo sint, et in creaturis secundum rationem majoris perfectionis et minoris; ex quo sequitur, cum non possint esse secundum unum esse utrobique quod sint diversae veritates.

ity among its species, expressed by their differences, but does not thereby cease to be a univocal term. The inequality (*non parificantur*) of the species is said to be *secundum esse*. It is not to be confused with the inequality, the order *per prius et posterius* of a plurality of meanings of a common term. Thomas's response comes down to this. The objector is confusing the *per accidens* and the *per se*. While in the example of "healthy" the quality health from which denomination is made exists in only one of the analogates, this is *per accidens* to being an analogous term.

Why? Because sometimes in things named analogously the *res significata* of the common term exists in only one of the analogates, whereas sometimes it exists in all of the analogates, though of course *per prius et posterius*. From this, one concludes not that there are two kinds of analogous name but that these variants are *per accidens* to analogous naming. To underscore this, Thomas points out that inequality *secundum esse*, an order thanks to which one of the things named is primary and another secondary, is compatible with the term's being univocally common to them.

In short, Cajetan embraces the fallacy Thomas is intent on dissolving, joins what Thomas is putting asunder, and defines the truly analogous name as one in which there is both an order among the meanings of a common term and possession of the denominating form by all the analogates. But what Cajetan calls true analogy is invariably illustrated, in the text of Thomas, by what Cajetan considers to be an analogous name only abusively.

What then is the meaning of the rule for analogous names in *ST* Ia.16.6: *quando aliquid dicitur analogice de multis, illud invenitur secundum propriam rationem in uno eorum tantum, a quo alia denominantur*: when something is said analogically of many things, it is found according to its proper notion in only one of them? It does not mean that the form from which denomination is made exists in only one of the analogates. The rule is not a rule for "healthy" alone but is meant to illuminate what is being discussed in the text where it is formulated, namely, "true" as analogically common to God and creature and, to underscore the relevance of this for our purposes, for "good" as common to God and creature. In names said analogously of God and creature, as in all analogous names, the *ratio propria* of the name is found in one of them alone.

The *ratio propria* is the way of signifying the denominating form that is controlling in understanding other, extended ways of signifying that form.[10] Whether the example be "law" or "virtue" or "healthy" or "being," the rule will always obtain. This is not the place to discourse on analogous names as such, but this much is enough to prevent us from thinking that the divine names involve some special kind of analogy invented for the purpose. If they did, Thomas would not illustrate by "healthy" what he means by saying that God and creature share a name analogously. Needless to say, our talk about God will, like the knowledge it reflects, reveal that we are at the very limits of our creaturely powers.

When we say of God that He is good or one or true or being, we are extending terms whose controlling meanings make them appropriate to creatures—their *rationes propriae* are rooted in creatures, not in God—and we use them to speak of the causative, creative source of these created perfections. The only way we can know God is via His effects; naming follows the path of knowing; the only way we can talk of God is to use of Him words whose proper meanings were formed in knowing creatures.[11]

The problem with which this chapter began will now be clearer. Unless we have a meaning or meanings for "good" appropriate to our ordinary commerce with creatures, the term cannot be extended to God with appropriate alteration of meanings. Is it fair to say that Boethius does not provide us with any such controlling meaning? Is it fair to suggest that for him the controlling meaning is the divine goodness and that only derivatively are creatures good, known to be good and called good?

10. In short, a *ratio nominis* is a compound of the *res significata* and a *modus significandi*.
11. These are of course commonplaces, but cf. *ST*, Ia, qq. 12 and 13.

A text as oblique and deliberately difficult as the *De hebdoma-dibus* obviously should not be queried as if it were MacGuffey's Reader. Indeed one reaction to this problem could be to say that if it is one for Boethius it is also one for Thomas.

After all, it is Thomas in his commentary who says that the *"esse primi boni est secundum rationem propriam bonum*: the existence of the First Good is good according to its proper notion" and that *"esse autem secundi boni est quidem bonum, non secundum rationem propriae essentiae*: for a second good to be is indeed good, but not because of the proper account of its essence." (n. 62) Is Thomas saying that God saves the *ratio propria* of the analogously common term "good" and that creatures do not, and that thus creatures are named good with reference to God's goodness, not the reverse?

The answer to the exegetical question is simple, but a wider question is raised. In the text, *"ratio propria"* means the essence or nature of the thing, what would be expressed in its definition, and the point is that goodness is identical with what God is, but this is not the claim made of the creature, *"quia essentia eius non est ipsa bonitas, sed vel humanitas, vel aliquid huiusmodi*: because goodness as such is not its essence, but rather humanity, or the like." (n. 62) In short, *ratio propria* is not to be understood here as it must be in the rule for things named analogously given in *ST,* Ia. 16. 6. That said, are we not told on considerable authority that it is from God that all fatherhood is named both in heaven and on earth?

Of course of the things named "good," God is ontologically first; if He were not good, nothing else would be. He is the source of all goodness, both in heaven and on earth. Even as we, or St. Paul, say such things, we are employing a human language whose first meanings and referents are the things of our experience, the things we see and touch and weigh and alter with our arts. The suppleness of language within even the most restricted range of "terrestrial" usage reveals the scale and order and unifying that characterize our efforts to know that world. Thomas was struck, in reading Aristotle's *Physics*, with how a term like *morphe*, whose obvious meaning is the external shape or contour of an object, is used in graded ways to mean any property of a thing, then its constituting essential element. All this in the first book of the *Physics*. And language so developed is the only one we have for speaking of God when knowledge of the things of this world enables us to come to knowledge of the invisible things of God. To speak of God's will and mind and ideas involves stretching our language to the breaking point. We come to do it with ease, as we learn easily to say the Lord's Prayer, but the Gospels knew we needed images and pictures of human fathers to catch this new meaning.

What is first in our knowledge and language may be last on the ontological scale, and vice versa. Aristotle had already suggested this. It is what characterizes names analogously common to God and creatures. The language as used of creatures controls its extension to speak of the divine. But that which is indicated in God, however imperfectly, is the source of the created perfections. This is captured by the distinction made between the order *secundum impositionem nominis* and the order *secundum rem nominis*.[12]

It seems clear enough that in *De hebdomadibus* Boethius adopts a sapiential viewpoint, the viewpoint of the theologian who would see everything with reference to God. In Thomas's words, the opusculum is concerned with the procession of good creatures from the good God: *de processione bonarum creaturarum a Deo bono*.[13] Nonetheless, like Thomas in *Summa theologiae*, Boethius has to rely on our knowledge of the contrast between good things and the First Good. It could be said that, to a great degree, though not exclusively, the axioms state that contrast.

In the *Disputed Question on Truth*, Thomas confronts the problematic of our discussion when he asks if all things are good because of the First Goodness. The Boethian tractate is referred

---

12. See Thomas *In V Metaphysicorum*, lectio 5, n. 824–826.
13. *In Boethii de trinitate*, ed. Calcaterra, prologus, n. 7.

to again and again, and becomes the source of the objection that creatures are extrinsically denominated good from the divine goodness. Isn't that what *De hebdomadibus* establishes by showing the incoherences that result from trying to understand created goodness without reference to the First Good? Having recalled this in q. 21, objection 1, the next objection continues:

> But notice that there is no goodness in creatures when the goodness in God is ignored because the goodness of the creature is caused by God's goodness, not because the thing is formally denominated good from God's goodness.[14]

Now this, as it happens, is Thomas's own view. The objector, however, continues by rejecting what I have just quoted and adding that when something is denominated solely with reference to another it is extrinsically denominated, that is, not denominated from a form intrinsically possessed. And the old stand-by healthy is invoked. Urine and exercise are denominated from the health in the animal, not from some intrinsic form of health in themselves. And isn't that the way creatures are denominated good from the divine goodness?

Thomas replies by distinguishing two ways in which a thing can be denominated something with reference to another. Sometimes it is the reference or relation itself which is the reason for the denomination, and that is the case with calling urine and exercise healthy with reference to the health of the animal.

> Something is denominated with respect to another in a second way when the cause and not the respect is the reason for the denomination; just as air is said to be illumined by the sun, not because air's being related to the sun is for it to be lit, but because the direct opposition of air to sun is the cause that it is lit; and this is the way the creature is called good with respect to Good. (*ibid.*, ad 2m)[15]

14. Sed dicendum quod ideo hoc contingit quod non intellecta bonitate in Deo non est bonitas in aliis creaturis, quia bonitas creaturae causatur a bonitate Dei, non quia denominetur res bona bonitate Dei formaliter.

15. Alio modo denominatur aliquid per respectum ad alterum, quando respectus non est ratio denominationis, sed causa; sicut si aer dicatur lucens a sole; non quod ipsum referri aerem ad solem sit lucere aeris, sed quia directa oppositio

God is the cause of the goodness of the creature but that is not the meaning of the term when the creature is called good, as if for the creature to be called good meant "is dependent on God." The creature would neither be nor be good if God did not cause it, but when we say that a thing is or is good, the meaning of these terms is not "is caused by God."[16]

A disputed question is always far more complicated and nuanced than a parallel discussion in the *Summa theologiae* but in neither case is what Thomas says of the goodness of creatures, while owing much to Boethius, confined to the crabbed coded Boethian doctrine. The *sed contra est* of Ia, q. 6, a. 4 (which asks the by now familiar question: *Utrum omnia sint bona bonitate divina*) provides a crisp summary of Thomas's view.

On the contrary, all things are good just insofar as they are. But all things are not called being from the divine existence, but from their own existence. All things are not good by the divine goodness, therefore, but by their own goodness.[17]

It is not God's goodness that is the goodness of creatures any more than His existence is theirs: there is created goodness and created existence thanks to which creatures are and are good. Thomas, in the body of the article, reminds us that Plato posited a realm of transcendental entities to which appeal had to be made to explain the fleeting things of this world. Odd as that sounds in the case of "man" and "white" and the like, Thomas says it makes a good deal of sense, even Aristotelian sense, to speak of something that is being as such and goodness as such.

---

aeris ad solem est causa quod luceat; et hoc modo creatura dicitur bona per respectum ad bonum.

16. At the end of *Q. D. de veritate*, q. 21, a. 5, Thomas gives this interpretation of Boethius's exercise in mentally separating creatures from God. "Dato igitur quod creatura esset ipsum suum esse, sicut et Deus; adhuc tamen esse creaturae non haberet rationem boni, nisi praesupposito ordine ad creatorem; et pro tanto adhuc diceretur bona per participationem, et non absolute in eo quod est. Sed esse divinum, quod habet rationem boni non praesupposito aliquo, habet rationem boni per seipsum; et haec videtur esse intentio Boethii in lib. de Hebd."

17. Sed contra est quod omnia sunt bona inquantum sunt. Sed non dicuntur onmia entia per esse divinum, sed per esse proprium. Ergo non omnia sunt bona bonitate divina, sed bonitate propria.

And how do created good things relate to God who is goodness itself?

Anything can be called good and a being by way of some assimilation, however remote and defective, insofar as it participates in that which is goodness and being in its essence, as the foregoing has made clear. In this way something is called good from the divine goodness as from the first exemplar, efficient and final cause of all goodness. Nonetheless, each thing is called good from a likeness of the divine goodness inherent in it which is the goodness formally denominating it. So it is that there is one goodness of all and many goodnesses.[18]

We have here an account which incorporates the Boethian account into a more comprehensive one, the final pay-off on the quasi demur registered in the exposition when, after analyzing Boethius's solution, Thomas notes that there is a *duplex bonitas*, a twofold goodness, in creatures. They are and are good thanks to the causality of the First Good, but as effects of the First Good they have their own existence and goodness thanks to which they are remotively and defectively like their cause. We of course are first aware of creatures and our notions of existence and goodness reflect this epistemological priority which grounds a priority of nomenclature. Only when creatures are seen to require a cause very different from themselves does the possibility arise of speaking of being itself and goodness itself as referring to a unique entity. Then it can be said that because He is we are, because He is good other things are good. In *De hebdomadibus*, Boethius favors this sapiential approach, the *via descensus*; it is thoroughly characteristic of Thomas that he should constantly remind us of the complementary *via ascensus*.[19]

18. "A primo igitur per suam essentiam ente et bono, unumquodque potest dici bonum et ens, inquantum participat ipsum per modum cuiusdam assimilationis, licet remote et deficienter, ut ex superioribus patet. Sic ergo unumquodque dicitur bonum bonitate divina, sicut primo principio exemplari, effectivo et finali totius bonitatis. Nihilominus tamen unumquodque dicitur bonum similitudine divinae bonitatis sibi inhaerente, quae est formaliter sua bonitas denominans ipsum. Et sic est bonitas una omnium; et etiam multae bonitates." *Ia*, q. 6, a. 4, c.

19. See Thomas *In Boethii de trinitate*, ed. cit. lect. 2, q. 2, a. 1 (= Wyser and Decker q. 6, a. 1, ad tertiam questionem), p. 382a-b.

If the problem of *De hebdomadibus* arises from the seeming impossibility of saying of a creature either that it is good substantially or that it is good accidentally, it generates a further problem as to the relation between divine and created goodness. The tractate concludes by referring created goodness to the First Good as if what it means to say of a creature that he is good is that his existence is caused by God in whom existence and goodness are identical. On the other hand, it seems clear that we can know the divine goodness only on an analogy with created goodness. The question then becomes precisely that Thomas asked in *ST*, Ia, q. 13. a. 6: Are names analogically common to God and creature said first of God or of creature?

If a term is used metaphorically of God, Thomas notes, it is clear that the creature would be the point of reference for understanding its use in speaking of God. Furthermore, if all divine names were negative or relative, the same would be true—the reference to the creature would be primary. But what of affirmative divine names, names like "wise" and "good?" When we say that God is wise or that God is good, we do not mean that He is the cause of created wisdom or goodness. What do we mean?

For when God is called good or wise this means not only that He is the cause of wisdom or goodness but that these preexist eminently in Him. On that account it should be said that with respect to the perfection meant by the name they are said first of God rather than of creatures, because these perfections emanate from God to creatures. But with respect to the imposition of the name, these are first imposed on creatures since we first know them.[20]

This does not mean that, contrary to the rule we discussed earlier, two of the analogates save the *ratio propria* of the com-

20. *Summa theologiae*, Ia, q. 13, a. 6. Cum enim dicitur *Deus est bonus* vel *sapiens*, non solum significatur quod ipse est causa sapientis vel bonitatis, sed quod haec in eo emenentius praeexistunt. Unde, secundum hoc, dicendum est quod secundum rem significatam per nomen, per prius dicuntur de Deo quam de creaturis: quia a Deo huiusmodi perfectiones in creaturas manant. Sed quantum ad impositionem nominis, per prius imponuntur creaturis, quas prius cognoscimus.

mon term, or that there are two *rationes propriae* of "good" according to one of which it is first said of creatures and according to the other first said of God. In order to say that God's goodness is a perfection He would have even if He had never created, we must mention created goodness. The relation of divine goodness to created goodness is not a real relation, but only one of reason. But it cannot be considered an epistemological prop we can dispense with so as to consider the divine goodness in itself. We have no such direct access.

When then it is said that God is good, the meaning is not that God is the cause of goodness, or that He is not evil, but rather this: *that which we call goodness in creatures preexists in God*, and indeed in a higher way. From this it does not follow that to be good pertains to God insofar as He causes goodness, but rather the reverse: because He is good, He diffuses goodness to things.[21]

Thus the *ratio boni* as said of God includes the *ratio propria* of created goodness even while expressing the fact that God's goodness is prior to created goodness.

But what then of the fact that created goodness is an effect of God's causality? Must this not be the meaning of "good" as said of creatures? The text we quoted earlier (*Ia*, q. 6, a. 4) provides the answer. God is the good of the creature as its first exemplar, efficient and final cause. That is the final word on created goodness. But it cannot be the first. The creature is called good by a similitude of the divine goodness inherent in the creature, which is its own goodness whereby it is formally denominated good. Only when this formal goodness is grasped, and understood in terms of what is intrinsic to the creature, can there be an ascent to the divine goodness. But that ascent can never let go of its

21. Cum igitur dicitur *Deus est bonus*, non est sensus *Deus est causa bonitatis*, vel *Deus non est malus*: sed est sensus, *id quod bonitatem dicimus in creaturis, praeexistit in Deo*, et hoc quidem secundum modum altiorem. Unde ex hoc non sequitur quod Deo competat esse bonum inquantum causat bonitatem: sed potius e converso, quia est bonus, bonitatem rebus diffundit. *Ibid.*, q. 13, a. 2. Thomas adds a quotation from Augustine's *De doctrina christiana*, I, 32: *inquantum bonus est, sumus*: because He is good, we are.

springboard, as Thomas makes clear in his account of "God is good."

Thus it is that Thomas's account of divine and created goodness incorporates but is not exhausted by the account he found in the *De hebdomadibus* of Boethius.

# Sine Thoma Boethius Mutus Esset

The thesis of this book is that Boethius taught what Thomas said he taught and that the Thomistic commentaries on Boethius are without question the best commentaries ever written on the tractates. The foregoing chapters have tried to establish the truth of that thesis. In this brief epilogue I shall summarize the results of the study and engage in reflections on the circumstances that made the proving of the thesis necessary.

Because Thomists came to insist on the originality and centrality of *esse* in the thought of Thomas, though they gave different accounts of that claim, as Fabro noted, there was a disposition to oppose Thomas's thought to that of his predecessors—and indeed to most of his followers.[1] Such Thomists were susceptible to and relatively untroubled by the claim of Duhem that there exists a chasm between what Boethius meant and what Thomas took him to mean.

So far as the commentary on *De trinitate* is concerned, the argument for the singularity of the position of St. Thomas goes far beyond the Boethian text, as indeed the commentary itself does, but we have seen that claims as to the uniqueness of Thomistic metaphysics departed from the context of the discussion in Boethius and in Thomas at its peril. Question Five of the Com-

---

1. Etienne Gilson has not been alone in criticizing the great commentators on St. Thomas, but he has certainly been the most vigorous. Indeed, as his letters to Henri De Lubac make clear, Jacques Maritain was the only Thomist Gilson seemed willing to be associated with. Ironically, Maritain, as we have had occasion to notice, was a grateful reader of such commentators as Cajetan, John of St. Thomas and the Dominicans of Salamanca. On Gilson, see *Letters of Etienne Gilson to Henri De Lubac*, translated by Mary Emily Hamilton (Ignatius Press, 1988). Cardinal De Lubac, in his lengthy comments on these brief and tendentious letters, delights in poking fun at Thomists and using *obiter dicta* of Gilson's in a way somewhat unfair to many.

mentary invoked a very precise doctrine on the subject and unity of a science and thus on how one science can be said to differ from another. Since St. Thomas himself uses these criteria to distinguish two different theological sciences, there is no prima facie reason why the claim that there are two formally different metaphysics, that of Aristotle and St. Thomas, could not be made. We concluded, however, that no coherent case has been made for a radically different Thomistic metaphysics in terms of the criteria Thomas himself recognizes for distinguishing sciences.

In the case of *De hebdomadibus*, the text of Boethius seems to be making an obvious point—it is explicitly said to be a *per se nota* one—when it states that *diversum est esse et id quod est*. But some Thomists had reached the point where they were saying that *no one* before Thomas had recognized this self-evident truth. What to do? Accept Duhem's claim that *esse* here means not existence but form or essence. If Duhem's interpretation had not appealed to the predisposition already noted it is doubtful that its manifest flaws would have been so universally overlooked. We saw that on facing pages Duhem equates *esse* and *forma* and *id quod est*, thereby depriving *diversum est esse et id quod est* of any consistent meaning whatsoever. He did this by regarding *De trinitate* and *De hebdomadibus* as parts of the same work, but even if one were to test his original suggestion that *esse* = *forma* by replacing all occurrences of *esse* in the axioms with *forma*, it would have been seen that it could not be done.

The significance of this is clear. To say that for Boethius *esse* means form or essence whereas for Thomas it means existence cannot be supported by the text of Boethius. Indeed, it runs afoul of it. Yet this untenable claim has been repeated by Thomists since 1926. There were few attempts to read as a whole the tractate from which the axiom had been taken in order to test its purported meaning. It was almost as if Thomists did not care what Boethius had meant.

One of the honorable but unnoticed exceptions to this grim

sameness was the 1960 dissertation written by Peter O'Reilly at the Pontifical Institute for Mediaeval Studies in Toronto. Not even Obertello took notice of this remarkable study. O'Reilly notes that to ask whether Boethius means essence or existence by *esse* presupposes that he recognized the distinction. But did he? How are we to understand the very question to which the tractate seeks to provide an answer: *Quomodo substantiae in eo quod sint bonae sint cum non sint substantialia bona*? O'Reilly suggests that this can be understood in either of two ways, depending on how we read *in eo quod sint*. That phrase can be taken either as "in that which they are" or "inasmuch as they are" and if the first is understood things will be taken to be good by reason of their essence, whereas on the second understanding they will be good because of their existence. "But would there be a serious difference in the two meanings for one who was unaware of the distinction?" [2] O'Reilly, apparently unique among Thomists, wished to defend his master as a commentator or expositor of Boethius. He did so by maintaining that Boethius neither distinguished nor identified essence and existence and that Thomas does not attribute the distinction to him in his exposition. Thus the commentary does not attribute to Boethius views he did not hold; equally, it does not tell us what Thomas himself thinks.[3]

Whereas the received opinion among other Thomists was that Thomas in the commentary gives us *his* views and not those of Boethius, O'Reilly takes the contradictory position that in the commentary Thomas gives us only Boethius's views and not his own.

Despite this dramatic difference, O'Reilly is himself an existential Thomist. For him, Thomas is "the man who has in our day become famous as the discoverer of this distinction." [4] For this reason, I shall not, certainly not in an epilogue, go more deeply into his reading of the exposition. But I should like to

2. Peter O'Reilly, *op. laud.*, p. 341.
3. *Op. cit.*, p. 398.
4. *Ibid.*, p. 341.

repeat that O'Reilly's is the most serious and sustained effort to understand the *De hebdomadibus* exposition I have seen and it is incredible that it has not figured in the discussions we have reviewed.

This study points to what would seem to be the underlying problem in what Thomists have been saying about the difference between Thomas's teaching and that of others. More and more, it appears that it is fantastic readings of the meaning of *esse* in Thomas which underwrite claims that no one else has said such things. The question arises whether Thomas himself did.

For Thomas it is true of any creature that to be is to be something or other. To be is read from form or essence and a thing is or exists in the primary sense thanks to substantial form and it is or exists in a secondary way thanks to accidental form. *Omne namque esse ex forma est.* It was self-evident to Boethius and Thomas that for a thing to be and what it is differ. And of course the things they first and chiefly had in mind were material substances, compounds of matter and form. A physical thing exists in the primary sense when its substantial form inheres in its matter. This is the *esse inhaerens* Thomas speaks of. For the form actually to be in the matter, for the composition to be actual, is what is meant by existence. Existence is the act of all acts even of forms precisely because the act that form is and its actually inhering in the matter are diverse. Both Boethius and Thomas are careful to establish the meanings of *forma* and *esse* with reference to physical substances. Unless this is first done, the extension of the diversity to subsistent forms cannot coherently be carried off. More importantly, this background is needed to grasp the significance of Thomas's description of God as *Ipsum esse subsistens*.

It is my view that Thomists have gotten into the habit of saying such extraordinary things about created acts of existence because they apply what is said of subsistent existence to created existence. I have argued elsewhere that this is the case with Fabro's notion of *esse ut actus intensivus*. Does the creature's *esse* include intensively all that it will be? Is its essence somehow drawn out of its *esse*? Surely not.

The difficult thing is not, as Existential Thomists put it, to isolate or segregate *esse* from essence. *Au contraire*. The heart of the matter is to establish that there is one in whom they are *not* distinct. That is the achievement. Only for creatures is it true that to be is to be something or other. God is not a being among beings, a kind of being, a thing for whom to exist is measured by a determinate form different from other determinate forms. In *De hebdomadibus*, Boethius does not consider subsistent forms, but his discussion of the First Good, of God, as beyond the distinctions that obtain in creatures, as not a particular kind of being, is gratefully endorsed by St. Thomas.

These are large questions and it may seem reckless to treat them so summarily here. Surely a good deal more work is needed to recover Thomas's own attitude toward his predecessors and mentors. If this is important in the case of Boethius, it is far more important in the case of Aristotle. The recent tendency to drive wedges between Thomas and the texts and thinkers without whom he is unintelligible must be reversed. Thomas's genius was not to develop doctrines unheard of before. His great accomplishment was akin to that of Boethius: to find similarities, to unify, to see diverse efforts converging on a comprehensive truth. The mark of genius, Aristotle said in the *Poetics*, is to find similarities among dissimilar things.

As the title for these final reflections, I have adapted a famous saying. Perhaps it is only with the help of Thomas's commentaries that Boethius can speak to us today. But it is equally true that Thomas can only be understood by seeing what he learned from Boethius, and from other Neoplatonists, but chiefly from Aristotle. It is time we stopped trying to imagine a Thomism unindebted to its sources.

# Chronologies of Boethius
# and St. Thomas

| | |
|---|---|
| 476 | Odoacre conquers Ravenna, deposes the last Roman Emperor, acknowledges Eastern emperor, becomes ruler of Italy. |
| 480 | Anicius Manlius Severinus Boethius is born in Rome. |
| 482 | Emperor Zeno, at behest of Acacius, Patriarch of Constantinople, publishes *Henoticon*, which attempts to reconcile Christological doctrines of Nestorians and Monophysites. |
| 483 | Pope Felix III is elected. |
| 484 | Pope Felix III excommunicates Acacius because of *Henoticon* and schism results. |
| 485 | Symmachus, future father-in-law of Boethius, is named consul. |
| 487 | Father of Boethius is named consul. |
| 488 | Emperor invites Ostrogoths into Italy. |
| 489 | Theodoric, King of Ostrogoths, becomes ruler of Italy. |
| 490 | Boethius's father having died, the boy is taken into household of Quintus Aurelius Memmius Symmachus, whose daughter Rusticiana he will eventually marry. |
| 491 | Anastasius I becomes emperor and acknowledges Theodoric, an Arian. |
| 492 | Pope Gelasius I is elected. |
| 496 | Pope Anastasius II is elected; he tries in vain to heal Acacian schism. |
| 497 | Theodoric is granted right to name consuls. |
| 498 | Pope Symmachus is elected. |

503      About this time Boethius composes *De arithmetica* and *De musica*, perhaps as well works on astronomy and geometry which are not extant.

504/5      First commentary on Porphyry.

505/6      Work on categorical syllogisms.

507/9      Second commentary on Porphyry.

509/10      Commentary on Aristotle's *Categories*.

510      Boethius is named consul.

512      Boethius composes tractate against Nestorius and Eutyches, a defense of Catholic orthodoxy against monophysite and Nestorian Christological heresies.

513      First commentary on *Perihermeneias*.

514      Pope Hormisdas elected.

515/6      Second commentary on *Perihermeneias*.

             After 516, work on hypothetical syllogisms.

518      Comments on Cicero's *Topics*. Justinian I becomes emperor and seeks conciliation with Pope.

521      The four other *opuscula sacra* are written.

522      The two sons of Boethius are named consuls. Boethius is named Master of Offices and writes work of topical differences.

523      Pope John I is elected.

524      Boethius is arrested, writes *Consolation*, is executed.

526      Deaths of John I and Theodoric.

### THOMISTIC CHRONOLOGY

1200      Charter of University of Paris.

1210      Prohibition against "reading" Aristotle at Paris.

1215      Founding of Order of Preachers. Council of Lateran. First statutes of University of Paris. Magna Carta.

1225      Birth of Saint Thomas at Roccasecca.

1230–39      Thomas at Monte Cassino.

1231      Lifting of ban on Aristotle at Paris.

1239–44      Thomas is a student at University of Naples.

1240      First works of Averroes become known.

| 1240–48 | Albert the Great comments on Aristotle at Paris. Roger Bacon comments on Aristotle. |
| 1244 | Thomas joins Dominicans at Naples. |
| 1244–45 | Detained by family. |
| 1245 | Deposition of Frederick II. |
| 1245–48 | Thomas is a student at Paris. |
| 1248 | Albert the Great founds Faculty of Theology at Cologne. |
| 1248–52 | Thomas is a student of Albert at Cologne. |
| 1248–54 | Crusade of Saint Louis. |
| 1248–55 | St. Bonaventure teaches at Paris. |
| 1250 | Death of Frederick II. |
| 1250/1 | Thomas is ordained a priest. |
| 1252–56 | Bachelor of *Sentences* at Paris. |
| 1256 | Thomas is named Master of Theology. |
| 1256–59 | First Paris Professorate. |
| 1259–68 | Thomas in Italy. |
| 1263 | William of Moerbeke translates Aristotle for Thomas. |
| 1264 | Thomas writes liturgy for feast of Corpus Christi. |
| 1266–70 | Averroist controversy at Paris. |
| 1268–72 | Second Paris Professorate. |
| 1270 | First Condemnation of Averroism. |
| 1272 | Thomas is named Regent of Theology at Naples. |
| 1273 | Thomas stops writing. |
| 1274 | March 7, Thomas dies at Fossanova. |
| 1274 | Council of Lyon unites East and West. |
| 1276 | *Roman de la Rose.* |
| 1277 | March 7, condemnation at Paris of 219 Averroistic propositions, including some Thomistic tenets. |
| 1323 | Canonization of St. Thomas. |
| 1325 | Revocation of Paris condemnation. |

# Bibliography

Bianchi, Luca. *L'Errore di Aristote: La Polemica contro l'eternita del mondo nel XIII secolo*. Florence, La Nuova Italia, 1984.

Bird, Otto. "How to Read an Article in the Summa." *The New Scholasticism*, 27, 2, 129–59.

Bobik, Joseph. *Aquinas On Being and Essence: A Translation and Interpretation*. Notre Dame: University of Notre Dame Press, 1965.

Boethius. *Anicii Manlii Severini Boetii commentarii in librum Periher-meneias*, ed. Carolus Meiser. New York, Garland, 1987 (Reprint of Teubner, 1880).

————. *Boethius, Anicius Manlius Severinus, Opera*. Corpus Christianorum, Series Latina, v. 94, ed. Ludovicus Bieler, Turnholt, Brepols, 1957.

————. *Boethius, Anicius Manlius Severinus, Opera*. Corpus Scriptorum Ecclesiasticorum Latinorum, v. 48, ed. Samuel Brandt. Vindibonae, Tempsky; Lipsae, Freytag, 1906.

————. *Consolatio Philosophiae and Opuscula*, ed R. Peiper. Leipzig, Teubner, 1860.

————. *Manlii Severini Boethii Opera omnia*. Patrologia Cursus Completus, Series Latina, ed. J. P. Migne, tomes 63–64, Paris, Apud Garnier fratres, 1847.

————. *Theological Tractates*, ed. and tr. H. F. Stewart, E. K. Rand, and S. J. Tester. Loeb Classical Library, Latin. Cambridge, MA, Harvard University Press, 1973.

————. *Die theologischen Traktates*, ed. and tr. Michael Elsasser. Hamburg, F.R.G., F. Meiner, 1988.

Bourke, Vernon J. *Aquinas' Search for Wisdom*. Milwaukee, WI, Marquette University Press, 1965.

Capua, F. di. "Il cursus nel De Consolatione philosophiae e nei trattati teologici di Severino Boezio," *Didaskaleion* 3, 1914, 269–303. (Reprinted in his *Scritti Minori*, Rome, Ateneo, 1959.)

Cappuyns, M. "The supposed commentary of John the Scot on the Opuscula sacra of Boethius," *Revue neo-scolastique* 36, 1934, 67–77.

Chadwick, Henry. *Boethius: The Consolations of Music, Logic, Theology, and Philosophy*. Oxford, Clarendon Press, 1981.

Chenu, M.-D. *Introduction à l'étude de St. Thomas d'Aquin*. Paris, J. Vrin, 1954.

Cobban, A. B. *The Medieval Universities*. London, Methuen, 1975.

Collins, James. "Progress and Problems in the Reassessment of Boethius." *Modern Schoolman* 23 (1945–46), 1–23.

Cooper, L. *A Concordance of Boethius: The Five Theological Tractates and the Consolation of Philosophy*. Cambridge, MA, The Mediaeval Academy of America 1928.

Courcelle, Pierre-Paul. "Boece et l'école d'Alexandrie." *Mélanges d'Archéologie et d'Histoire*, 52 (1935), 185–223.

_____. "Boece," in *Dictionnaire des Lettres françaises*, Le moyen âge (Paris, 1964), 139–141.

_____. *Late Latin Writers and Their Greek Sources*, trans. Harry E. Wedeck, Cambridge, MA, Harvard University Press, 1969.

Courteney, William. *Schools and Scholars in Fourteenth Century England*. Princeton, 1987.

Crocco, Antonio. *Introduzione a Boezione*. Naples, Empireo, 1970.

Degli'Innocenti, M. "Nota al De Hebdomadibus di Boezio" *Divus Thomas* 42, 1939, 397–399.

Dondaine, Antoine. *Secrétaires de Saint Thomas*. 2 vols. Rome, Editori di S. Tomaso, S. Sabina, 1956.

Draseke, J. "Uber die theologischen Schriften des Boethius," *Jahrbucher fur protestantische Theologie* 12, 1886, 312–333.

Duhem, Pierre. *Le Système du Monde*. Paris, 1917.

Evans, G. R. "More Geometrico: The place of the axiomatic method in the twelfth century commentaries on Boethius' opuscula sacra," *Archives Internationales d'histoire des sciences* 27, 1977, 207–221.

Fabro, Cornelio. *Participation et causalité selon S. Thomas d'Aquin*. Editions Nauwaelerts, Louvain, 1961.

_____. *La nozione metafisica de partecipazione*, 3 rev. ed. Turin, Societa Editrice Internazionale, 1963.

_____. *Esegesi Tomistica*. Rome, Libreria Editrice della Pontificia Universita Lateranense, 1969.

_____. *Tomismo e Pensiero Moderno*. Rome, Libreria Editrice della Pontificia Universita Lateranense, 1969.

Ferrua, Angelico, O.P. *Thomae Aquinatis Vitae Fontes Precipuae*. Edizione Domenicane. Alba, 1968.

Gabriel, Astrick L. *Garlandia: Studies in the History of the Medieval University*. Notre Dame, The Medieval Institute, 1969.

Galdi, M. *Saggi boeziani*. Pisa, 1938.

Geiger, L.-B. *La Participation dans la philosophie de S. Thomas d'Aquin*. Paris, J. Vrin, 1953.

———. "Abstractio et séparation d'après S. Thomas: in de trinitate, q.5, a.3." *Revue des Sciences Philosophiques et Théologiques*, XXXI, 1947, 206–223.

Gersh, Stephen. *Middle Platonism and Neoplatonism: The Latin Tradition*, 2 vols. Notre Dame, University of Notre Dame Press, 1987.

Gibson, Margaret, ed. *Boethius, His Life, Thought and Influence*. Oxford, Blackwell, 1981.

Hadot, Pierre. "Un fragment du commentaire perdu de Boece sur les Catégories d'Aristote dans le codex Brenensis 363," *Archives d'histoire doctrinale et littéraire au moyen âge* 26, 1959.

———. "La distinction de l'être et de l'étant dans le De Hebdomadibus de Boece," in *Miscellanea Mediaevalia*, ed. P. Wilpert II, 147–153. Berlin, Walter De Gruyter, 1963.

———. "Forma essendi: interprétation philogique et interprétation philosophique d'une formule de Boece," *Les Études Classiques*, 38, 1970, 143–156.

Haring, N. M., ed. *The commentaries on Boethius by Gilbert of Poitiers*. Toronto, Pontifical Institute of Mediaeval Studies, 1966.

———, ed. *Commentaries on Boethius by Thierry of Chartres and his school*. Toronto, Pontifical Institute of Mediaeval Studies, 1971 (1960), 134–136.

———. *Life and Works of Clarembald of Arras*. Toronto, Pontifical Institute of Mediaeval Studies, 1965.

Lewis, C. S. *The Discarded Image: An Introduction to Medieval and Renaissance Literature*. Cambridge, Cambridge University Press, 1964.

Liebeschutz, H. "Boethius and the legacy of antiquity," in A. H. Armstrong (ed.), *The Cambridge History of Later Greek and Early Medieval Philosophy*. Cambridge, Cambridge University Press, 1967.

Maioli, Bruno. *Teoria Dell'Essere e dell'Essistente e Classificazione delle scienze in M. S. Boezio*. Arezzo, Ucello, 1977.

Mansion, A. *Introduction à la Physique Aristotélicienne*. Louvain, Presses Universitaires, 1945.

McInerny, R. *A History of Western Philosophy* III. Notre Dame, University of Notre Dame Press, 1970.

———. *Logic of Analogy*. The Hague, M. Nijhoff, 1961.

———. *Studies in Analogy*. The Hague, M. Nijhoff, 1968.

———. "Boethius and St. Thomas Aquinas," *Rivista di filosofia neo-scolastica* 66, 1974, 219–245.

———. *Rhyme and Reason: St. Thomas and the Modes of Discourse*. The Aquinas Lecture. Milwaukee, WI, Marquette University Press, 1981.

Merlan, Philip. *From Platonism to Neoplatonism*, 2nd rev. ed. The Hague, M. Nijhoff, 1960.

Minio-Paluello, L., ed. *Aristoteles Latinus*, vols. I, II, III, V, VI. Leiden, E. J. Brill, 1961–1975.

———. *Opuscula: The Latin Aristotle*. Amsterdam, M. Nijhoff, 1972.

———. "Boethius," *Encyclopaedia Brittanica* (1968).

———. "Boethius," *Dictionary of Scientific Biography* II, New York, 1970, 228–236.

Nedoncelle, M. "Les Variations de Boece sur la personne," *Revue des sciences religieuses* 29, 1955, 201–238.

———. "Proposon et persona dans l'antiquité classique," *Revue des sciences religieuses* 22, 1948, 227–299.

Neumann, Siegfried. *Gegenstand und Methode*. Munster: Aschendorffsche Verlagsbuchhandlung, 1965.

Obertello, Luca, ed. *Atti del congresso internazionale di studi Boeziani*. Rome: Editrice Herder, 1981.

———. *Boezio: la Consolazione della filosofia, gli opuscoli teologici*. I classici del pensiero, sezione II, Medioevo e rinascimento. Milan, Rusconi, 1979.

———. "Boezio, le scienze del quadrivio e la cultura medioevale," *Atti del'Accadamia Ligure Scienze di scienze e lettere* 28, 1971, 152–170.

———. *Severino Boezio*. 2 vols. Genoa, Academia Ligura di scienze e lettere, 1974.

O'Donnell, J. J. Review of revised Loeb edition of Boethius by S. J. Tester, in *American Journal of Philology* 98, 1977, 77–79.

O'Reilly, Peter. *Sancti Thomae de Aquino Super Librum Boetii "De Hebdomadibus," An edition and study*. Dissertation. Toronto, Pontifical Institute, 1960.

Pattin, A. *Le liber de causis*. Louvain, n.d. (1966).

Pera, C. *Le fonti de Pensiero di S. Tommaso D'Aquino nella somma teologica*. Con presentazione di M.-D. Chenu, O.P., et aggiornamento Bibliografico di C. Vansteenkiste, O.P. Turin, Marietti, 1979.

Pieper, Josef. *The Silence of St. Thomas*. New York, Pantheon, 1957.

Powicke, F. M. and Emden, A. B., eds. *Rashdall's Medieval Universities*. A new edition in three volumes. Oxford, The Clarendon Press, 1936.

Rand, E. K. "Der dem Boethius zugeschriebene Traktat *De fide catholica*." *Jahrbucher fur classiche philologie*, Suppl. 26, 1901, 401–61.

———. "The supposed commentary of John the Scot on the Opuscula sacra of Boethius," *Revue neo-scolastique* 36, 1934, 67–77.

_____. *Johannes Scottus*. Munich, C. H. Beck, 1906.

_____. Review of V. Schurr, *Die Trinitatslehre des Boethius*, in *Speculum* 11, 1936, 153–156.

Riche, P. *Éducation et culture dans l'occident barbare VIᵉ–VIIᵉ siècle.* Patristica Sorbonensia 4. Paris, J. Vrin, 1979.

_____. *Les écoles et l'enseignement dans l'occident chrétien de la fin du Vᵉ siècle au milieu du XIᵉ siècle.* Paris, J. Vrin, 1979.

Rijk, L. M. de. *Logica modernorum,* 2 vols. Assen, Van Gorcum, 1962, 1967.

_____. "On the chronology of Boethius' works on logic," *Vivarium,* 2, 1964, 1–49, 125–162.

Robert, J. D., O.P. "La métaphysique, science distincte de toute autre discipline philosophique selon Saint Thomas d'Aquin." *Divus Thomas,* Piacenza. Vol. L, 1947, pp. 206–223.

Roland-Gosselin, M.-D., O.P. *Le De ente et essentia de Saint Thomas d'Aquin.* VIII. Paris, Bibliothèque Thomiste, 1926.

_____, ed. *De ente et essentia.* Paris, J. Vrin, 1948.

Rovighi Silvia Vanni. "La filosofia di Gilberto Porretano," *Miscellanea del Centro di Studi Medievali.* Milan, 1955, pp. 8–18.

Schrimpf, G. *Die Axiomenschrift des Boethius (de Hebdomadibus) als Philophisches Lehrbuch des Mittelalters.* Leiden, E. J. Brill, 1966.

Schurr, V. *Die Trinitatslehre des Boethius im lichte der 'Skythische Kontroversen.'* Forschungen zur Christlichen Literatur und Dogmengeschichte 18, I. Paderborn, 1935.

Stewart, H. F. *Boethius, An Essay.* Edinburgh and London, W. Blackwood and Sons, 1891.

_____. "A Commentary by Remigius Autissiodorensis of the De consolatione philosophiae of Boethius," *Journal of Theological Studies* 17, 1915, 22–42.

_____. and Rand, E. K. Edition of *Consolatio* and *Opuscula* in Loeb Classical Library. 1st ed., 1918. (Revised 1973 by S. J. Tester.)

Stryker E. "La notion aristotélicienne de séparation dans son application aux Idées de Platon." *Autour d'Aristote.* Louvain, Publications Universitaires de Louvain, Lovain, 1955.

Stump, Eleonore, tr. *Boethius's De topicis differentiis.* Ithaca, NY, Cornell University Press, 1978.

_____. *Boethius's In Ciceronis Topica.* Ithaca, NY, Cornell University Press, 1988.

_____. "Boethius' Works on the *Topics*," *Vivarium.* XXII 2, 1974, 77–93.

Tester, S. J., with H. F. Stewart and E. K. Rand. *Consolation of Philosophy and Theological Tractates.* Loeb Classical Library, Latin. Cambridge, MA, Harvard University Press, 1973. (Revision of 1918 edition by H. F. Stewart, E. K. Rand.)

Thomas Aquinas. *Sancti Thomae de Aquino Opera Omnia Iussu Leonis XIII P.M.* Edited by the Leonine Commission, Roma, ongoing.

_____. *Expositio super librum Boethii De Trinitate*, ed. Bruno Decker. Leiden, E. J. Brill, 1955.

_____. *De ente et essentia*. ed. Roland-Gosselin. Paris, 1948.

_____. *De ente et essentia*, In *Opuscula Philosophica*, ed. R. Spiazzi, O.P. Taurini, Marietti, 1954, 1–18.

_____. *In Boetium De trinitate et de hebdomadibus expositio*, ed. M. Calcaterra, O.P., In *Opuscula Theologica II*. Taurini, Marietti, 1954, 291–408.

_____. *In Librum Boethii De trinitate quaestiones quinta et sexta*, ed. Paul Wyser, O.P. Fribourg, Société Philosophique; Louvain, Nauwelaerts, 1948.

_____. *In Librum de causis expositio*, ed. C. Pera, O.P. 2nd ed., Taurini, Marietti, 1972.

_____. *Scriptum Super libros Sententiarum*. Eds. Mandonnet and Moos. Paris, Lethielleux, 1929–33.

_____. *Super Librum de causis expositio*, ed. H. D. Saffrey. Textus Philosophici Friburgensis, 4/5. Fribourg, Société Philosophique; Louvain, Nauwelaerts, 1954.

_____. *Thomas von Aquin in librum Boethii de Trinitate Quaestiones quinta et sexta*. Fribourg, Paulusverlag, 1948.

Usener, H. *Anecdoton Holderi, ein Beitrag zur Geschichte Roms in Ostgothischer Zeit*. Bonn, 1877.

Vogel, Cornelia de. "Boethiana." I and II. *Vivarium* 9, 1971, 49–66, and 10, 1972, 1–40.

Wagner, David, ed. *The Seven Liberal Arts in the Middle Ages*. Bloomington, Indiana University Press, 1983.

Weisheipl, James, O.P. *Friar Thomas D'Aquino*. 2nd ed. Washington, DC, The Catholic University of America Press, 1983.

# Index